Global Social Policy

112, 141
109, 104 : system matters

116
123-24, 127 ideology matters

137: dissent w/in orgs →
how much is intellectual debate,
fighting who has better argument
→ how much is care about
country's transition?

Global Social Policy

International Organizations and the Future of Welfare

Bob Deacon

with

Michelle Hulse and Paul Stubbs

SAGE Publications

London • Thousand Oaks • New Delhi

First published 1997

SAGE Publications Ltd
6 Bonhill Street
London EC2A 4PU

SAGE Publications Inc.
2455 Teller Road
Thousand Oaks, California 91320

SAGE Publications India Pvt Ltd
32, M-Block Market
Greater Kailash – I
New Delhi 110 048

British Library Cataloguing in Publication data

A catalogue record for this book is available from the British Library

ISBN 0 8039 8953 9
ISBN 0 8039 8954 7 (pbk)

Library of Congress catalog card number 97–068534

Typeset by Mayhew Typesetting, Rhayader, Powys
Printed in Great Britain by Biddles Ltd, Guildford, Surrey

Contents

idea: there is global. of soc. pol. except EU?

Should point to different effects of econ. ? in devel. countries

Why has rapid transition to market econ. in former comm.
46 countries not led to good welfare results?

subjective nature : 80-9, some loaded summary, others
didn't → right way of

Figures

Tables

Preface

This book is a textbook based on original research and develops an important thesis. It concerns the globalization of social policy and the socialization of global politics. The book demonstrates first that national social policy is increasingly determined by global economic competition and by the social policy of international organizations such as the World Bank, and secondly that the substance of social policy is increasingly transnational. Global social policy is constituted of global social redistribution, global social regulation and global social provision and empowerment. This textbook reviews for students the state of the world's welfare in terms of how far human needs are met. Trends in global inequity, and the diverse experiences of different kinds of welfare regime North, South, East and West, are summarized. The social policies of international organizations are reviewed systematically for the first time. The book is also a report of two major research projects which focused on the making of post-communist social policy and the role played in this by international organizations in Bulgaria, Hungary, Ukraine and the post-Yugoslav countries. The research which documents the global discourse taking place within and between international organizations about the future for welfare policy reinforces the thesis concerning the globalization of social policy.

The book is primarily addressed to students of social policy but it is also intended that it should be read by other colleagues and students in academia, government and international organizations. Development studies specialists would benefit from the comparisons and connections made between social policy in developing and developed countries. Students of international organizations and international relations will find the book informs the debates concerning the future of these areas of study. Economists should read it because it demonstrates that choices between economic and social policies are a matter not of mathematical modelling but of political values. Political scientists should read it because it demonstrates that the locus of key policy decisions lies far from national governments and inside global banking organizations. Soviet and East European area studies specialists should read it to appreciate the importance of external influences on the region. Sociologists should read it as an example of an attempt to study the social relations of power and the nature of discursive practices at a global level. Social policy makers and their advisers should read it to locate the institutions within which it might be most appropriate to apply their skills.

The book is the culmination of almost four years' work. It has been informed by research undertaken by myself and my research assistant Michelle Hulse into the role played by international organizations in shaping post-communist social policy. For Michelle's support and companionship on numerous trips to Eastern Europe I am grateful. The completeness of the references has depended on her. Chapter 5 has been informed by research undertaken by Paul Stubbs into social development and social reconstruction in post-Yugoslav countries. Paul wrote the first draft of this chapter. We are all three grateful to Leeds Metropolitan University social policy research fund, the Nuffield Foundation small grants scheme, the Ford Foundation grant scheme administered by the British Association of Soviet and East European Studies, and the Overseas Development Administration of the UK government for financial support. At the same time the book has been informed by my involvement, at various points in the life of the project, with some of the international organizations that are the subject of the research. This involvement has included acting as a social policy consultant on an ILO project in the Czech and Slovak Republics, on a World Bank funded project in Bulgaria, on an UNPREDEP mission in Macedonia, on an UNRISD project for the UN World Summit on Social Development, on an ODA funded project in Beijing, as an expert for EU TACIS, and as an expert for the Directorate of Economic and Social Affairs of the Council of Europe. Such involvement has sharpened my insight into the role being played by these organizations in shaping social policy but also, of course, detracted from the time available to complete this book.

I discussed some of the ideas in this book at an early stage of development with Fiona Williams. Those early conversations have continued to inform the book. I am indebted also to my students who have responded positively when they have had the book tried out on them in lectures, including especially my 'most enthusiastic student' Ruth. Michelle's role I have already acknowledged. Paul, while formally only responsible for a draft of one chapter, has become a valued collaborator and a most enthusiastic publicist for the cause of international social policy analysis. I am indebted to several people who have commented on drafts of chapters, helped me formulate ideas, or answered detailed questions by fax or e-mail. Among these are Alastair McCauley, David Donnison, Branko Milanovic, Michael Cichon, Sandor Sipos, Guy Standing, Mita Castle and Dharam Ghai. My newest research student David Chandler has been important in challenging some ideas and his fellow student Zoe Irving has contributed ideas also. For putting up with me being boring about the topic over several pints of beer or glasses of wine I have been grateful at different times to Gerry Lavery, Gordon Johnston, Alan Ward and Joan Forbes. For being a supportive friend who has encouraged me to stick at the task of keeping the flag of research going in the ex-polytechnics I must thank Alison Ravetz. For word processing the final draft thanks to Marilyn Harrison. Of immense value to the book have been the small army of ministers, officials and professionals Michelle and I have interviewed in international organizations and governments in Kiev, Budapest, Sofia, Paris, Strasbourg, Brussels, Geneva, New York and Washington. Paul would want to acknowledge the contribution of many working in the NGOs in post-Yugoslav countries who have helped formulate ideas about the region. He would also want to thank Jasmina for her support. I reserve my most grateful appreciation for Lynda who has been unswervingly loving and loyal and proven for me that it is possible to write a book and remain human.

Bob Deacon

Abbreviations

APEC	Asian Pacific Economic Co-operation
BWI	Bretton Woods institutions
CEE	Central East Europe
CEET	Central and Eastern European Team (ILO: Budapest)
CCET	Centre for Co-operation with Economies in Transition (OECD)
CEF	Social Development Fund (COE)
CIS	Confederation of Independent States
COE	Council of Europe
DGI	External Relations Directorate (EU)
DGV	Directorate of Employment, Industrial Relations and Social Affairs (EU)
EBRD	European Bank for Reconstruction and Development
EC	European Commission (EU)
ECHO	European Commission Humanitarian Office
ECHR	European Charter of Human Rights
ECOSOC	Economic and Social Council (UN)
ECU	European currency unit
ESC	European Social Charter
EU	European Union
FSU	Former Soviet Union
FYROM	Former Yugoslav Republic of Macedonia
GATT	General Agreement on Tariffs and Trade
GDP	gross domestic product
GNP	gross national product
G7	Group of Seven (industrialized countries)
G77	Group of Seventy-Seven
HDI	human development index
IBRD	International Bank for Reconstruction and Development
ILO	International Labour Organization
IMF	International Monetary Fund
ISSA	International Social Security Association.
NAFTA	North Atlantic Free Trade Area
NGO	non-governmental organization
NIS	new independent states (of the FSU)
ODA	Overseas Development Agency

OECD	Organization for Economic Co-operation and Development
OSCE	Organization for Security and Co-operation in Europe
PAYG	pay as you go
PHARE	assistance for economic restructuring in Central and Eastern Europe (initially only Poland and Hungary) (EU)
PIT	Partners in Transition (OECD programme)
TACIS	Technical Assistance Programme to the former republics of the Soviet Union (EU)
TNC	transnational co-operations
UNCTAD	United Nations Conference on Trade and Development
UNDP	United Nations Development Programme
UNECE	United Nations Economic Commission for Europe
UNESCO	United Nations Educational, Scientific and Cultural Organization
UNIDO	United Nations Industrial Development Organization
UNHCR	United Nations High Commission for Refugees
UNICEF	United Nations Children's Fund
UNPREDEP	United Nations Preventive Deployment Force
UNPROFOR	United Nations Protection Force
UNRISD	United Nations Research Institute for Social Development
WB	World Bank
WHO	World Health Organization
WTO	World Trade Organization

1

Globalism and the Study of Social Policy

The globalization of social policy and the socialization of global politics

Traditionally social policy has been the subject concerned with those state and non-governmental activities within one country that are designed to intervene in the operations of the free market in the interests of social protection and social welfare. Central to social policy has been the income transfer mechanisms whereby the employed support those excluded from work through age, infirmity, family responsibilities and the failures of the market.

In the present phase of world economic development however social policy activities traditionally analysed within and undertaken within one country now take on a supranational and transnational character. This is so for several reasons. Economic competition between countries may be leading them to shed the economic costs of social protection in order to be more competitive (social dumping) unless there are supranational or global regulations in place that discourage this (Kosonen, 1995). International migratory pressures generate the political logic that there could be income transfers between nations to stave off the political consequences of mass migration (Castles, 1993). Similarly common markets in capital and labour between countries give rise to the possibility of a supranational authority providing at a supranational level the social citizenship rights denied or threatened at national level (Baubock, 1994).

The implications for national, supranational, and transnational social policy of this present phase of globalization is an under-theorized and under-researched topic within the subject of social policy. Whereas globalism has received considerable attention recently from scholars working within the discipline of political science (Held, 1991; 1995), sociology (Featherstone, 1990; Sklair, 1991), economics (Griffiths and Wall, 1993; Hirst and Thompson, 1996; Strange, 1994; Stubbs and Underhill, 1994) and international relations (Halliday, 1994; Shaw, 1994) this has not been the case for social policy. Supranationalism in the context of Europeanization is, of course, an exception. Kleinman and Piachaud (1993) and Liebfried (1994) among others have usefully reviewed work in this subglobal context. Huber and Stephens (1993) have speculated on the future for Scandinavian social democracy in the light of increased global economic competition and Europeanization. Esping-Andersen (1996) has similarly reviewed comparative welfare trends in a global context. Abram de Swaan (1994) has advanced furthest the case for social policy analysis to shift gear to the global and transnational.

The relative decline of the power of national governments in the face of globally mobile capital challenges the traditional frameworks of social policy analysis in a number of ways.

First, it suggests that the *supranational and global actors* need to be given more attention in explanations of changing social policy. Because social policy's analytical frameworks have derived from work on economically privileged North and West welfare states they have tended to downplay the importance of background institutions like the IMF and the World Bank. Now that social policy analysis (Esping-Andersen, 1996) is encompassing less economically privileged South and East welfare states, and because the sustainability of the welfare states of Europe is questioned by global economic competition, this relative neglect of these institutions is no longer justified. As will be demonstrated in Chapter 4 they are now important influences on national social policy.

Secondly it introduces a new field of enquiry into the subject. This field encompasses what we call the supranationalization or globalization of social policy instruments, policy and provision. This supranationalization of social policy takes three (at least) forms. These are supranational regulation, supranational redistribution and supranational provision.

The first form embraces those mechanisms, instruments and policies at a supranational and global level that seek to regulate the terms of trade and the operation of firms in the interests of social protection and welfare objectives. At a global level such instruments and policies are at a primitive stage of development. The key issue here is whether the social regulation of capitalism practised by the European Union can and will be elevated to the global playing field. It is argued by some (Lang and Hines, 1996) that the General Agreement on Tariffs and Trade and the new World Trade Organization should embrace social and environmental concerns. These concerns are, of course, the stock-in-trade of development studies. It is scholars working in that field who have argued the case for the shift from free market structural adjustment to a socially regulated adjustment with a human face (Cornia et al., 1987). Our point is that with the collapse since 1989 of the state bureaucratic collectivist alternative to capitalism and the increasingly intense nature of global economic competition, these issues traditionally associated with development studies and poor countries should become also the concern of analysts of developed welfare states. The obverse argument, that development studies should emerge from its ghetto and address the implications of its analysis for global processes, has been made recently by Foster-Carter (1993) and echoed by Duffield (1996b).

The second form that supranational social policy can take is that of redistribution between countries. At a subglobal level this operates effectively already within the European Union through the structural and associated funds that ensure a degree of support for poorer regions by richer ones. Once again the overlap with development studies and those scholars concerned with the emergence of global governance is obvious. The valued United Nations *Human Development Report* suggested that 'Human society is increasingly taking on a global dimension. Sooner or later it will have to develop the global institutions to match . . . a system of progressive income tax [from rich to poor nations] . . . a strengthened UN' (UNDP, 1992: 78).

The third form of supranational and global social policy is that of social welfare provision at a level above that of national government. This refers to the embryonic measures so far almost exclusively developed only at the subglobal, especially European, level whereby people gain an entitlement to a service or are empowered in the field of social citizenship rights by an agency acting at a supranational level. The United Nations High Commission for Refugees acts in the welfare interests of stateless persons and refugees. The Council of Europe empowers the citizens of member states to take their governments to the Strasbourg Court of Human Rights if they believe their rights have been circumscribed. Weale (1994) has argued that the EU could develop a European safety net social assistance policy that applies in all countries, to counter the xenophobic concerns with 'welfare tourism'.

The other side of the coin of the globalization of social policy is the socialization of global politics. In other words the major agenda issues at intergovernmental meetings are, now in essence social (and environmental) questions. The G7 summit in June 1996, with the Presidents of the IMF, World Bank and World Trade Organization and the UN Secretary-General in attendance, resolved, for example, to discuss the relationship between free trade and the 'internationally recognized core labour standards' at their Singapore meeting in the autumn of 1996 (the outcome of this meeting is reported in Chapter 6). In the example of UN preventive intervention in Macedonia (Deacon, 1996) a focus of concern is to find social policy mechanisms that increase co-operation across ethnic divides (Chapter 5). Figure 1.1 captures this shift in the content of global politics.

With the collapse of the cold war, the rise of international migratory pressures, and the human suffering arising from social instability in many parts of the globe, the security that faces world leaders is, in effect, social security. Cancellation of debts arising from the ill-informed period of structural adjustment, transnational humanitarian aid to create global political security, and the 'threat' to economic competitiveness posed by the 'social protectionism' of European welfare states, are today's top agenda items. The 1995 UN World Summit on Social Development merely echoed this.

In the remainder of this chapter we first review the globalization process in a little more detail through the eyes of social science disciplines other than social policy. Then we focus on the argument as to whether developed welfare states are threatened by the increased intensity of global economic competition already referred to. We then set out in more detail the terrain of global social policy analysis.

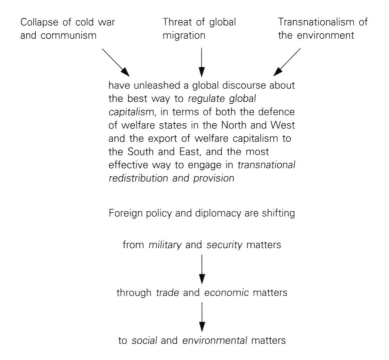

| Collapse of cold war and communism | Threat of global migration | Transnationalism of the environment |

have unleashed a global discourse about the best way to *regulate global capitalism*, in terms of both the defence of welfare states in the North and West and the export of welfare capitalism to the South and East, and the most effective way to engage in *transnational redistribution and provision*

Foreign policy and diplomacy are shifting

from *military* and *security* matters

through *trade* and *economic* matters

to *social* and *environmental* matters

Figure 1.1   *The globalization of social policy and the socialization of global politics*

Globalism, the social sciences and social policy

With the collapse of the cold war and the historic defeat of a particular statist and command economy version of 'socialism' the world has entered a new phase. On the one hand, there are possibilities of the emergence of numerous national rivalries, or regional trade wars, and of the growth of racism and illiberalism. This pessimistic scenario has been painted by, for example, Chomsky (1993). On the other hand there is now the opportunity for the emergence of an effective global politics that will be concerned not so much with the protection of national sovereignties but rather with intervention in the global economic system to improve the well-being of the world's population. Beyond the crippling ossification of the claims and counter-claims of existing capitalism and existing 'socialism' that have marked the past 70 years, there is now a chance for the search for global and social justice and for the meeting of more of the human needs of more of the world's population.

Factors other than the collapse of the cold war impel this development. An increasing global concern with sustainable growth that no longer threatens the environment and the future is one important factor. The cultural consequences of globalization include the contribution of world media expansion. It is possible to detect, we suggest, not only the development of racist sentiments within Europe and the developed world, but also an increasing compassion towards and concern to alleviate the suffering of the world's poor. Indications of this might be the growth of the work of non-governmental organizations in addressing issues of global redistribution and development, the strengthening of UN specialist agencies, and the rhetoric of world agencies such as the World Bank which is increasingly concerned with the alleviation of poverty in developing countries (World Bank, 1990; 1992a). Recent UN summits in 1995 focused on social development and the position of women. The forward looking report of the Commission on Global Governance (1995) is indicative. Whether it is through humanitarian compassion or the protective self-interest of the developed economies of Europe and elsewhere, we could see in the next decade the strengthening of the hand of global social reformists against the hand of global *laissez-faire* economists. The threat posed by global economic competition and global economic migration to the social democratic and social market economy achievements of Europe and elsewhere might impel an articulation of global reformism, just as the threat posed by the poor within one nation to the stability of capitalism impelled national social reformism a century ago. Charity as a means of relieving world poverty and starvation could give way to systematic transnational intergovernmental intervention.

Within this context social scientists have begun to attempt to make sense of the new processes of globalization and offer alternative social, economic and political strategies for acting in the new world (dis)order. *Economists* have already charted the globalization of the economic system (Carnoy et al., 1993; Stubbs and Underhill, 1994). With the collapse of the Soviet Union the logic of capital accumulation and the imperatives of competition will have extended to the whole globe. The managed economic reform going on behind the veil of undemocratic government in China is leading to an effectively competitive state capitalism (Cornia, 1994; Kelly, 1992). The teaching of the Koran against money lending will continue to be circumvented within those countries of Asia and the Middle East who, despite the anti-western rhetoric, will continue to wish to develop economically. Transnational corporations are assuming a larger share in global investment. As a result of these economic processes the nation state has become less important in shaping global economic activity, although the extent of this is disputed (Hirst and Thompson, 1996; Picciotto, 1991). A separate section of this chapter develops the point further in terms of the economic analysis that suggests developed welfare states might be threatened by the forces of global economic competition.

Political scientists have embarked on two new fields of study that reflect these economically driven changes. On the one hand there is the opening up of the field of *comparative* politics to include a huge number of newly emergent nation states and, very often, subnational regional claims for autonomy. On the other hand there is a renewed interest in the processes of the globalization of politics with its consequences for the possible decline of national sovereignty (Camillieri and Falk, 1993; Smith, 1995). Evan Luard (1990) first addressed this theme systematically. David Held (1995) in a major text is concerned with the chances for democracy as politics becomes globalized. Held notes a disjuncture between the needs of the time for a cosmopolitan democracy and the laggardness of the national political institutions. On the one hand a threat to democracy is posed by the existence of non-democratic politics and nations on the world stage. Equally he notes that little progress has yet been made to democratize global institutions such as the World Bank. The possible strengthening of democracy can be envisaged on the other hand by the development of parallel systems of local, national and supranational decision making. Each level of government could act as a check on the potential abuse of power by the others. Within this new paradigm of political science, tiers of government in effect give way to spheres of influence of complementary and contending local, national, supranational and global political forums. This is evident within the workings of the European Community. It is in this context that socialists have argued that democratic planning bodies need to be established at a global level as well as within Europe (Blackburn, 1990; Panitch and Mandel, 1992). It is no longer a matter of being 'in and against' the state but of being 'in and against' international organizations.

Allied to the work of political scientists concerned with the challenges to democracy of the growth of supranationalism are the ongoing debates within the field of *international relations*. Neo-realists have continued to contend (Gilpin, 1984; Waltz, 1986) that global politics remains a matter of the compromises worked out between sovereign states who remain the key actors. Supranational bodies such as the ILO or the World Bank continue to be the instruments of state policy (Ruggie, 1993). Others have suggested that this may have been the case in cold war days but is now giving way to a situation in which international organizations are either a means of transforming international society or, at least, a reflection of a pluralistic world community (Boardman, 1994). Others have gone further. Strang and Chang, in a study of the ILO, concluded that

> Social welfare, and domestic policy more generally, is an increasingly trans-national business. Global standards and agenda setting play roles in the rapid expansion of programs of some states . . . It seems useful to conceptualise part of the discourse generating the 'welfare state' as global in scope, and emerging out of the normative models and formal organisations that span national societies. (1993: 259)

This book will reinforce this conclusion and as such might be regarded as an example of a global policy study which is a study not of comparative politics or of international relations but of a policy area that is trans-national (Nagel, 1991).

Fred Halliday has set out a new research agenda for the subject of international relations which includes 'the manner in which agency operates transnationally . . . e.g. the international organisation of hegemonic groups'

(1994: 242). Susan Strange has appealed to her realist friends that 'international political economy . . . becomes much more interesting to teach, research and write about when you drop the idea that the states are the unit of analysis and that war is the main problematic of the international system' (1994: 218). Martin Shaw has argued that 'the development of global society requires a new politics of global responsibility' (1994: 187). In this context it has to be asked if the international organizations such as the World Bank and international NGOs are on the side of the angels in their concern to eradicate world poverty or on the side of the imperialist gangsters cloaking western interventions in a new moral garb (Chandler, 1996). This new turn in the understanding of the subject of international relations has indeed generated an intense controversy as to the ethical claims of this emergent international society or world community and the intergovernmental organizations through which it operates (Wheeler, 1996). This controversy will be evaluated in Chapter 6.

An important feminist contribution (Tickner and Morgenthaus, 1991) to the renewal of international relations theory argues that international relations needs redefining as food, health and environmental security and hence as the business largely of women. Empowerment and shared human values would mark this view of the subject. In the same volume O'Keohane (1991) argues that the feminist contribution to international relations theory is to challenge the 'male' notions of sovereignty and power and replace them by networking and facilitation.

Sociologists, or at least those who have been influenced by the claims of postmodernism, in the context of globalism, are faced with a tension in their analysis and, where they wish to put their analysis to use, prescription. The postmodernist analysis and argument lead to a celebration of the diversity and difference within and between societies. In an age of doubt, contingency and uncertainty, all world redeeming and transcendental projects are jettisoned. Neither capitalism, nor communism, nor rational philosophy can provide the answer to the world's problems. For Bauman (1991) the best there can be is a counter-culture to the capitalist project that will, if not challenged, turn tolerance into neglect, diversity into indifference, and freedom into the shopping mall. Sociological theory needs, we suggest, to escape both the 'cynical gaze of Marxism' (Lee and Raban, 1990) which suggests nothing can be done until everything is done and the paralysing gaze of postmodernism which suggests there are no grounds for action, and utilize instead its substantive insights into how the world system works to better it in the future. Work by Wallerstein (1991) and particularly Sklair (1991) on transnational power structures could be a basis upon which this project might be built. This, in turn, may enable us to answer the central question posed by the present turn of world events: can the benefits of a socially regulated capitalism be extended globally given environmental constraints and the political problems posed by global inequity (Sklair, 1992)? McGrew et al.'s (1993) discussion of globalism reviews the same theoretical ground and interestingly gives concluding prominence to Margaret Archer's (1991) address to the Twelfth World Congress of Sociology in which she argues that 'international sociology aims at no less than the mobilisation of Humanity itself as one self-conscious social agent.' This study is situated in this tradition of sociological analysis which, rather old-fashioned as it is, seeks to better understand the world so that we might change it for the better. De Swaan, writing in this spirit, suggested that

> sociology, if it is to remain true to its mission as a synthetic science of human society, has arrived at a point where it must transcend the institutionalised disciplinary limits of national and area studies and even go beyond comparative research in order to confront the emerging reality of world society. This vast task should be taken up by focusing on the study of the transnational relations that increasingly link human beings in a global network. (undated: 25–6)

This study is a small contribution to this project.

Social policy as an academic discipline or field of study has, we suggest, been rather slower to wake up to the impact of the new world (dis)order on its subject matter than some economists, political scientists, international relations students and sociologists. On the other hand, because of its commitment to welfare and the concern of its practitioners to not only analyse existing policy but prescribe better ways in which human needs might be articulated and met, its potential contribution to the new global politics is immense. The subject did break out of its Fabian reformism and national ghetto some years ago with the development of comparative analysis. Studies that have focused on the diverse ways in which developed western societies provide for social needs have multiplied in recent years (Castles and Mitchell, 1990; Esping-Andersen, 1990; Ginsburg, 1992; Mishra, 1990). The worlds of welfare capitalism in the West can now be divided into liberal (free market) regimes (USA), conservative corporatist or social market economy regimes (Germany), social democratic regimes (Sweden, as was), and the hybrid liberal collectivist or labourite regimes (UK, Australia). The feminist inspired contribution to the literature has suggested criteria of women friendliness against which to compare welfare states. Siaroff (1994) has concluded that there are four OECD regime types: three that are similar to Esping-Andersen's and one, 'late female mobilization welfare states', which neither encourages women's work nor supports women's caring (e.g. Spain, Switzerland, Japan). Systematic comparison of the ethnic minority friendliness of welfare regimes has yet to be concluded but Williams's (1995) work is relevant here.

To these western regimes must be added the now collapsed regimes of state bureaucratic collectivism and their replacements which elsewhere (Deacon, 1992) we have argued include not only regimes similar to those in Western Europe, but also a new post-communist conservative corporatism. Very recently comparative social policy has also begun to describe the distinctive state management features of South East Asian welfare regime types (Goodman and Peng, 1996; Jones, 1993). The countries of Latin

America have been shown to offer a choice between neo-liberal and social democratic models (Huber, 1996).

Within the European context it is now being recognized that the future of welfare state diversity within the European Community will be affected by the supranational social policies of the Commission. The levelling down and up towards a social market economy regime type (rather than liberal or social democratic) is suggested together with an appreciation that redistribution of resources for meeting needs is now taking place between member states. Offe (1991) has argued that changing patterns of work within Europe suggest the need for the social policy of the Community as a whole to break from a work based entitlement to a citizenship entitlement of basic income or social dividend. A similar case has been put to encourage a flexible labour market in the former USSR (Standing, 1991).

Despite these useful excursions into *comparative* and European analysis, social policy writers have had little to say about the globalization phenomenon. George (1988) did begin to address the issue of wealth, poverty and starvation on an international scale and MacPherson and Midgley (1987) addressed issues of social policy in the Third World. Some time ago Deutsch addressed the idea that we should move from national welfare states to an international welfare system and concluded optimistically that the trends 'moving towards . . . [an] international welfare system are larger and stronger than the forces moving in the opposite direction' (1981: 437). Townsend (1993) has more recently contributed to the analysis of poverty on an international basis. In a subsequent paper with Donkor he concluded rather polemically that

> Far from scrapping the institutions and services which have become known as the 'welfare state' or targeting them in ways currently recommended by monetarists they should be improved and modernised, and the most vital parts of the basic infrastructure extended by stages to the poorest countries . . . The problems of the industrial revolution and exploitative forms of capitalism led in the late nineteenth century to the establishment of the welfare state in one country after another. The problems in the late twentieth century of the international market and the replacement of sovereignty and empire by international hierarchical power will demand the establishment of forms of an international welfare state. (1995: 20)

There has not yet been a sustained intellectual political project in this area. It is our argument that the collapse of the cold war, the consequent proliferation of little states, and the consequential increase in the importance of supranational, regional and global economic and political processes lead now to the need for social policy analysis to change gear from a focus solely on national and comparative social policy to a focus that gives equal weight to supranational and global social policy.

To embark on the study of the globalization of social policy the intellectual resources of social policy analysis need to join forces with those active in development studies in order to further the analysis of the obstacles to and the prospects for the better meeting of the human needs of everyone. The work of Doyal and Gough (1991) represents potentially the meeting point of comparative social policy with development studies upon which the further development of the study of the globalization of the social policy could be based. Their elaboration, within the subject of social policy, of the concept of basic human needs as being constituted of the twin elements of health and autonomy parallels the emergence within the United Nations Human Development Project of a human development index constituted of the three elements of income, longevity and literacy (UNDP, 1990). Although there is still controversy over the ways of defining and measuring human needs we do have useful frameworks for both measuring and comparing how good different types of welfare regimes are at enabling those needs to be met. In principle, therefore, we should be able to work, through appropriate mechanisms of transnational redistribution, regulation and provision, to increase the number of good welfare regimes in the world.

In another sense the tools of the subject of development studies need now to be used by social policy analysts if the discipline is to embrace the globalization process. The social policy of a country or locality is no longer wholly shaped (if it ever was) by the politics of the national government. It is increasingly shaped, as was suggested earlier, by the implicit and explicit social policies of numerous supranational agencies, ranging from global institutions like the World Bank and the International Monetary Fund, through supranational bodies such as the OECD and the European Commission, to supranational non-government agencies like OXFAM. These agencies, as we shall see in Chapters 3, 4 and 5, work in contradictory directions and are, we shall argue, increasingly the locus of the future ideological and political struggles for better global and national social policies. The lessons learned from the African and Latin American experience of structural adjustment policies need to be appreciated by analysts of the social policy of developed economies.

The discipline or academic activity of social policy has made a considerable contribution to the understanding of the processes that have hitherto shaped national social policy. In turn these analyses have contributed to effective political action either through institutional processes or through engagement in social movement activity. The discipline, in association with development studies specialists, should now embark on an analytical and political project focused on the globalization of social policy. The project should embrace, as we have already suggested, both the emergence of a global social policy between nations (transnational redistribution, regulation and provision) and the intervention in national social policy of global supranational agencies. This book is a contribution to that project. At the same time the book, by reporting the empirical study of the role of international organizations in the making of post-communist welfare, is also a contribution to the sociology of international relations and to the understanding of economic processes as the outcome of political choices made within supranational forums and organizations.

Welfare states and global economic competition

If there were no other reason for exploring the implications of the global-ization process for social policy, both as an academic discipline and as a field of political practice, the fact that, through global economic com-petition, welfare regimes of different kinds are pitted against each other would be reason enough.

A vast literature, of which perhaps Esping-Andersen (1994), Kosonen (1995), Scharpf (1995), Gough (1996) and the earlier Pfaller et al. (1991) are the most useful examples, points to the possible problems posed to the social democratic and conservative corporatist welfare states of Europe by the freeing of global regulations on finance capital and the increased free trade negotiated through GATT in the 1970s and 1980s. All concur that the golden age of the western welfare state was a consequence, under conditions of protected economies after the Second World War, of Keynesian economic management combined with the power of trade unions and social move-ments to shift resources either from capital to labour or from wages to welfare. While competition between firms was largely within one geographi-cal boundary the same rules could apply concerning the social costs to be borne by enterprises. Equally the techniques of economic management, such as changing interest rates on capital to encourage real job creation kinds of investment, could be used. Once global movements of capital took place and once governments consequently lost control of investment policies through Keynesian economic management, capital could in principle go 'regime shopping' and engage in 'social dumping' whereby firms leave areas where the taxation (for social purposes) is high.

Three kinds of response to this openness of economies to global trade have been identified (Esping-Andersen, 1994). Some social democratic welfare states like Sweden have attempted to maintain the commitment to welfare through job creation in the public sphere but doubts are increas-ingly raised about how viable this is as a permanent solution. At the other extreme liberal welfare states have embarked quite enthusiastically on deregulation and wage lowering to attract global investment in lower wage jobs. The USA, which opens its borders to low wage workers from the Third World, has gone furthest down this road. Conservative corporatist regimes like Germany have shed jobs in the less productive sectors and have, in effect, gone for a strategy of jobless growth with investment in high producing firms. A dualization of society has of course ensued. Gough (1996) has suggested that in understanding the impact on welfare policy of competitiveness it is necessary to examine the impact of the welfare effort on the supply of capital, the supply of labour and the productivity of capital and labour. At the same time the welfare effort should be unpicked and the impact of taxation should be considered separately from the nature of particular programmes and separately from the outcomes of welfare expenditure. If analysed in this way the relationship between welfare effort and competitiveness is seen to be complex. One outcome of little welfare effort could be crime and the consequential costs to firms of security. As an example pointing in the opposite direction, payroll taxes (e.g. social insurance contributions) will be a disincentive to invest. Pay-as-you-go (PAYG) pensions might reduce personal savings and, therefore, new investment.

Kosonen (1995) has concluded that there are two choices to be made in response to the competitive pressures. One is to follow the low wage, low social costs, inequality generating strategy of deregulation. The other is to invest in welfare for a productivity advantage.

> Comparative evidence demonstrates that high-productivity countries may uphold competitiveness despite high wages and employers' social costs . . . higher productivity of the workforce makes accidents, absenteeism and turnover more expensive and encourages an increase in social welfare programmes to strengthen the internal labour markets. In addition increased social welfare provisions may increase worker motivation and generate greater social consensus, both of which are conducive to further productivity gains. (1995: 15)

A likely outcome of both strategies – the low wage, low unemployment strategy and the high wage, high productivity, higher unemployment strategy – is however a dualization of the workforce, certainly globally and often within one country. On the one hand are those still protected in terms of insurance based benefits and on the other those exposed to a Hobson's choice between low wages and parsimonious means tested social assistance – at best. This increasing flexibilization of the workforce (Burrows and Loader, 1994), the shift towards shedding the low wage periphery, the casualization of work contracts, are generating a challenge to the traditional social security structures and mechanisms that lie at the heart of many European welfare states. The danger is that the workplace based social insurance systems, if they can be adapted to new circumstances, become a privileged possession of the insiders and that a residualized means tested assistance becomes the lot of the outsiders. Alternative strategies for social policy in the income maintenance field have therefore emerged for serious discussion in recent years. Two examples might be given at this point. One is the citizen's or participation income which would provide for all a minimum, guaranteed social entitlement. Having dispensed this, governments would then be free to wash their hands of further social obligations in the income maintenance field. Citizens would find what casualized or non-casualized employment they could to supplement this minimum and provide privately for additional benefits in times of sickness and old age. An alternative strategy, but one that is equally far removed from the Bismarckian employment based social insurance system, is that adopted in Australia. Here adequate tax based benefits (and services) are provided but better-off citizens are targeted out via means and assets tests which are set at a fairly high level, thus retaining some middle class attachment to welfare policy.

What is being hinted at in this very cursory and introductory exploration of the subject is that global capitalist economic competition may indeed have eroded for all time the conditions that generated the universalistic welfare states of social democracy or conservative corporatism. The ethnically homogeneous social democracies of Scandinavia, and the workplace certainties of conservative corporatisms, have gone. The danger is that we are faced with a world of liberalism and residualism, consequent inequality, and low pay for many. Two, at least, alternative strategies for welfare might present themselves: (1) a citizenship income entitlement as some kind of concrete welfare foundation (set at a level appropriate to the country) upon which flexible inequality could be built; or (2) a liberalism with a human face, a social liberalism with means and assets tested tax based social provision. In the chapters that follow we shall attempt to discover what possible futures for welfare are being hatched in the forums that now make global social policy and whether these two number among them.

The terrain of global social policy analysis

We have argued in the previous section that the focus of the discipline of social policy should shift from *comparative* to *supranational* or *global* social policy. In doing this it should combine its intellectual resources with those of the discipline of development studies. Together this could lead to a more effective intervention by experts within these disciplines within the supranational and global forums where issues of social policy are increasingly decided. Together they could better act as interpreters of need between social movements and supragovernmental agencies. The thrust of this argument is that the better focus of the (flawed) universal class of intellectuals is no longer the nation state but global institutions.

This section sets out in a little more detail the terrain of global social policy analysis. A systematic analysis of the phenomenon of global social policy could be constructed by proceeding through the following six steps:

1 *Pressures for globalization* and supranationalism and the consequent reduction of national sovereignty in the shaping of social policy could be investigated and analysed.
2 Traditional practical and analytical *issues* within the practice and study of social policy such as those of social justice could be reconceptualized at a global level.
3 A *typology* of supranational and global social policy *mechanisms* could be constructed for analytical purposes.
4 Possible *goals for global reformists* wishing to increase global justice might be formulated.
5 The *obstacles* to both the processes of globalization and the realization of a global social reformist project could be delineated.
6 The alternative *political strategies* available to global actors shaping global social policy could be distinguished.

All of these empirical, analytical, theoretical and political endeavours in the new terrain of global social policy would have implications for the analysis of national and comparative social policy. This new intellectual activity should enable hypotheses to be constructed and tested regarding not only the emergence of transnational social policy but also the possible futures of diverse welfare regimes. In this section a few of these parts of the map (i.e. steps 1, 2 and 3) of a global social policy analysis will be elaborated in more detail. Brief comments on steps 4, 5 and 6 will be made but these are explored in more detail in Chapter 6.

Pressures towards the globalization of social policy

Pressures leading to the globalization of social policy have already been reviewed in the first section of this chapter. They included the end of the cold war, increased global economic competition, and the challenge now posed to global capitalism to regulate itself in the interests of human need. Also of importance is the dissolving frontiers phenomenon analysed elsewhere by Vobruba (1994). He points to the pressures for economic migration and the emergence of common transborder environmental threats leading to the necessity of formulating transnational social policy. As we have seen, however, these pressures do not lead automatically to the adoption of supranational or global solutions. National and regional self-interest and protectionism are alternative strategies available to governments. Supranationalization can be resisted. There might not be any global political actors of vision to seize the opportunity. These obstacles to global policy making are examined later.

Social policy issues in a global context

Standard texts within the subject of social policy not only describe and analyse particular social services such as medical care, housing and income maintenance and the social problems within these fields, but also address at a higher level of abstraction a number of social policy issues. The way these issues have been formulated and the exact nuances given to their analysis vary according to the theoretical framework of the policy analyst. Nevertheless, cutting through and across the liberal, social democratic, Marxist, feminist, anti-racist and post-structuralist perspectives on the 'welfare state' are a number of issues about which all the perspectives have something to say. These may be listed as:

Social justice   What is meant by this concept and how might governments and other political and social actors best secure it? Trade-offs between social justice and economic competitiveness are a central concern here. Processes and mechanisms of rationing also feature.

Citizenship   What is meant by, especially, the social elements of citizenship rights and entitlements and what are the processes of inclusion and exclusion at work?

Universality and diversity   How might social justice and social citizenship be secured for all universally while, at the same time, acknowledging and meeting the very diverse needs of different social groups? Issues of discrimination and equal opportunities arise here.

Autonomy and guarantees   To what extent do economic, political and social arrangements facilitate the autonomous articulation and meeting of social needs by individuals and groups from below and at a local level, and how might this autonomy trade off against social guarantees through social provision from above? Issues of subsidiarity and regionalism arise here.

Agency of provision   Should the state, the market, the organizations of civil society, the family provide for the welfare needs of the population, and in what mix? The vexed questions of the level of public expenditure and the proportion of GNP devoted to the welfare effort feature here.

Public and private   A subtheme of this concerns the extent to which the business of care is and should be a private matter (more often than not undertaken by women for men) or a public matter (within which the gendered division of care becomes a matter of political debate). There is often an ethnic dimension to this analysis too.

Different social policy analysts might organize the list slightly differently but there would be a fair measure of agreement that these issues are the stock-in-trade of our field of study and our political concern.

If the state is withering in importance, if the power of supranational agencies is increasing, if, through migration and global economic inter-connectedness, the world is becoming one place how then should we reconceptualize these issues at a supranational and global level? Let's take each in turn.

Justice between states   At one level this provides no major conceptual problems. Social policy analysis, thinking globally, would simply join forces with development studies specialists and analyse the extent to which the world was a 'fair' place. Data concerning social inequalities within and between nations are now much more accessible and will be reviewed in Chapter 2. Here we will be able to describe the extent to which the welfare needs of the world's population are increasingly being met but also the extent to which they are being met inequitably.

At another level, however, the issue of transnational justice raises difficult analytical and political questions. The Rawlsian conception of justice appropriate to a capitalist state (whereby that inequality is justified that raises the level of the poorest) becomes problematic at a global level. Attempts have been made to reformulate this principle between states (O'Neill, 1991). Equally the political processes of democratic class struggle within small relatively homogeneous states in parts of the North and West that have secured a degree of social justice are not easily replicable on a global terrain, and moreover competition between such relatively just states and those not 'burdened' with the same degree of social justice is, as we have seen, in danger of undermining the local social justice achievements of parts of the North and West.

Put simply, how can an alliance be constructed between the poor of the South and the better-off poor of the North that struggles to achieve an improvement in the conditions of the poor of the South without unacceptably undermining the relatively better-off poor of the North and in ways which are economically and ecologically sustainable? How, in other words, will the social commitments of European social and economic policy not only, as they are doing, secure a greater degree of justice within the territory of the EU but also secure this commitment in other parts of the globe? By what social and political processes will the uncertain global alliances from below translate into the construction of global political institutions that seek to secure an acceptable measure of global justice? Daunting as this prospect might seem, it is part of the argument of this book that we are already witnessing this process and the progress it is making. The World Bank is beginning to be concerned to secure a fairer world. The discourse between the Commission of the EU and the Directorate of the World Trade Organization is about regulating capitalism globally to prevent social dumping, to minimize global economic migration and to secure, therefore, greater global political security. The analysis of the emergence of a global social policy concerned with transnational justice is dealt with in Chapter 3. The future prospects for this process and the alternative political strategies that are available are addressed again in the concluding chapter of the book.

Supranational citizenship   Thinking about the concept of citizenship in a globalizing world only serves to highlight the double-sidedness of the concept. On the one hand citizenship within the context of democratic capitalist society is about securing rights and entitlements for all within a state. On the other hand it is about excluding from the benefits of citizenship those outside the state. In the last years of the twentieth century we have seen a simultaneous deepening and strengthening of citizenship rights and entitlements within some states and tightening of restrictions on migrants seeking access to the citizenship rights of many of those same northern and western countries. Overlaying this development has been the emergence of supranational citizenship rights and entitlements within subglobal regions, notably Europe (Meehan, 1993). At the same time such subglobal regions act in an exclusionary way towards complete outsiders (Sivanandan, 1993).

To begin the process of reconceptualizing citizenship at a supranational level it is useful to return to Marshall's division of the concept into the components of political rights (the right to vote), civil rights (the right to equal treatment before the law) and social rights (the right to a fair share of the nation's resources). While these rights and associated duties were developed historically in capitalist societies within one state, the globalization process is generating the emergence of supranational citizenship entitlements of all three kinds. This process has developed furthest in the

European context. The 30-odd member states of the Council of Europe provide for their citizens the right to equal treatment before the Court of Human Rights in Strasbourg with regard to human rights issues. No supranational political and social rights are guaranteed for the citizens of the member states of the Council of Europe but states are encouraged to ratify (and most have ratified) the Council of Europe's Social Charter which lays down a range of minimum social rights and entitlements (see Chapter 3). For the smaller number of states of the EU a plethora of political, civil and social rights now exists and is enshrined in the supranational law of the community (Meehan, 1993). Sceptics of the supranationalization of social citizenship rights at a European level point however to the impossibility of a supranational body declaring such rights without it also at the same time having the power to direct and redirect economic resources to secure those declared social rights in reality (Closa, 1995).

At a global level the UN Declaration of Human Rights embraces social questions but as yet there is no legal enforcement of these rights in member states of the UN and no individual rights of petition. The International Court of Justice at The Hague serves so far only to regulate disputes between states and not between individuals and their state.

There are other ways in which the social aspects of citizenship are, in a piecemeal way, developing an international dimension. Numerous bilateral agreements exist between states regarding the reciprocal recognition of social security and other social rights (Chapter 4). At a global level the United Nations High Commission for Refugees assumes responsibility for the livelihood of stateless persons. At the same time as this process of the supranationalization and globalization of social citizenship rights gathers pace there are many examples of the tightening of access to national citizenship Within the process of the emergence of new states in Eastern Europe and the former Soviet Union there are several examples (Estonia, the Czech Republic, the former Yugoslavia, etc.) where citizenship laws have been drawn up to exclude either former colonizing citizens (Russians in Estonia) or oppressed minorities (Romany population in the Czech Republic) from access to some of the benefits of citizenship. An important factor here is the possible consequential exclusion from social assistance rights.

These issues flowing from the reconceptualization of social citizenship at a supranational level will be developed further in Chapters 4 and 5. There it will be argued that two parallel processes are taking place. Within the realm of insurance based social rights and entitlements an internationalization is taking place to accommodate a globally mobile skilled workforce, whereas in the realm of means tested social assistance a Poor Law localizing process is taking place where not only supranational bodies but states are shedding responsibility onto impoverished localities.

Global universality and diversity   Within the context of the analysis of social policy within one country the contemporary problematic was expressed recently as 'how to facilitate the universal meeting of diverse human needs' (Williams, 1994). This cogently captures the tension between the continued commitment to a morality of universalism typical of social policy analysts and the new sensitivity to diversity and difference that critical and post-modern social policy analysis has emphasized.

Projected onto a supranational and even global scale the problematic is further complicated. In the first place we can't readily assume a global commitment to the values of universalism which policy makers might use to guide their thinking in the context of diversity. Gellner (1994) has suggested that three competing world views presently vie for ascendancy. First is ethical relativism, very much a reflection of the collapse of the certainties of the socialist project. Second is fundamentalism of various kinds where place and reward are largely prescribed. Third, and only one among the three, is liberalism which still seeks after some notion of truth and within which paradigm the rationale discourse concerning justice, equality and universalism can take place.

While the search for rational truth and the assertion of fundamentalism do seem implacably opposed as world views, there is a dialogue between relativists and rational truth seekers. Within this context Bauman (1993) has recently argued that the new epoch of postmodernism creates a new space for moral discourse. Modernism of the capitalist and state socialist kind had dispensed with moral judgements and discourse. The best order would follow inexorably from the pursuit of one of these mirror image modernist projects. With the crisis in both projects the moral purpose of policy reasserts itself. Policy making, the regulation of capitalism globally, is called upon to justify itself against ethical concerns.

If this is so it explains the re-emergence, after a silence of decades, of scholarly and political interest in the charters of human rights. Regardless of the dispute between relativists, fundamentalists and rational truth seekers, the fact is that the emerging supranationalism of the current period is rationalist and is concerned to inject a morality of universalism into supranational and global policy making. The UN Charter of Human Rights and the much expanded Council of Europe's Charter of Human Rights are now taking on a character against which capitalism East and West, North and South, should be judged. Member states must pass these tests for full world membership.

Taking this one step further it can be argued that social rights are now on the supranational agenda. Where once the capitalist West could focus only on political and civil (legal) rights in its challenge to the 'communist' East which discounted these rights in favour of social rights, now, with the collapse of the 'communist' project, global capitalism is being called upon to be judged by its capacity to secure legal, political *and* social rights universally (albeit in diverse ways). In Chapter 3 we shall review the development of social rights as an issue being addressed by supranational agencies. This is not to suggest the project is plain sailing. Clearly the phenomenon of ethnic cleansing and the rise of xenophobia pull in the opposite direction (Chapter 5). At the same time this makes even more urgent the need to secure the power of international regulatory authority to intervene when political, civil and social rights are denied because of ethnic or cultural difference.

Subsidiarity and supranationalism: autonomy and guarantees Before the collapse of 'communism', standard texts comparing western capitalism and state socialism (Davis and Scase, 1985) used to point to the apparent trade-off between individual autonomy, that is the right to articulate social needs from below, on the one hand (a feature of capitalism) and social guarantees, that is the universal commitment of the often paternalistic state to provide for social needs from above, on the other (a feature of communism). Projected onto a transnational terrain the same dichotomy might be observed. The more states have the autonomy to determine what and how social needs might be met within the country, the less there is the guarantee of their meeting those needs, and vice versa. Within the context of European supranationalism the debate is currently expressed in terms of the concept of subsidiarity. Subsidiarity, a principle now enshrined in the post-Maastricht policy making process, provides for decisions to be taken above a particular local, regional or national level only if they can better be made above that level. Conversely decisions (and often provision) should be as local as possible.

The principle of subsidiarity only serves, however, to beg the question as to which bits of social policy making *are* best determined supranationally. The choice between a policy of providing transnationally the means by which states can guarantee certain social rights, and a policy whereby states have the autonomy to make their own policy and provision, exemplifies the point. Any policy which provides for transnational redistribution and for the cross-national regulation of the rules of capitalist competition *must* be better taken *above* the level of the state if guarantees of subsidy to impoverished areas and guarantees against social dumping are to be secured. Moreover it should be possible to construct decision making processes to connect the local (articulation of need) to the supranational (provision of resources and rules) which aim at simultaneously guaranteeing provision and facilitating autonomy.

This process of the erosion of the autonomous power of states to determine policy in favour of the guarantees of supranational intervention and regulation is taking place not only within the region of Europe but also, as this book demonstrates, at a global level. The recent questioning by UN bodies of the previously hallowed right of sovereignty is but one expression of this. This returns us to the debate signalled earlier and reported in Chapters 5 and 6 as to whether the supranational interveners are on the side of the civilizing angels or the global imperialist gangsters.

Global welfare mix (Agency of Provision) In the preceding sections we have tried to show how the policy issues with which social policy analysts

are concerned take on interestingly different dimensions when transposed
from the national to the supranational and global terrain. Social justice
becomes transnational redistribution, citizenship issues become a matter of
social exclusion, the search for universalism in the context of diversity turns
into a global codification of human and social rights, the guaranteeing of
social rights becomes an issue of supranational regulation against social
dumping. Does the policy issue of the agency mix in social provision take
on a new dimension when examined in a supranational context?

This brings us back to the question of global competition between kinds
of welfare states. One paradigm that still has purchase on policy makers is
that economic competitiveness and welfare state expenditure are trade-offs.
The more economic competition takes place in an unregulated way, therefore, the less state welfare expenditure there might be. This paradigm seems
especially to connect to policy debates about the level of taxation on firms
and the costly regulations under which they have to work. If this paradigm
prevails as a result of increased global competition then the development of
supranational regulation will be slow and the welfare mix is likely to shift
away from the state. There is evidence, as we noted earlier, that a competing paradigm might replace the previous one. This argues that certain
kinds of state expenditure are beneficial to capital either in terms of
investment in education, or in terms of the multiplier effect of the con-
sumption of social security recipients, or in terms of securing political
stability. This would lead to greater government intervention. In Chapter 3
we will examine the extent to which this paradigm shift is taking place
within and between global agencies such as the IMF, the World Bank and
the OECD. One conclusion from this debate will be that welfare state
expenditure might be affordable if consumers and not firms pay for it
(Scharpf, 1995). This either leaves each country to its own devices in terms
of whether it agrees to trade wages for welfare or, alternatively, suggests
that a welfare orientated global regulation that did not want to damage the
competitiveness of firms is likely to focus on the level of public not
enterprise taxation.

The process of globalization is also likely to support the tendency away
from national provision to local and regional. We have already explained
this pincer movement of global and local eroding the state. Within this
process there might be a case for the social policy obligations of states and
firms to be carried out by the locality. Greater moves to federalism are a
likely consequence of this process. The erosion of state and workplace
welfare might also lead to the strengthening of civil society. More non-
governmental organization activity seems to be a consequence of the
process of the erosion of the state. The case studies in Chapters 4 and 5 will
demonstrate how far these expectations are being realized in practice.

Who services whom globally   Social policy analysis has demonstrated the
gender and racial divisions of caring (Williams, 1987). Women care for men
and black people service white. In general women do more of the care for

men and dependants when it is provided in the home (although there are exceptions both between countries and in terms of the category of person cared for). In general there is a slight shift in the gendered division of care if it takes place in public institutions. Class and ethnic differences between women become important here. Some analysis of especially western welfare states has pointed to the role of black minorities and migrant workers in undertaking a greater share of the lower skilled caring jobs in public institutions.

The globalization process is leading to the further widening of the gender, class and racial division of caring. In the USA (an example of a liberal regime towards which the world might be being impelled) white middle class professional men and women have their caring duties undertaken by black migrant (often illegally migrant) women from the poorer South. The analysis would apply equally for the public (and regulated private) institutions that provide for the care of dependants. The other side of the coin of this phenomenon of mobile, usually black, labour meeting the welfare needs of white people in privileged countries is the remittances returned to the South (and East) by these mobile workers. The remittances can contribute a significant percentage of the GNP of labour exporting countries. Families likely to be in receipt of such remittances may well be debarred from receipt of local social assistance.

This brief exposition serves to show how complex the question of caring relationships becomes once transposed onto a global terrain. The question is posed as to how, if it is desired, might regulations, transnational redistributions, or other policies be fashioned to lessen these global inequities in caring.

In this section we have reviewed the ways in which the policy issues of interest to social policy analysts might need to be reconceptualized in the light of the globalization process. Certain policy prescriptions at transnational level have been hinted at. In the next section we conceptualize three kinds of global social policy response.

Global social redistribution, regulations and provision

A very simple *typology of global social policy responses and mechanisms* would first separate out global intervention in *national* social policy and secondly distinguish three forms of global social policy, namely transnational *redistribution*, supranational *regulation* and global or supranational *provision*. All three types of supranational activity already take place but often these are confined within one regional economic trading bloc such as the European Union. Elements of all three are, however, to be found at a global level. The economic assistance from the West to the East may fall short of a Marshall Plan but it is motivated in part by the wish to secure social stability in the former Soviet Union. Concern to prevent social dumping by multinational capital does now appear on the agenda of the World Bank. The United Nations High Commission for Refugees does operate an elementary system of global citizenship entitlements for stateless persons. Within this intellectual map the scholarly work presently being undertaken on the emerging social policy of the European Union could be a special case and exemplar of a future global social policy analysis and practice. Recent work by Kleinman and Piachaud (1993) discussing the issues of subsidiarity, citizenship rights and democracy in the emerging supranational European social policy can be transposed onto a global terrain. The same concerns apply: at what level can policy best be formulated; how can national citizenship be reconciled with supranational mobility; and how can national democratic constituencies be recast to ensure meaningful accountability at supranational level?

Fleshing out this initial conceptualization requires us to analyse which supranational and global agencies are actors in the emerging processes of influencing national policy and engaging in transnational *redistribution*, supranational *regulation* and supranational and global *provision*. Coupled with this we need an analysis of the *instruments* with which agencies and organizations acting above the level of the state can redistribute resources, influence and regulate national social policy and international competition, and contribute to supranational and global policy and provision. A moment's reflection on this topic leads to the appreciation that the subject matter is extraordinarily complex and that it is in a very rapid process of evolution. There are a very large number of agencies using a variety of instruments to push and pull country social policy and practice in often very different directions and seeking to impose very different degrees of regulation on international competition.

Table 1.1 which focuses on global intervention in national policy, captures the idea of the web of interconnectedness that, say, an East European country wishing to join Europe finds itself within in the sphere of income maintenance policy. This clearly demonstrates the contending influences of say the IMF, concerned to balance the state budget, with say the ILO concerned to seek the adoption of decent social security conventions. The tension between the budget balancing requirements of the IMF and the expenditure requirements of the Social Charter of the Council of Europe is another example. These examples and others will, of course, be developed in more detail later in the book (Chapters 3 and 4).

Table 1.2 focuses on the global social policy mechanisms of redistribution and regulation and provides an initial indication of the most important global and regional agencies engaged in those aspects of supranational policy and the instruments with which they either facilitate redistribution or regulate activity. An important contrast is shown up here between the EU, where between-country redistribution accompanies free trade, and the North American Free Trade Association, which while freeing trade doesn't engage in compensatory social redistribution (or even significant social regulation) (Grinspin and Cameron, 1993). Of note also in

Table 1.1 *Some contending influences on national income maintenance policy in the European region*

Agency	Type of influence
All countries	
International Monetary Fund	Public expenditure limitations as loan conditions affects income maintenance budget
World Bank	Advice on social 'safety net' policy and social security expenditure; loans on condition of social reform
International Labour Office	Conventions on social security systems; advice on tripartite forms of government
Countries within the Council of Europe	
Council of Europe	Obligatory Charter of Human Rights; subject to Strasbourg Court of Human Rights
	Optional Social Charter; subject to independent expert judgements
	Optional conventions on social security
Countries within the EU	
EU	Obligatory Social Chapter; subject to Luxembourg Court of Justice
	Participation in Social Exclusion Project
	Net loser/winner in redistribution of Structural Funds

this table is the lack of power the World Trade Organization has in the social redistribution or social regulation field. The comments in the table indicate where current international debate and discussion on the issue of developing global social regulatory mechanisms have reached. These issues, of course, will be dealt with in greater detail in Chapters 3, 4, 5 and 6.

An important complexity arises if we turn to the *social provision* afforded by supranational and global authorities and agencies. Little direct provision of services yet operates at supranational level although the work of the UNHCR is an exception. We can however speak of the *empowerment* of citizens that some supranational bodies facilitate. One of the supranational instruments, identified in Figure 1.2, operates through the rights conferred on individual citizens by legal authorities existing at supranational level. Government policy and practice within the European region, for example in the spheres of social security, the right to social assistance, the equal treatment of men and women as well as human rights generally, has now to take account of the legal judgements of both the European Court of Justice in Luxembourg and the Council of Europe's Court of Human Rights in Strasbourg. Elizabeth Meehan (1993) has documented the impact of the Luxembourg Court on aspects of the social rights of citizens of the European Union. Davidson (1993) has recently reviewed some of the judgments with human rights implications of the Strasbourg Court. As yet individual citizens globally do not have recourse to the UN International Court of Justice in The Hague. This is reserved for disputes of a territorial kind between states or for war crime tribunals. In principle, however, and not

Table 1.2 *Supranational and global redistribution and regulation*

Agency	Instrument					
	Raise revenue from citizens or business	Raise revenue from states[1]	Expend money on some basis of social need	Lend money on non-market terms	Capacity to influence national social policy	Social regulation of trade
UN[2]	✗ (not yet)	✓	✓	✗	✓	✗ (not yet)
World Bank	✗	✓	✓	✓	✓	✗ (not yet)
IMF	✗	✓	✗	✗	✓	✗
OECD	✗	✗	✗	✗	✓	✗
WTO	✗	✗	✗	?	✗ (not yet)	✗ (not yet)
EU	✗	✓	✓		✓	✓
NAFTA	✗	✗	✗	✗	✗	✗
ILO	✗	✗	✗	✗	✓	✓ (aspires to)

[1] By this is meant revenue over and above that needed just to fund the running of the organization.

[2] At this stage the UN is taken to be an umbrella body for all its social and other agencies, unless indicated separately. Chapter 3 analyses components of UN activity in more detail. The most important agencies through which the UN redistributes resources for social welfare purposes are UNICEF, UNDP, UNFAO, World Food Programme and UNHCR.

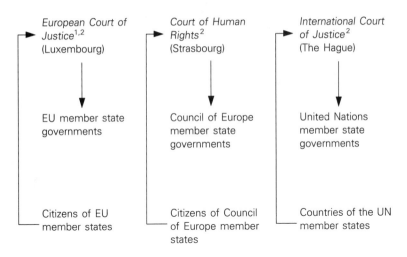

European Court of Justice[1,2] (Luxembourg)

Court of Human Rights[2] (Strasbourg)

International Court of Justice[2] (The Hague)

EU member state governments

Council of Europe member state governments

United Nations member state governments

Citizens of EU member states

Citizens of Council of Europe member states

Countries of the UN member states

[1] Competencies in the social rights sphere,
[2] Competencies in the human rights sphere

Figure 1.2   *The emergence of supranational citizenship in the sphere of human and social rights*

just as a utopian vision, such a court could in due course adjudicate on aspects of human and social rights of global citizens. Figure 1.2 captures this evolving situation.

Supranational and global agencies already, therefore, contribute to the shaping of national policy and the terms of international competition by laying down social policy conditions on governments for the receipt of financial assistance, or by redistributing resources between governments, or by establishing conventions and offering technical advice and assistance as a step towards legal social regulation. Also as individual citizens are empowered to appeal to an authority above the state, a world within which universal human and social rights are recognized and reinforced is in principle already possible. This book is concerned to document, through the case studies of Eastern European and post-Yugoslav countries, just how far these globalizing trends have reached and to argue in Chapter 6 the future direction they yet might take.

A global social reformist project: goals, obstacles and political strategies

Having identified the *pressures* and forces leading towards the globalization of the making of social policy, and explored the *issues* with which the subject is concerned transposed onto a global terrain, and noted the mechanisms of redistribution regulation and provision available to the supranational actors shaping social policy, it is appropriate to turn to the possible goals that might be aimed at by those working within and around these agencies.

At one level the global reformist project might be simply expressed as the further development of those systems of redistribution, regulation and provision just described. A global progressive taxation policy that levied disproportionally from the richer countries to fund social security schemes in the poorer would be an example of the first. An extension of the European project to socially regulate capitalism in all of the globe would be an example of the second. The increasing of the powers of supranational courts and the greater empowerment of citizens to use these against governments would be an example of the third. The extent to which these are emerging as identified goals of global reformists will be discussed in Chapter 3. The possibility of the realization of such goals in the context of a discussion of obstacles and alternative political strategies will be the subject of Chapter 6. At this stage we should simply note that the obstacles to the global social reformists' project of seeking to provide, regulate and redistribute at a global level are manifold. An initial short-list of the most obvious might be: national self-interest, to which democratic structures are still largely attached; subglobal regional economic trading competition with an associated drive to cost cutting and deregulation; the failure to agree globally on what might constitute global social progress; and the very real problems of sustainability. Social welfare achievements in the North and West may not be replicable on a global scale given finite energy and other resources. These obstacles may, of course, in turn generate the attempt by collective actors and social movements to find solutions to them. The obstacles and their possible solutions will be elaborated in Chapter 6.

It is one of the contentions of this initial exploration of the emerging field of global social policy analysis that implicitly, if not explicitly, alternative *political strategies* for global social reformism are being articulated and struggled over. *Free trade* and the breaking down of trade barriers in the interests of the economic growth of developing countries is a strategy favoured by some. The *reform of the World Bank* and the IMF so that these Bretton Woods agencies adopt a more thoroughgoing strategy of *social conditionality* in their lending strategies is another. Social intervention of this kind by supranational agencies to secure poverty programmes, to secure human and political rights and to protect minorities is a growing phenomenon. Others, not imagining that the world's paramount regulator of global capital can also secure the interests of the world's poor, are adopting the political strategy of the *struggle between global agencies*. To check the power of the Bank greater emphasis needs to be put on the work and power of the United Nations social agencies such as the ILO and the WHO to help governments shape social policy. Some argue the Bank and the Fund should be subject to UN authority.

Whether the reforming of the World Bank or the struggle between global agencies is regarded as the most appropriate strategy, both would depend on the development of *international social pressure* for the global reformist project to succeed. Whether this will be strengthened in the foreseeable future or whether there will be a collapse into identification with local and ethnic groupings is of course a fundamental question upon which any talk of a progressive global social policy depends. In Chapter 6 we will, in effect, identify the possibilities for *the construction of a global hegemonic project* that links social pressures across borders with actors in global and supranational agencies in the project of creating sustainable global social justice.

2

The State of the World's Welfare

This chapter presents an accessible summary for students of social policy of the state of the world's welfare. It captures the extent to which the welfare needs of the citizens of different countries of the world are met, the progress that has been made in this respect over the past decades, the extent of remaining and continuing inequalities North, South, East and West, and the degree to which these measures of welfare progress may or may not be associated with measures of economic development and political freedom. More than this, however, the chapter also attempts to capture the differences in the way the major developed countries of the world organize their strategies for meeting the needs of their citizens. The broad policy choices and welfare models that appear to operate in different kinds of developed countries are described. The connection between the first point – how far the world's welfare needs have been met – and the second – the different strategies for welfare adopted by different kinds of society – will be demonstrated. A key issue historically has been whether capitalist or socialist societies have better met the welfare needs of their citizens. In the current period this, of course, becomes an issue about whether those societies in the process of transforming themselves from 'socialism' to 'capitalism' are improving the welfare of their citizens. This issue is the third to be developed in the chapter.

Each of these three points could be and indeed has been the basis of whole texts. The aim here, however, is to bring together in one place the diverse strands of comparative social policy literature and development studies research as a backcloth for the discussion about the global discourse on the future of welfare that is reported in the subsequent chapters. This chapter, unlike the others which report original research and develop the subject matter conceptually, is entirely derivative of published sources. It draws heavily on Doyal and Gough's *Theory of Human Needs* (1991) on the annual *Human Development Reports* of the United Nations Development Programme, and on parallel state of the world reports of the World Bank, ILO and UNICEF. The comparison of developed welfare states is derivative of the work of Esping-Andersen (1990; 1994; 1996) among others. For the account of the social impact of economic restructuring on former socialist economies the chapter is heavily indebted to the work of the UNICEF Child Development Centre in Florence (UNICEF, 1993a; 1994; 1995b).

Charting welfare progress: basic needs and universal rights

To measure the extent to which a given country is making progress in terms of meeting the welfare needs of its citizens we need some indicators upon which broad agreement can be reached between countries and cultures. First let us reject measures of economic growth alone as necessarily measures of social welfare progress. Measures such as gross domestic product (GDP), it has long been argued, fail to count many activities that contribute to human welfare such as subsistence economic activity, informal economic activity, and the unpaid work of the domestic economy mostly done by women (Mies, 1986; Miles, 1985). Equally economic indicators include humanly wasteful activities such as warmongering and war preparation, questionably useful activities such as corporate advertising, and decidedly humanly harmful activities such as the production of pollutants and the operation of environmentally damaging processes. Recently a genuine progress indicator (GPI) has been constructed on an experimental basis which adds to the GDP the value of housework and subtracts from it the cost of pollution, loss of leisure, and resource depletion. By this indicator genuine progress has *not* been made in the USA since 1965 (New Economics Foundation, 1989). Second only to the issue of the shortcoming of economic measures is the issue of cultural relativity. Can a concept of human and social progress be agreed upon across the paradigms of fundamentalism, ethical relativism and rationalism? Doyal and Gough (1991) attempt to suggest that such a concept is possible. It is argued by them that in all cultures there is a basic human need to act effectively within one's culture and society. To do this individuals need a measure of health and autonomy. Health and autonomy are secured in culturally diverse ways through the meeting of intermediate needs for shelter, clothing, food, lovingness, security, education and so on. To this core argument about health and autonomy they add the case for critical autonomy which would enable individuals not only to act effectively in their own culture but also to critically challenge it or opt out from it. Multicultural education, for example, would be an intermediate need that would need to be satisfied to ensure the development in individuals of critical autonomy. Armed with some composite measure of the healthiness and capacity for autonomous action of citizens, countries could in principle be compared. Equally they could be compared in terms of the extent to which various intermediate needs are satisfied. While we are sympathetic to and use the Doyal and Gough analysis it is by no means clear that they do resolve the problem of whether societies working within different paradigms can agree on this question. In slave-owning society the welfare of slaves did not contribute to aggregate welfare. It is arguable that in Islamic states the welfare of women counts for less than that of men. In Soviet-style socialism, certainly in the 1920s and 1930s, the welfare of workers counted for more than the welfare of hostile classes. Equally critical autonomy may be regarded as a 'bad' rather than a 'good' in certain fundamentalist societies.

The United Nations Development Project devised in 1990 a measure of human progress that takes account both of the critique of economic activity as not necessarily, above a certain level, contributing much to human needs and of the central importance of health and autonomy (redefined as educational attainment) as measures of progress. The human development index (HDI) is a composite of longevity, educational attainment (made up of mean years of schooling and literacy rates), and a modified GDP which discounts most of the further growth of GDP above a certain level (UNDP, 1993a: 104). Countries are located on a relative scale within which comparisons can be made. The HDI does not readily capture the critical autonomy that is of concern to Doyal and Gough. Recent annual *Human Development Reports* have, however, experimented with a political freedom index (PFI) (UNDP, 1992) which is constituted of a number of variables such as freedom of expression, freedom to organize political parties, freedom of movement, equal treatment before the law, etc. The human development index can be disaggregated for gender, ethnicity and region where health, education and economic data that differentiate on these dimensions are available. It is this UN defined measure of social progress that we shall use, among others, when comparing the social progress of different kinds of developing and developed welfare states later in this chapter.

It might still be objected that the HDI measure and more surely the PFI measure are constructs of a particularly rationalist paradigm and ought not to have purchase in fundamentalist societies. In the last analysis this argument can't be won on rational grounds but must be won on the grounds of value choices about desirable social and political goals and processes. The Universal Declaration of Human Rights was adopted in 1948 without a dissenting voice. There is, however, a contradiction within the UN system whereby many member countries both belong to the UN which promulgates these human rights and also operate themselves under laws and customs that are derived from religious and other traditions that oppose them. While the HDI, and more surely the PFI, are open to the criticism that they are western liberal constructs, the response can only be either that there are value choices to be defended or, pragmatically, that for the moment the world, with the significant exception of Islamic fundamentalist states, is (a) moving in the direction of using these criteria to evaluate itself and (b) succeeding gradually in advancing human welfare according to these criteria. It is to these measures of progress that we now turn.

Progress and disparity in meeting human welfare needs

There is a vast and complex literature on the subject of the extent to which human and social progress is being made globally as measured by the kinds of criteria discussed above. There is contestation regarding evidence which suggests that societies organized economically and politically in particular

Table 2.1   *Social development in representative countries, 1990*

Regime type	Example country	GDP per capita (US$)	Life expectancy at birth (years)	Adult literacy (%)	Human development index
Developed countries					
Liberalism	USA	21,449	75.9	99.0	0.976
Conservative corporatism	France	16,051	76.4	99.0	0.972
Social democracy	Sweden	17,014	77.4	99.0	0.977
Late female mobilization	Japan	17,616	78.6	99.0	0.983
Former communist Eastern Europe	Hungary	6,116	70.9	97.0	0.887
Former communist Soviet Union	USSR	7,968	69.3	94.0	0.862
Developing countries					
Liberalism	Brazil	4,718	65.6	81.1	0.730
Social liberalism	Costa Rica	4,542	74.9	92.8	0.852
Pluralist democracy	India	1,072	59.1	48.2	0.309
Socialist authoritarian	China	1,990	70.1	73.3	0.566
SE Asian state managed capitalism	Malaysia	6,140	70.1	78.4	0.790
Islamic	Iran	3,253	66.2	54.0	0.557
Sub-Saharan Africa	Angola	840	45.5	41.7	0.143

Source: UNDP, 1993a

Table 2.2   *Gender and income inequality adjusted human development index for representative developed countries, 1990*

Country	HDI	Gender disparity adjusted HDI	Income distribution adjusted HDI
USA	0.976	0.824	0.943
France	0.972	0.864	0.938
Sweden	0.977	0.921	0.958
Japan	0.983	0.763	0.981

Source: UNDP, 1993a

ways are more successful than others in achieving human development goals. There have been innumerable theses written on the way in which the imperialist history of most of the world had locked certain developing societies into a dependency on the developed. Despite the enormity and complexity of the issues involved it is nonetheless possible to discern some identifiable trends and truths which this and subsequent sections of this chapter attempt to capture. There is no better attempt to affirm the sense of continuing global progress coexisting with continuing global shortcomings than the UN's *Human Development Report*. Key conclusions regarding the developing and developed world are captured in Tables 2.1 and 2.2, reproduced from the 1995 report (UNDP, 1995a). From the report it can be seen that the life expectancy of the world's population is increasing, that school enrolment rates are increasing, that in most regions of the world gross domestic product is increasing. In sum, with a few exceptions, notably in sub-Saharan Africa (which we will discuss below) and since 1989 in much of Eastern Europe and the former Soviet Union, in almost all countries of the world life is longer, more literate, and lived in the context of a greater abundance of resources. Equally this social progress coexists with enormous global economic inequity, which is widening between developed and developing countries, with the continued danger of starvation and food deprivation in many regions, and alongside new global social problems of forced migration, increased physical insecurity and exposure to organized crime. Inequalities within many countries are also increasing (UNDP, 1996).

A sense of the disparities between countries in terms of indicators of social progress can be seen from Table 2.1. This selects countries which, as we shall see later in the chapter, have significance in terms of their representation of kinds of developing and developed society. A number of features of this table are of note. First it is evident that, at the highest stages of human development, indicators of longevity and literacy do not enable us to distinguish finely between more or less successful types of developed welfare state. Some interesting differences are, however, shown up when the similar aggregate human development indices for the USA, France, Sweden and Japan are disaggregated by gender, as in Table 2.2.

It can be seen that Sweden, as a social democratic regime, is more successful at meeting the human development needs of women than the liberal USA regime or Japan. Similar differences are found if the country HDI is adjusted for a measure of income inequality in the country. Sweden meets more of the human needs of its citizens more equitably than the USA. This is also shown in Table 2.2.

Of significance is the figure for the USA disaggregated by ethnicity (not shown). Whereas the HDI for all citizens is 0.976, the index for white citizens is slightly higher and the index for black citizens is 0.880. This reflects among other things a differential life expectancy between white and black Americans of about six years. A more complex comparison and contrast between the welfare states of the USA, Sweden, France and Japan will be provided in a later section of this chapter.

The second observation is that the progress made in human development terms of the former Second World, the Soviet Union and Eastern Europe, was less than in the equivalent capitalist West. This will be explored further in a later section. By contrast a comparison between China, a developing country adopting a socialist strategy of development, and nearby India, adopting in the British image a pluralist democratic form of government, shows the clear advantage in human developmental terms of the socialist path at that level of development. Obviously the HDI does not capture the political unfreedoms of China.

On the South American continent there are clear contrasts between countries like Brazil or more especially Chile, under IMF pressure, adopting a more fundamentalist free market approach with minimum state regulation as a development strategy, and countries like Costa Rica with a greater continuing universalistic commitment of the state to welfare inter- vention (Esping-Andersen, 1994; 1996; Huber, 1996). As with social democracy in the developed world, so some social intervention by the state (which we will later define as social liberalism) pays off in terms of human development.

Malaysia, but it could have been Singapore, stands out as an example of what have come to be known as South East Asian tigers (Goodman and Peng, 1996; Jones, 1993; Richard et al., 1992). A high level of investment, particularly in education and training but also in health care and social security for the employed, has characterized the social policy of the tigers. Family networks of support underpin the system. There are clear pay-offs in both economic and social terms. By contrast our representative examples of Islamic states and sub-Saharan African states represent a less satisfactory picture. The male–female inequity of Islamic states and sub-Saharan African states represent a less satisfactory picture. The male–female inequity of Islamic states goes some way to explain the level of human development. The female literacy rate is 42 per cent compared with a country average of 54 per cent (UNDP, 1993a). The bleak situation in sub- Saharan Africa is a consequence of a compound of post-colonialism, intervention by the former racist South Africa in wars of liberation, ill- conceived structural adjustment policies of the 1980s, and unfavourable climatic conditions.

Narrowing social inequalities, widening economic inequalities

The picture painted in the previous section was very much a static one, a snapshot of the current situation. Charting economic and social develop- ment over time better enables us to get a sense of the narrowing inequalities in the world – which exist in the social and political spheres – and the widening inequalities in the sphere of economics. Table 2.3 summarizes some changes over two or three decades for our typical countries. Some points stand out. Everywhere life expectancy has lengthened although later data from much of the former Soviet Union and Eastern Europe since 1989 show a worsening situation (UNICEF, 1994). Everywhere educational enrolment at either secondary or tertiary level has increased. With extreme variations in rate GDP has grown everywhere except in our typical example of a sub-saharan country. Later data (UNDP, 1996) demonstrate, however, that between 1980 and 1993 there was a small decline in GDP per capita not only in sub-Saharan Africa (–1.0 per cent) but also in Latin America (–0.3 per cent), Eastern Europe and the former Soviet Union (–1.8 per cent), and among Arab states (–0.9 per cent). The greater social achieve- ments of Costa Rica compared with Brazil, of China compared with India are evident from this data set.

Table 2.3 *Social and economic trends in representative countries*

	Life expectancy at birth (years)		Education enrolment[1] (%)		Real GDP per capita (US$)	
	1960	1990	1965–70	1990	1960	1990
USA	69.9	75.9	40	70	9,983	21,449
France	70.3	76.4	18	37	5,344	16,051
Sweden	73.1	77.4	13	33	6,483	17,014
Japan	67.9	78.6	13	31	2,701	17,616
Hungary	68.1	70.9	13	15	–	6,116
Soviet Union	67.7	69.3	–	45[2]	–	7,968
Brazil	54.6	65.6	65	91	1,404	4,718
Costa Rica	61.6	74.9	76	77	2,160	4,542
India	44.0	59.1	49	68	617	1,072
China	47.1	70.1	66	88	723	1,990
Malaysia	53.9	70.1	62	75	1,783	6,140
Iran	49.5	66.2	52	83	1,985	3,253
Angola	33.0	45.5	–	–	1,308	840

[1] Primary and secondary for developing countries, tertiary for USA, France, Sweden, Japan, Hungary and Russia.
[2] 1993.

Source: UNDP, 1993a

The world is becoming a more equal place in terms of certain social indicators. A narrowing of the gaps between North and South is evident in terms of life expectancy under-five mortality rates, daily calorie supply, adult literacy and access to safe water (UNDP, 1993a). Even in those countries where GDP is now declining, the quality of life as measured by the HDI is increasing. As we explore in detail later, Eastern Europe and the former Soviet Union are exceptions to this. The relative HDI for the region has fallen by seven per cent between 1980 and 1993 (UNDP, 1996).

With 100 as the index for the North, average life expectancy in countries of medium human development shifted between 1960 and 1990 from 70 to 91. For countries of low human development the shift over the same period was from 62 to 76. Similar progress is charted in the other indicators mentioned.

There has however been a widening of the gap between the North and South in terms of GDP per capita. If 100 is the index for the North, real GDP per head shifted in countries of medium human development from 19 to 18, and in the case of countries of low human development from 11 to eight. Sub-Saharan Africa experienced the worst fall, from 14 in 1960 to eight in 1990. In this sense, the North is getting richer and the South poorer. The percentage of the world's GNP available to the North has shifted from 30 per cent in 1960 to 59 per cent in 1989. The poorest 20 per cent of the world's population in 1996 had access to only 1.4 per cent of the world's income, while the richest 20 per cent had access to 85 per cent of it (UNDP, 1996). The widening economic inequality between countries is accompanied by a widening of economic inequality within countries. The growth of economic inequality within countries has been particularly evident in countries following a neo-liberal path of economic development. Within the UK, now the most unequal country in the developed world, the real income of the poorest 10 per cent of the population fell by 20 per cent between 1979 and 1993 (UNDP, 1996). For some 14 East Asian countries the obverse was true. In Japan the share of the national income enjoyed by the poorest 20 per cent of the population doubled between 1960 and 1980.

The correlates of welfare progress: economic preconditions, economic overkill and political choice

If the world is becoming more equal in social and human development terms but is yet becoming more unequal economically, what does this say for the connection between social and economic progress? In one sense it simply reinforces the point made at the opening of this chapter regarding the uselessness of economic indicators as measures of human development. In this section we explore the relationship between economic growth and social welfare in more depth and the issue of the relationship between social and human development and political freedom.

A very early study of the comparative development of welfare states (Wilensky, 1975) correlated the relationship between welfare state effort and economic growth. The measure of welfare state effort – percentage of GNP spent on social security – was open to the charge that it measured also non-progress like the increased expenditure on unemployment benefit. The result was a direct correlation between the two. Economic growth was a precondition of social welfare, it was concluded. However at the higher end of economic development there were clearly problematic cases, in particular the USA which despite further economic growth was clearly a 'welfare state laggard'. Subsequent comparative social policy analysis has demonstrated that beyond a certain economic precondition level there is no necessary association between the nature of a country's welfare effort, its form of welfare organization and its welfare outcomes and economic level. Political choices matter and make a difference. The *Human Development Report* (UNDP, 1993a) has also concluded that there is, above a minimum level, no automatic link between GDP and human development. Several countries stand out as having a human development index far above that which would be suggested by their GNP. Among these are China and Costa Rica. Table 2.4 summarizes for our typical countries.

At the other end of the spectrum of economic growth it has, of course, been argued that there may be considerable diswelfare consequences of too much growth. New welfare problems such as the diseases of development,

Table 2.4   *The non-association between human development and economic development*

Country	GNP per capita rank minus HDI rank[1]	Performance on HDI relative to GNP
USA	4	
France	5	
Sweden	0	
Japan	2	
Hungary	24	Good
Russia	10	
Brazil	−17	Poor
Costa Rica	34	Good
India	12	
China	41	Good
Malaysia	9	
Iran	−44	Poor
Angola	−34	Poor

[1] The larger the rank number of GNP or HDI for a country, the *lower* it is in the league table of countries. The smaller the rank number of GNP or HDI, the *higher* it is in the league table of countries. A high positive figure therefore indicates a country whose human development outstrips its economic development. A high negative figure indicates a country whose economic development outstrips its human development.

Source: UNDP, 1992

the threats to life from disorder and crime, and the damaging consequences of environmental degradation are only a few of these. These issues of global importance will be addressed briefly at the end of this chapter and again in Chapter 6.

A feature of the relationship between economic growth and social welfare that has received attention recently is the link between economic growth and inequality within a country. The economic orthodoxy of the 1970s and 1980s has argued that greater income inequality within a country is the trade-off for greater economic growth: the more unequal a country the richer it is and, in consequence, the better off everybody is. This orthodoxy is now being challenged not only by the UNDP (1996) but also by the OECD (1996). After reviewing the extent of widening within-country inequality discussed earlier, the 1996 report of the UNDP concludes that there is a positive correlation between economic growth and income equality. Equality works by giving everybody a stake in the economy. The growth of the South East Asian states is seen as predicated upon this. Social policy that aims to give everybody a fair distribution of assets and resources may benefit economic growth. The OECD (1996) report concludes, rather iconoclastically, that future prosperity depends in some instances on reducing growing inequality in income and earnings. This is a further twist in the complexity of the argument, reviewed in Chapter 1, concerning the relationship between welfare states and competitiveness.

If the link between economic activity and human welfare has been problematized, so has the link between political freedom and human welfare. Obviously if basic human needs are defined, after Doyal and Gough, as including *critical* autonomy, then countries without certain political freedoms would, by definition, not meet the needs of their citizens. If this element is excluded, however, and the focus is only on longevity, educational attainment and other indicators of access to welfare, the situation looks different.

There are a few attempts to locate countries on a spectrum of more or less freedom according to criteria which reflect the UN Declaration of Human Rights. As previously mentioned, the UN *Human Development Report* experimented in 1992 with a political freedom index (PFI) constituted of a number of elements which included measures of personal security, the rule of law, freedom of expression, political participation and equality of opportunity. When the PFI index of a country was compared with the human development index there was a clear distinction between high HDI countries which equally had high PFIs, and both medium and low HDI countries which were associated with only the same medium level of political freedom. This begged the question as to whether political freedom followed or facilitated economic and human development. Humana's (1992) index of human rights is a comparable attempt to locate countries on a scale of adherence to the UN Declaration and comparable conventions. Again countries with high human development are shown to have a high respect for human rights and political freedoms.

The conclusions of these investigations are problematic for those wishing to see an automatic link between human and social progress and democracy within the still developing world. Political pluralism and the *democratic* regulation of markets are far from automatic indicators of success in meeting aspects of human needs. Over the 30 year period 1960–90 one of the most successful regimes in improving human development was South Korea (UNDP, 1990). Through sustaining social programmes and developing new ones it saw its under-five mortality rate fall from 120 per 1,000 live births in 1960 to 33 in 1988 and its adult literacy rise significantly. This achievement by a regime that doesn't guarantee some human rights and whose democratic institutions are shaky suggests that this and the parallel successes of China and Cuba that some have put down to their socialist ideology might be better attributed to the state management of economic and social development. Of course, if human needs are defined as the right to pluralist politics and free speech, the rank order of regime success changes. If human needs are defined as health (longevity) and autonomy is measured only as access to income and literacy, then pluralist political democracy in the underdeveloped world does not appear to be a precondition for the meeting of human needs. India has had a long tradition of democracy but lags far behind other developing countries in

terms of human needs indicators. On the human development index it
scores 0.439 compared with South Korea at 0.903 (UNDP, 1992).

The literature on the contested question of the relationship between
democracy and development is extensive. Healey and Robinson (1992)
concluded recently that 'There is no evidence that [developing] countries
that are more democratic are better at producing either economic growth
or reduced income inequality . . . effective leadership, clarity of decisions,
and political stability are more important factors.' The UN *Human
Development Report* of 1992 also acknowledged that 'it is true that auto-
cratic governments can sometimes engineer fundamental reforms and
promote social concerns' but that equally 'it is difficult to establish a
durable connection between authoritarian rule and economic or social
development.' Over the long haul, however, greater economic growth and
human development are paralleled by greater political freedom. Those
countries with a higher score on the human development index (HDI) are
also the countries with a higher score (84.1) on the political freedom index
(PFI) (UNDP, 1992: 32). This conclusion is somewhat modified when
comparing countries of medium and low HDI. Those with medium HDI
score 49.6 on the PFI and those with low HDI score a similar 48.2. For
the countries of Central and Eastern Europe, the focus of Chapter 4, it
might be that the ideal combination of democratic politics and the meeting
of human needs, as represented by Sweden for example, are for economic,
cultural and historical reasons simply unobtainable. Choices between
democracy and human development might constantly be present. It could
be that the lessons from the developing world are more relevant. Pluralist
politics might need to be dispensed with in favour of the state
management of development. This point will be returned to later in this
chapter.

Diversity among developed capitalist welfare states: socially regulated capitalism does best

We saw earlier that simple measures of human development such as the
HDI did not enable us to enter into a sophisticated comparison and
contrast of the workings and outcomes of highly developed capitalist
welfare states. To effect this comparison and contrast we need to turn to
the literature that has constructed ideal types of welfare regimes and
evaluate their capacity to meet welfare needs. Before doing so, however, we
may note that it is of significance that Doyal and Gough (1991) did attempt
to apply their concept of basic human needs, and their analysis of the
intermediate needs that should be satisfied (in culturally diverse ways) to
secure the meeting of these needs, to a range of countries. Their summary
comparison of the First World, the Second World (of former socialist
states) and the Third World (deconstructed into medium income and

low income countries) and with China and India analysed separately is reproduced in Table 2.5.

Among many conclusions Doyal and Gough drew from this study was that China and India, as we have already seen, represent very different rates of success in meeting basic needs. China is a 'star performer among low income countries' (1991: 270) but has a poor record of human rights abuse. In terms of the developed capitalist world they proceeded to refine the comparison by isolating the UK, the USA and Sweden as examples of different kinds of welfare state. Supporting some of the points we have made earlier they concluded that 'Sweden . . . emerged as the global leader, the country most closely approximating optimum need satisfaction at the present time' (1991: 290). Subsequently in the Deutscher lecture given by Doyal and Gough in 1994 they, after further analysis of the data (Gough and Thomas, 1993), concluded unequivocally that 'socially regulated forms of capitalism do best' in terms of meeting human needs, defined to include critical autonomy as one element. Putting this differently they concluded that 'economic development contributes most to welfare when guided by effective public authority that guarantees civil, political and social rights to all and is thus open to pressures by effective political mobilisation'.

Subsequent comparative analyses of welfare states which have demonstrated by cluster analysis that there are distinct types or families of nations have, for the most part, only reinforced these conclusions. The seminal text of Esping-Andersen (1990), which distinguished between liberal welfare states like the USA, heavily reliant on private welfare and residualist means tested provision for the poor, conservative corporatist welfare states like Germany, reliant on work based social insurance schemes, and social democratic welfare states like Sweden which are high taxation redistributive states, has been subject to a variety of criticisms. It wrongly attributed the UK to the liberal camp (Castles and Mitchell, 1990); like Australia, it is better regarded as a labourite regime embodying an unresolved tension between liberalism and collectivism. The Southern European welfare states were a separate category, the Latin Rim (Leibfried, 1990). Feminists (Orloff, 1993; Sainsbury, 1995; Shaver and Bradshaw, 1993) have focused on the limitations of the class redistribution focus of Esping-Andersen's study and sought to suggest that different criteria are required to evaluate welfare states from the standpoint of meeting women's needs. Lewis (1992) identified dual breadwinner and single breadwinner regimes. Siaroff (1994) has provided perhaps the most satisfying cluster analysis of developed welfare states in terms of the extent to which they meet women's needs. If countries are measured on three criteria – the family welfare orientation of policy, the desirability of female work (i.e. how easy it is for women to work on equal terms with men), and which parent receives benefits for children – then a close fit is demonstrated with Esping-Andersen's trilogy of regimes, with a fourth, rather like the Latin Rim, added. Siaroff labels these Protestant liberal welfare states (UK), advanced Christian democratic welfare states (Germany), Protestant social democratic welfare

Table 2.5 *Substantive need satisfaction in the Three Worlds*

		Third World			Second World	First World	World
		China	India	Other Low income	Medium income			
1	Pop., 1986 (m)	1,054	781	663	1,230	396	742	4,885
2	GNP/head, 1986	300	290	242	1,330	(2,059)	12,964	2,780
3	GDP/head PPP, 1980	–	573	(760)	(2,594)	–	9,699	(3,879)
Survival/health								
4	Life expectancy, 1986	69	57	50	61	72	75	64
5	Infant MR, 1985	36	105	119	66	23	9	61
6	Under-5 MR, 1985	50	158	193	108	27	12	94
7	Low birth weight (%)	6	30	24	12	6	6	14
Autonomy								
8	Literacy, 1985 (%)	69	43	46	73	(c. 100)	(c. 100)	–
Water/nutrition								
9	Safe water, 1983 (%)	–	54	33	59	(c. 100)	(c. 100)	–
10	Calories, 1982	111	96	92	110	132	130	111
Housing								
11	Overcrowding, 1970s (%)	–	–	–	(61)	13	2	–
Health services								
12	Pop./phys., 1981	1.7	3.7	11.6	5.1	0.34	0.55	3.8
13	Access, 1980–3 (%)	–	–	49	(57)	(c. 100)	(c. 100)	–
Security								
14	War dead, 1945–85 (%)	0.2	0.1	1.0	0.4	0.0	0.0	0.3
15	Homicide, 1987	–	–	–	(8.3)	1.9	3.8	(4.6)
16	Poverty, 1977–84 (%)	–	48	(55)	(33)	–	–	–
Education								
17	Adults: sec. ed. (%)	16	14	(9)	10	42	30	16
18	Adults: post-sec. ed. (%)	1.0	2.5	(1.4)	4.8	(8.9)	11.7	3.7
19	Students: sec. ed. (%)	39	35	23	47	92	93	51
20	Students: post-sec. ed. (%)	–	–	3	14	20	39	19
Reproduction								
21	Contraception, 1985 (%)	77	35	21	50	—— 66 ——		50
22	Maternal MR, 1980–7	44	340	510	130	—— 10 ——		250

Notes to Table

The definition of 'low' income, 'medium' income and 'industrial market' economies follows the World Bank (1988: 217). However data for the state socialist countries have been recomputed to include eight countries: Albania Bulgaria, Czechoslovakia, German Democratic Republic, Hungary, Poland, Romania and the USSR. Four high income oil-exporting nations in the Middle East are excluded from these country groups, though they are represented in the global averages. There are many problems in equating 'development' with income per head (Thirlwall, 1983: Chapter 1), but the organization of world statistics makes it difficult to present the data

Table 2.5 *(continued)*

organized according to some other variable. Countries in groups are weighted by population except where noted. Numbers are in brackets when data are available for fewer than half the countries in that group.

Since there are well known problems in comparing per capita incomes across nations, two separate measures are provided. Row 2 shows average GNP per head in US$ at current exchange rates, whereas row 3 shows average GDP per head (unfortunately only for 1980) in US$ at 'purchasing power parities' which reveal differences in national real incomes more accurately (World Bank, 1987: 268–71). Unfortunately this information is not yet available for all nations.

Definitions and sources (by row numbers):
1 Total population, 1986, millions (World Bank, 1988: Table 1).
2 Gross national product per head in 1986 in US$ using average exchange rates for 1984–6 (World Bank, 1988: Table 1).
3 Gross domestic product per head in 1980 in US$ at 'purchasing power parity' (PPP) (World Bank, 1987: Box A2).
4 Life expectancy at birth in years. 1986 (World Bank, 1988: Table 1).
5 Infant mortality before one year of age, per 1,000 live births, 1985 (UNICEF, 1987: Table 1) (MR: mortality rate).
6 Mortality of children under 5 years of age per 1,000 live births (UNICEF, 1987: Table 1).
7 Proportion of babies weighing under 2,500 g (UNICEF, 1987: Table 2).
8 Percentage of persons aged 15 and over who can read and write, 1985 (UNICEF, 1987: Table 1).
9 Access to drinking water, as defined by WHO, 1983 (UNICEF, 1987: Table 3).
10 Daily calorie supply per head as percentage of requirements, 1983 (UNICEF, 1987: Table 2).
11 Percentage of housing units with more than two persons per room, various years 1970s (UN, 1987: Table 4.5).
12 Population (thousands) per physician, 1981 (World Bank, 1988: Table 29).
13 Percentage of population with access to health services as defined by WHO, 1980–3 (UNICEF, 1987: Table 3).
14 War deaths between 1945 and 1985, as percentage of population in 1986 (UN, 1987: Table 9.11).
15 Homicides per 100,000 population (WHO, 1989: Table 10).
16 Percentage of population with incomes below that where a minimum nutritionally adequate diet plus essential non-food requirements is affordable, as estimated by world Bank (UNICEF, 1987: Table 6).
17 Proportion of adults who have ever entered secondary education, various years between 1970 and 1982 (UNESCO, 1989: Table 1.4).
18 Proportion of all adults who have entered post-secondary education, years between 1970 and 1982 (UNESCO, 1989: Table 1.4).
19 Number of secondary school pupils of all ages as percentage of children of secondary school age (generally 12–17 years), around 1985 (World Bank, 1988: Table 30).
20 Number of students enrolled in all post-secondary education, schools and universities, divided by population aged 20–4, around 1985 (World Bank, 1988 Table 30).
21 Percentage of married women of childbearing age who are using, or whose husbands are using, any form of contraception. whether traditional or modern methods (UNDP, 1990: Table 20).
22 Annual number of deaths of women from pregnancy related causes per 100,000 live births (UNDP, 1990: Table 11).

Source: Doyal and Gough, 1991

Table 2.6   *Welfare regimes in OECD countries and Eastern Europe*

Welfare regime type	Typical country	Entitlement basis of benefits	Distributional impact of benefits	Extent of meeting women's needs[1]
Liberalism (Protestant liberal)	USA Australia	Commodified	Inequality	2
Conservatism (advanced Christian democratic)	Germany France	Semi-decommodified (insurance)	Status differential maintained	2
Social democratic (Protestant social democratic)	Sweden Denmark	Decommodified (citizenship)	Redistribution	3
Late female mobilization	Japan Spain	Semi-decommodified (insurance)	Status differential maintained	0
State bureaucratic collectivism	Bulgaria Russia	Decommodified (work loyalty)	Proletarianized but privileges	2/3

[1] The scale of 0 to 3 is an approximate linear description of the extent to which the different regimes meet fully or partly the needs of women as defined by Siaroff's (1994) threefold criteria.

states (Sweden), and late female mobilization welfare states (Spain, Japan, Switzerland, Greece).

Deacon (1992) attempted to locate the earlier state bureaucratic collectivist regimes of Eastern Europe and the former Soviet Union alongside these typologies in order to predict the directions they were likely to take as these societies embraced some version of capitalism.

Table 2.6 summarizes these attempts at typology as far as the welfare regimes of Europe, including Eastern Europe before transformation, North America and a limited number of the developed Pacific countries (Japan, Australia and New Zealand) are concerned.

Not only do we know that developed welfare states are different; that they are funded and organized in different ways; that the impact of the benefits available on distribution differs; and that they are differentially friendly to women; but we also know the factors that go some way to explaining the variation. In sum, from numerous studies (Castles and Mitchell, 1990; Esping-Andersen, 1990; Gough and Thomas, 1993; Hubers and Stephens, 1993) we know that:

1   Social democratic regimes are associated with a high degree of working class mobilization and political representation.

2 Conservative corporatist regimes are heavily influenced by catholicism.
3 Liberal regimes are associated with the absence of these two factors and, possibly, with upwardly mobile societies.
4 Late female mobilization regimes are obviously a reflection of the small part played by independent women's movements in politics.
5 State bureaucratic regimes are a particular product of the expropriation of capital and the paternalistic management of the state.

Other factors have been shown to have a bearing on regime differentiation. These include the degree of federalism of government (associated with liberalism), the ethnic homogeneity of society (associated with social democracy) and the lateness of overcoming absolutism (associated with conservatism).

Complex as the picture is now becoming it still does not adequately describe all the welfare regimes that we are interested in, or adequately explain their variation, or adequately address other dimensions upon which we might distinguish regime types. In summary some of the shortcomings of the literature reviewed so far might be noted as follows.

First the extent to which different regimes meet equitably the welfare needs of ethnic minorities and migrant labourers is not yet adequately addressed Ginsburg (1992) began the task of describing the variation between the USA, the UK, Germany and Sweden in this respect. He was able only to conclude that 'racial inequalities in access to and needs for welfare benefits and services remain acute in all four states, and the evidence suggests that these have probably worsened in the past two decades' (1992: 193). Williams (1995) has begun to chart the differential extent to which different welfare regimes address the needs of their racialized minorities. At this stage it is not entirely clear whether there is a neat parallel whereby those regimes which are more women friendly are also more ethnic minority friendly or whether, to the contrary, some of the greater success of, say, social democratic regimes is attributable precisely to their ethnic homogeneity, and the relative welfare failure of the liberal regimes is attributable to their ethnic complexity. Certainly it is possible to suggest a range of overarching social policy responses to the presence of ethnic minorities. At one extreme is ethnicized nationalism which defines citizenship in racial terms and seeks only to provide for the welfare of those citizens; at the other extreme is an assimilationist policy which, while providing for the welfare needs of all denies the differences. Somewhere in the middle are multicultural strategies respecting minority rights while providing equitably for diverse needs, and anti-racist strategies which seek positively to discriminate in favour of racialized minorities. Systematic comparative welfare regime analysis along this dimension is awaited.

Secondly, the underdevelopment of the analysis of the emerging South East and East Asian economies in terms of their particular welfare orientation is noteworthy. Jones (1993b) has classified a new Confucian welfare state. Gould (1993) has described in some detail the particular characteristics of Japanese welfare. Goodman and Peng (1996) have reviewed social policy in Japan, Korea and Taiwan, concluding that learning from elsewhere in the context of nation building is the way to characterize social policy developments in the region. The success of some of the South East Asian tigers has, as we shall see in Chapter 3, clearly impressed the OCED and some in the World Bank. Investment in welfare infrastructure which is applauded in these regimes contrasts sharply with the 'welfare as burden' mentality associated with liberalism. It isn't entirely clear what the key welfare characteristics of this diverse set of countries is. At the risk of oversimplification we could list: (1) a large role for the state in centrally directing and regulating capital investment; (2) a willingness on the part of the state to invest in *some* aspects of welfare infrastructure, particularly, education, training, and *work* related social security; (3) a high level of personal saving encouraged by private pension schemes; but on the other hand (4) an approach which leaves the care of dependants and those who fall outside the category of socially secure workers to the extended family. Social assistance is rarely given if a family exists to offer support.

 Thirdly, the category of liberalism used above to encompass the USA, Canada, the UK and Australia is a rather mixed bag. In particular this grouping tends not to give the prominence that is due to the Australian welfare state. Unlike in the USA which operates a residualist version of the welfare state with, in general, public benefits available only on the basis of stigmatizing tests for the poor, the means testing in the Australian model is very much a means and assets testing of the better-off. A large tranche of welfare benefits to most Australian citizens is means and assets tested and, in that sense, Australia is different from either insurance based developed welfare states or means tested residualist welfare states. Gough concluded, as a result of a survey of means testing in OECD countries, that Australia represented the unique category of a 'selective welfare system' within which 'asset and earnings disregards are relatively generous and stigma is relatively slight' (1995: 24). This he distinguishes from the 'public assistance state [USA]'. As we shall see in Chapters 3 and 4, the Australian model is one that finds some favour in World Bank circles.

 Fourthly, the welfare policy of the Islamic family of states is an under-researched and under-reported aspect of comparative social policy. Dean and Khan (1995) have shown how through the Muslim principle of Zakat, the religious duty imposed on Muslims to give a proportion of their disposable wealth to members of their community, the Ummah provides an organizing principle for welfare equivalent to those in Protestant and Catholic states. The levy varies between 2.5 per cent for Sunni Muslims and five per cent for Shiah Muslims, and the detailed questions of what wealth can be disregarded for such tax purposes are complex and disputed. The poor have a right to the receipt of money so collected in the interests of social justice. There are presently about one billion Muslims in the world, and some 38 countries have Muslim majorities. However 'Muslim countries exhibit extraordinary diversity. They range from oil rich states like Saudi Arabia which retains essentially feudal political relations, through large poverty stricken "developing" democracies like Pakistan, to revolutionary Islamic states like Iran. There is considerable unrealised scope for comparative empirical studies of the substantive welfare institutions to be found in such countries' (1995: 8).

Fifthly, most of the comparative analysis reported so far has excluded, because they are not yet within the OECD club, the variations on the theme of developing welfare states in South and Central America. In general these have been heavily influenced by the liberal approach of the USA. Direct political intervention (as in Chile), and indirect influence through the mechanism of the USA training economics graduates who then return to work for their governments and readily accept liberal World Bank advice, have secured an orientation to the free market, funded pension schemes and the like. In consequence South America provides the world with some of its most unequal societies and with examples of absolute deprivation and poverty living cheek by jowl with affluence. The few work-based corporatist social security mechanisms benefit only a small privileged workforce. However, within this sea of fundamentalist liberalism regimes there are exceptions. We refer not to the obvious state bureaucratic collectivist regime of Cuba, which has secured longevity and education levels unattained elsewhere (at the price of political freedom), but to Costa Rica, which represents at the lower level of economic development typical of Latin America an orientation to social justice, public provision and social regulation, especially in terms of universal health care, more familiar in Europe (Esping-Andersen, 1994). Maybe Costa Rica can be dubbed liberalism with a human face or social liberalism. Evelyne Huber (1996) similarly applauding the Costa Rica model, even calls it an example of social democracy operating in the Latin American context.

Despite these shortcomings of existing comparative welfare state analysis and the work yet to be undertaken, we are able, as Doyal and Gough asserted, to identify those policies and practices in developed capitalist welfare states that better secure the meeting of welfare needs.

Socialist development and the transition to markets: the social costs of liberalism, the social achievements of managed capitalism?

Before the collapse of the communist project in Eastern Europe and the former Soviet Union, a key question for comparative social policy was how the 'socialist' countries compared with capitalist ones in terms of social welfare development. A key question for comparative analysis now is how far have the transitions to market mechanisms and the different ways they have been undertaken helped or hindered the meeting of social welfare objectives and human needs in those ex-socialist countries.

The answer in the past (Deacon, 1983; White et al., 1983) is similar to the answer today (Cornia, 1994; Deacon, 1992; UNICEF, 1993a; 1994). In the past those less developed countries such as China, Cuba and Mozambique that had adopted, following popular revolution, a state socialist path of development outstripped equivalent countries that hadn't in terms of health, health care, education, sanitation and much else besides. The exceptionally high position of China and Cuba in the league table of human development is testimony, at the price of political freedom, to this. At the same time those more developed state socialist countries like Russia, Hungary and Bulgaria seemed to have exhausted any further potential for improvements in human welfare. The inefficiency of the state economy combined with the absence of articulation of needs from below had led to an ossified state bureaucratic set of paternalistic welfare provisions which in many ways was no longer improving the welfare of their citizens. By comparison with western welfare states longevity was stagnant if not declining, education participation at tertiary level was low, and services such as housing and health care, although freely or cheaply available, were badly funded, organized and delivered. Social security benefits were high, however and non-workers shared in the relative impoverishment of the whole country. A balance sheet of this state bureaucratic collectivist period is provided in Deacon (1992).

Today, as a provisional judgement, it can be concluded that the impact, certainly in the short term, of the rush since 1989 in Eastern Europe to both capitalism and pluralist democracy has been at a high social cost. Liberalism has given birth to high levels of unemployment, a drop of about one-third in living standards, a significant rise in poverty, and for most countries worrying mortality rates. By contrast the slower managed introduction of capital investment and market mechanisms since 1979 within an undemocratic context in China has led to a continued rise in living standards, a minimal level of open unemployment, and a reduction in poverty levels. There are signs of regional inequity, however, and the lot of migrant peasants seeking work in the new development zones is a major and growing problem. In other words socialist development was good in the past for meeting human needs in China (and Cuba and elsewhere). A managed, if undemocratic, introduction of market forces seems, for now, to be good there too. Equally the bureaucratic state collectivist variant of socialist development that had ossified in Russia and Eastern Europe was no longer good for its citizens. The equally rapid rush there to unmanaged, pluralistically democratic liberal capitalism is of no short term benefit either. This sharp contrast between the negative post-communist experience in Russia and much of Eastern Europe and the positive managed socialist transformation in China is echoed by a study undertaken under the auspices of the UN University's World Development Institute. Blaho concluded: 'China's approach – economic incrementalism and limited political change – has produced an outstanding economic advance . . . the transition in Russia has so far brought about desperately poor short term economic results' (1994: 49).

Table 2.7 *The social impact of transition in selected former socialist societies*

Country	Change in real income per capita %	Change in poverty rate %	Change in infant mortality rate %	Change in school enrolment rate %
China	+40 (1982–90)	–35 (1990–92)	–25 (1978–89)	+29 (1982–90)
Russia	–38 (1989–93)	+36 (1990–92)	+13 (1989–93)	–5 (1989–92)[2]
Bulgaria[1]	–39 (1989–92)	+4 (1989–90)	+8 (1989–93)	–7 (1989–92)[2]
Hungary[1]	–3 (1989–93)	+4 (1989–90)	–15 (1989–93)	+3 (1989–95)[2]
Ukraine[1]	–4 (1989–92)[3]	–	+16 (1989–93)	–

[1] These countries are included because they are the case studies used in Chapter 4.
[2] Secondary school.
[3] The basis of this calculation is suspect.

Source: recalculations from Table 6 and Table II in Cornia, 1994 (see notes to those tables for detailed explanation of data source)

Table 2.7 clearly demonstrates that for Russia, Bulgaria, the Ukraine and to a lesser extent Hungary the short term social impact of the political and market reforms has been injurious to the population. Data for other countries in the region support this. The Czech Republic is, in general, an exception to the trend. By contrast the social indicators in China through this period of transition are, so far, almost universally positive. The bleak picture for the former Soviet Union and Eastern Europe is captured in Table 2.8.

The World Bank, reviewing outcomes of the reform process, notes similar differences: 'In CEE and NIS . . . the combination of falling output and rising income inequality has led to large increases in poverty and growing insecurity in many countries . . . Living standards have risen sharply in the growing Asian reformers; the first stage of reform in China lifted almost 200 million people out of absolute poverty, a massive achievement' (1996: 18–19). The Bank stresses however that the preconditions in, say, Russia and China were very different, so that 'the right reform mix cannot simply be transplanted between such starkly different countries as Russia and China' (1996: 21). In general it concludes that the real difference has been between those CEE and NIS countries that have consistently embraced economic reform and, slowly or more quickly, are now rebuilding their economies despite the short term human suffering, and those CEE and NIS countries that have prevaricated or blocked reform and are now starting to suffer for even longer.

While it is clear that the social costs of the transition in Eastern Europe and the former Soviet Union are high, what can be said about the kind of welfare state that is emerging in the region? Is any model of western capitalism being followed? Gotting (1995) concludes that the social costs have not so much been a result of changes in welfare policy but rather the consequences of changes in price subsidy policy – the rapid removal of

Table 2.8 *Summary of welfare changes in 18 Central and Eastern European countries, 1989–95*

Indicator	Unit	Czech R.	Slovakia	Hungary	Poland	Slovenia	Albania	Bulgaria	Romania	Estonia	Latvia	Lithuania	Belarus	Moldova	Russia	Ukraine	Armenia	Azerbaijan	Georgia	CE	SEE	Balt.	W FSU	Cauc.
																					Subregional Summary			
Income and consumption based indicators																								
Real wage	%	—	-21.7[a]	-21.6	-24.6	-23.1	-85.0[b]	-40.6	-30.9	-40.0[b]	-41.4	-64.4[c]	-39.0	-79.9	-54.9[d]	-61.4	-85.6[d]	-88.3[c]	-56.0[e]	-22.8	-52.2	-48.6	-58.8	-76.6
Poverty rate	%	1.2[f]	5.9[g]	5.0[g]	5.1[f]	1.6[h]	—	30.7[i]	22.1[g]	26.0[g]	32.2[g]	37.6[g]	—	38.2[e]	—	—	25.4[e]	51.4	—	3.8	26.4	31.9	38.2	51.4
Food share	%	-1.7	3.9[g]	2.4[g]	-6.4	-3.2	—	7.2	5.5	-0.9[m]	15.5[g]	21.6	24.1	24.8	13.9	25.7[g]	25.4[e]	18.8	38.8	-1.0	6.4	12.1	22.1	27.7
Calorie consumption per capita	%	—	-0.3[g]	-10.7[e]	-13.2[g]	—	-16.4[g]	-18.2	-2.6[g]	—	-12.4[g]	—	1.7[j]	-24.6	-9.8	-21.4[g]	-33.5[e]	-22.9[g]	-28.6	-8.0	-12.4	-12.4	-13.5	-28.3
Demographic indicators																								
Crude marriage rate	%	-32.1	-26.1	-15.9	-19.4	-14.3	-24.1[e]	-38.0	-11.7	-42.0	-52.2	-36.2	-21.9	-18.5	-23.4	-11.6	-46.2	-43.3	-42.9	-21.5	-24.6	-43.4	-18.8	-44.1
Remarriage rate	%	-25.0	-46.2	-27.8	-30.0	-14.3	-50.0[e]	-44.4	-7.1	-22.7[g]	-60.0	-45.0	-15.8	-6.3	-24.0	—	—	-56.3	-50.0[e]	-28.6	-33.9	-42.6	-15.3	-53.1
Crude divorce rate	%	0.0	6.2	-4.2	-16.7	-27.3	-0.0[e]	-7.1	-16.7	31.6	-23.8	-15.2	20.6	17.2	15.0	0.0	-41.7	-52.9	-64.3	-8.4	-7.9	-2.5	13.2	-53.0
Crude birth rate	%	-25.0	-24.8	-6.8	-24.8	-18.8	-6.5[g]	-32.3	-35.4	-41.3	-41.1	-26.5	-34.7	-31.2	-35.6	-27.8	-40.1	-26.5[c]	-33.5	-20.1	-24.7	-36.3	-32.3	-33.4
Mortality indicators																								
Life expectancy, males	years	1.9	1.5	-0.1	0.8	1.5	-0.1[g]	-1.4	-0.9[g]	-4.0	-5.5	-3.0	-3.9	-3.7	-5.9	-3.2[g]	-0.9[g]	-3.2[c]	—	1.1	-0.8	-4.2	-4.2	-2.1
Life expectancy, females	years	1.5	0.9	0.7	0.9	1.1	0.1[g]	-0.2	0.7[g]	-0.4	-2.6	-1.0	-2.1	-2.6	-2.8	-1.8[g]	0.2[g]	-0.7[c]	—	1.0	0.2	-1.3	-2.3	-0.3
Infant MR	%	-23.0	-18.5	-31.8	-28.8	-32.9	-40.3[g]	2.8	-21.2	0.0	64.0	15.9	12.7	3.9	-1.1	10.8	-30.4	-13.7	-28.6[g]	-27.0	7.3	26.6	6.6	-5.2
1–4 MR	%	-19.5	-17.1	-30.6	-28.4	-35.0	-38.2[c]	3.8	-24.9	5.8	28.3	13.3	6.5	1.1	3.6	11.4[g]	-21.0[g]	-3.1	-30.1[f]	-26.1	5.7	15.8	5.7	-18.1
5–19 MR	%	18.2	-5.6	-12.2	-12.2	-2.6	—	0.0	-3.1	-9.6[k]	-25.3	-18.2	0.0	-7.4	15.9	10.2[g]	71.4[g]	90.4	0.0[f]	-2.9	-1.6	-17.7	4.7	53.9
20–39 MR	%	-5.4	-15.4	-7.0	-7.4	-18.8	—	6.6	-1.1	50.8	75.7	29.8	39.9	23.1	63.9	41.1[g]	41.7[g]	126.0[g]	23.4[f]	-10.8	2.7	52.1	42.0	63.8
40–59 MR	%	-13.5	-19.1	6.3	-11.6	-16.4	—	7.2	18.6	41.2	93.9	38.2	30.8	25.8	58.5	37.2[g]	-5.1[g]	13.5[g]	-4.8[f]	-10.9	12.9	57.6	38.1	1.2
60 MR	%	-9.7	-3.8	0.0	-5.2	-5.6	—	22.4	1.2	2.4	20.8	3.9	17.8	34.2	19.5	22.2[g]	6.1[g]	6.0[g]	-5.6[f]	-4.8	11.8	9.0	23.4	2.1
Maternal mortality rate	%	-77.4	62.0	-28.6	-6.6	26	-46.9[h]	-12.8	-71.8	25.2	-60.9	-40.8	-44.4	-63.6	5.7	10.1	-15.3[g]	53.1[g]	-22.9[g]	-4.9	-43.9	-25.5	-23.0	5.0
Health indicators																								
Abortion rate	%	-35.0	-4.7	-6.3	-99.3	-16.1	48.0[g]	11.2	307.0	14.8	-4.7	4.1[l]	14.1	4.1	-1.0	-5.2	72.3[g]	-2.8[g]	-12.1[g]	-32.3	122.1	4.7	3.0	19.1
Live birth weight	%	5.8	16.1	-9.8	-11.8	-5.5	-17.6[g]	29.0	20.5	25.0[g]	8.9	10.5	19.0	-14.9	10.5	—	8.8[g]	-1.8[g]	37.7[g]	-1.0	10.6	14.8	4.9	14.9
Tuberculosis cases	%	4.4[g,n]	20.3[h,n]	13.9[g,n]	2.7[e,n]	-20.3[g,n]	—	-7.7[g,n]	48.6[g,n]	28.5[g,n]	66.4[g,n]	38.3[g,n]	15.8[g,n]	-3.2[g,n]	100.0[g,n]	1.4[g,n]	27.6[g,n]	-5.3[g,n]	—	-12.3	28.2	44.7	30.1	11.2

Social cohesion and protection indicators

Indicator																								
Births to mothers under 20 years %	-2.6	0.4	-0.5	0.6	-3.0	4.7[e]	1.7	2.2	3.2	-0.2	3.6	5.1	8.7	7.2	5.4[g]	9.5[g]	3.3	1.5[f]	-1.0	2.9	2.2	6.6	4.8
No. of adoptions %	-0.5[s]	34.6	-4.3	-28.4[g]	-51.9	—	87.0	—	8.4[m]	-34.3	62.0[o]	60.5	—	9.7[p]	16.9[q]	-68.8[g]	-43.2	—	-10.1	87.0	-29.3	29.0	-56.0
Crime rate %	212.0	143.0	130.0	63.0[g]	-3.9	—	269.0	—	-118.0	40.0	93.5	95.7	-6.2	69.5	77.7[g]	12.7	27.2	-21.2	108.9	269.3	84.0	59.2	6.2
Youths sentenced %	18.4	68.8	37.1	-14.4[g]	-67.4	—	135.0	212.0[g]	106.0	0.3	134.0	89.0	37.4	70.1	63.9[g]	196.0[g]	90.2[g]	40.6[g]	8.5	173.7	80.1	65.1	108.9
Homicide rate %	119.8	117.0	51.8	—	23.3	—	5.8[r]	—	242.0	57.9	224.0	—	50.6	134.0	—	31.8	83.4	—	78.0	5.8	174.4	92.3	57.6

Child education indicators

Indicator																								
Crèche/parental leave coverage %	-1.0[e,s]	—	3.6[e]	-23.6[e]	—	—	-18.8[g]	-1.2[g,t]	-12.0[g,t]	29.2[g]	-15.2[g,t]	-21.7[g,t]	-16.1[g,t]	-14.9[g,t]	-13.8[c,t]	-15.2[g]	-1.3[g]	—	-7.0	-10.0	0.7	-16.6	-1.3
Pre-primary enrolment rate %	-10.7	-20.7	1.2	-4.4[g]	6.4	-4.0[h]	-7.6	-24.5	1.1	-15.6	-27.7	-1.2	-16.0	-15.3	-17.2[g]	—	-3.0	-16.3[g]	-5.6	-16.1	-14.1	-12.4	-11.5
Primary enrolment rate %	0.4	1.8	0.1	-0.9	2.0		-4.7	2.2	-1.4[k]	4.2[l]	3.6[k]	2.9	2.0[l]	-3.0	2.2[g]	—	17.0	-12.3[g]	0.7	-2.2	2.1	-0.1	2.3
Secondary enrolment rate %	17.8[k]	3.0	16.2	4.2	3.2		-2.1	-14.2	-10.2[k]	-3.7	-8.0[k]	-4.3	0.0	-4.3	-7.4[g]	—	-8.0	-18.2[g]	8.9	-8.2	-7.3	-4.0	-13.1

Total number of observations	28	28	29	28	27	15	29	26	28	29	28	27	28	28	25	24	29	22	29	29	29	29	29
of which:																								
no. of deteriorations	13	16	15	13	8	11	24	18	23	22	24	22	21	25	22	18	22	14	12	24	24	27	25
no. of improvements	15	12	14	15	19	4	5	8	5	7	4	5	7	3	3	6	7	8	17	5	5	2	4
Percentage of deteriorations	46.4	57.1	51.7	46.4	29.6	73.3	82.8	72.0	82.1	73.3	85.7	81.5	75.9	86.2	88.0	75.0	75.9	63.6	41.4	82.8	82.8	93.1	86.2

a Average.
b Estimate.
c 1995, preliminary data.
d 1993–5 UNECE.
e 1989–93.
f 1989–92.
g 1989–94.
h 1990–3.
i 1990–4.
j 1993–5.
k 1990–5.
l 1991–5.
m 1992–4.
n Newly registered cases. Source WHO Health for All Database.
o 1992–5.
p Total number of children entering guardian families annually.
q Stock.
r 1991–4.
s Only parental leave care included.
t Only crèche enrolment rate included.

Source: UNICEF, 1997

subsidy on food, housing and transport – which have led to impoverishment, and changes in the labour market which have generated unemployment that the existing welfare system had not been designed to deal with.
She charts, in other words, rather small changes in social policy – in
pension policy, health care policy, etc.: 'While almost all political and
economic institutions of the communist regime were fundamentally
challenged in the first five years of transition, the social protection systems
were largely maintained. Despite strong reformist ambitions at the
beginning, post-communist governments did not bring about major shifts
in social policy' (1995: 1). This position gains some support from the
analysis of the World Bank (1996: 17) where it concludes that for both slow
and fast reformers within CEE and the NIS the index of social policy
reform (pensions, subsidy reduction, targeting of benefits, divestiture by
firms of social assets) is lower than the index of legal institutional reform,
banking reform, and other roles of government. While this is true there
have been some changes in welfare policy, as we describe and analyse
below.

On the basis of the welfare regime characteristics summarized earlier in
Table 2.6 it has been possible to construct four propositions about the
likely future of state bureaucratic collectivism. First, the work based
system of welfare characteristic of state bureaucratic collectivism, combined with the pre-existing status differentials reflected in the privileges
available not only to the *nomenklatura* but also to those workers who were
highly regarded under the system, suggests a relatively smooth and logical
transfer to a German-like system of conservative corporatism via the
establishment of a wage related social security policy. Secondly, social
democracy, which requires a productive economy that is willing to be
heavily taxed to facilitate significant social redistribution, was unlikely to
be a short term viable option. Thirdly, in direct contrast to state bureaucratic collectivism the impoverishment and indebtedness of the countries
were likely to expose them to strong pressures from the IMF and the
World Bank towards liberalism. Fourthly, the high involvement of women
in the workforce would suggest that a retraditionalization of these societies
is unlikely.

On the basis of these propositions and an analysis of those factors known
empirically to be associated with different kinds of welfare state, together
with new factors which were seen as likely to affect the outcome of the
transition, namely the character of the transition process (mass or quietude)
and the nature of the transnational impacts from the West (high if
indebted), Deacon hypothesized that we would see the emergence not only
of some liberal regimes (Hungary) and some conservative corporatist
regimes (East Germany) but also of a new variant which was labelled post-
communist conservative corporatism:

> To the extent that it is difficult or not desired [by the *nomenklatura* to convert
> themselves into capitalist entrepreneurs] then we may witness in some countries

the emergence of a modified form of conservative corporatism in which a 'deal is struck between some elements of the old *nomenklatura* and some elements of the working class to modify the free play of market forces, at the price of less economic growth, in order to secure a greater degree of state protection of both *nomenklatura* and skilled worker. (1992: 174)

It was also predicted that 'the future for Central Asian republics . . . is less clear. Here the model of a . . . South East Asian statist capitalist development which has little regard for democracy may prove to be necessary' (1992: 189). This particular book did not deal with China but the same point might well have been made if it had.

What can be said at this moment at this level of generality about the emerging world(s) of post-communist welfare? Are the propositions and predictions upheld? There has not yet been undertaken a systematic comparative description and analysis of post-communist social policy. Gotting (1994) has usefully compared developments in Bulgaria, Hungary and Czechoslovakia. Individual country reports have appeared on Poland (Ksiezopolski, 1993a) and the Baltics (Simpura, 1995). Some recent accounts of Russian social policy have been made by Manning (1994) and Shapiro (1995b). The International Social Security Association (ISSA, 1994a; 1994b) has monitored developments. The Child Development Centre of UNICEF in Florence has provided, as we have seen, an excellent service in monitoring *outcomes* of policy in three Regional Monitoring Reports (UNICEF, 1993a; 1994; 1995b). The World Bank (1996) has reviewed developments in all transition economies.

Cichon (1994b) working for the ILO, claims that there is a general pattern of development in the income maintenance sector leading to the establishment of a three pillared system of *social insurance* (for pensions, short term benefits), social *support* from taxes (for child benefits), and *social assistance* for those exhausting entitlement to benefit or not otherwise covered. To the extent that this is true – and certainly Polish, Hungarian, Czech, Slovak, Slovene, Lithuanian and Bulgarian policy is moving partly in this direction – then the logic of the transformation of state bureaucratic collectivism to conservative corporatism is being followed through. At issue, of course, is the level of benefits, the extent to which state pensions are wage related or only minimum flat rate guarantees, the adequacy at a local level of nominal state commitments to social assistance, and the extent to which the state support system is universal or targeted. Because in many cases it is only the minimum pension that is being guaranteed, and because support systems are increasingly means tested, the reality begins to look much more like a variant of liberalism – a liberalism with a human face, a social liberalism – rather than conservative corporatism. The struggle, influenced by external actors, between the two tendencies continues and this will be discussed in more detail in Chapters 4 and 5.

There is a distinction between those countries that have more readily embraced the Bismarckian social insurance system with independent funds and those that have dragged their feet on this and continue to see a closer link between the state budget and benefit funds. It is the latter type of country that is also more concerned to conserve industrial enterprises, and to temporarily lay off workers without pay rather than establish adequate unemployment benefits. This predicted post-communist conservatism (of Bulgaria, Romania and the Ukraine) is however being encircled within its own borders by a new unregulated private, semi-legal capitalism that refuses to be taxed. In these countries therefore the tension is not so much between conservative corporatism and social liberalism as between post-communist conservatism and an extreme unregulated liberalism.

The extreme version of this tension is being played out in Russia and some other countries of the former Soviet Union. Shapiro (1995b) has demonstrated that the trajectory of Russia in terms of income inequality and effective social policy making is much more towards a Latin American scenario of welfare collapse than towards any of the variants of western welfare capitalism. This gloomy picture in Russia in the income maintenance sphere is reinforced by a comparative analysis of health policy and mortality outcomes (Shapiro, 1995b). The life expectancy for males in Russia was (1994) 57.3 years (Field, 1995). The Gini coefficient in Russia has moved from 260 in 1991, through 289 in 1992 and 398 in 1993 to 409 in 1994. As one World Bank professional put it:

> I would add another item to your classification [of welfare futures]. It is actually a system of social neglect or disregard in countries at middling levels where the poor are not a very important constituency (they don't vote or their votes are stolen), the middle class is not big enough (and it has definitely shrunk in Russia), and the role of the state is highly uncertain (meaning that the state can expropriate all contributions, or inflate them away or simply cease to exist). (private communication)

In sum, therefore, we can conclude that diverse welfare regimes can now be found in Eastern Europe and the former Soviet Union. These include the existing western welfare model of Bismarckian conservative corporatism and the new post-communist conservatism which is always in danger of giving way to welfare collapse. A new social liberalism (liberalism with safety nets) is also evident and, as we shall see in Chapters 3 and 4 is one of the World Bank's preferred solutions.

China, however, continues to be a different story. This book and chapter cannot address this issue adequately but as mentioned earlier there is evidence that while maintaining post-communist conservative features (bankruptcies of old industries have not yet taken place) China also embraces, in its new zones of development, a distinctly South East Asian managed capitalism with, for example, individual social insurance accounts as the preferred social security system. China's move to an undemocratic market economy doesn't appear to be in the direction of Europe (Deacon, 1995; White and Shang, 1995).

The lessons and limits of comparative social policy analysis: globalism again

In this chapter we have reviewed very rapidly the state of the world's welfare in terms of how different countries and groups of countries compare one with another in meeting basic human needs. We have also reviewed the ways in which types of developed and developing welfare states compare with each other in terms of the nature and the social impact of their social policy. We have shown that for the developed world neither bureaucratic state collectivism (as in the former Soviet Union) nor free market liberalism (as in the USA) best meets human and welfare needs. A socially regulated system which embodies either corporative forms of tripartite government or a high commitment to a redistributive tax and benefit policy is the form of welfare capitalism that is most successful in these terms. For developing countries either the continuation of some kind of state socialist planning combined with a regulated market (as in China) or managed capitalist development (as with the South East Asian tigers) seems to best secure improvements in welfare. Some of the negative consequences in Eastern Europe of a rapid transition to democracy and free market capitalism have been highlighted.

In this chapter we have also learned something of the social, political, religious and other factors which explain variation between welfare regimes and therefore enable us to predict the circumstances within which certain kinds of welfare policy emerge. This is important when it comes to the process whereby countries might learn one from the other about the best welfare strategy to adopt in the future. While it is entirely possible for, say, the World Bank to argue for the export of liberalism to countries where the political, social, cultural and other circumstances are inappropriate, it makes more sense if the aim, as in the case of the ILO, is to secure the adoption of sound and well funded social policies (Cichon and Samuel, 1995) in order to seek to influence the political context of countries and to encourage them to adopt kinds of governance (in this case tripartite) that are the best breeding ground for social democracy or conservative corporatism. We can learn from comparative social policy analysis which social policy strategy, which welfare regime, works best by our agreed universal criteria and we can hope to influence countries in that direction if there is sensitivity to the constellation of factors that are more likely to ensure the replication of the desired policies. This is the subject matter of Chapter 4 where we shall examine the attempts by several international organizations to influence the direction of post-communist social policy.

There are however severe limits to comparative social policy analysis. As we argued in Chapter 1, the globalization process has shifted both the locus of social policy making and the location of the issues which a globalized social policy is increasingly being called upon to address. A globalized economy sets welfare regimes in competition with each other and, as we described in Chapter 1 the socially best welfare regime may not win unless the social regulation of that competition is managed globally. A globalizing policy shifts the locus of policy making both down to the local and up to the supranational and global. For this reason we defined the scope of global social policy as encompassing global social redistribution, global social regulation, and global social provision and empowerment. Equally the making of national social policy is increasingly the business of supranational actors. In terms of social structure and social problems the globalizing process generates in turn a new set of issues that are themselves transborder issues which states are only partially able to handle by themselves. In this sense globalizing tendencies generate states of disarray. The social effects of globalization have been well documented recently by the United Nations Research Institute for Social Development (UNRISD, 1995b). Here it is argued that globalization generates pressures for international migration, increases the capacity of criminals to network transnationally, generates a global drug trafficking problem, and exacerbates the fluidity and lack of certainty about identity. Added to this are the problems associated with the rise of transnational corporations who have freedom (from state legislation) without responsibility (for citizen's social welfare), and the ecological agenda which might set sustainable limits to growth globally that no one nation needs to heed locally.

Comparative social policy analysis reaches the limits that national social policy makers reach. It can't, within its paradigm, address the transborder social policy issues of the new world disorder. This is not to say that some of the analytical frameworks developed to make sense of one country within the social policy literature can't be adapted to fit the global picture. Class struggles can and do take on cross-border dimensions; the social movements of women are now largely global; the legacy of imperialisms and the racist policy consequences of this assert an influence between states as well as within them. Policy paradigms of incrementalism or of a power resource kind have purchase upon supranational policy making. In this context the analytical framework provided by Williams, (1987) of a racially structured, patriarchal capitalism, which was effectively used by Ginsburg (1992) to engage in the comparative analysis of the divisions of welfare, of class, gender and ethnic kinds in different countries, could be adapted to the analysis of the global interconnectedness of social policy issues and strategies. Williams's triangular framework as in Figure 2.1a, reflecting the struggles shown in Figure 2.1b, can in principle be adapted to the global terrain where, it would be hypothesized, supranational actors allied with these several conflicting interests would take part in the global policy making process. Crudely we might suggest the potential line-up of forces depicted in Figure 2.1c.

The next chapters of this book attempt to begin the task of global social policy analysis informed by this paradigm, aiming to capture not only the class struggles suggested above but also the struggles between fractions of global capitalism (EU, NATFA), the range of positions on the continuum from fundamentalist liberalism to social reformist capitalism likely to be

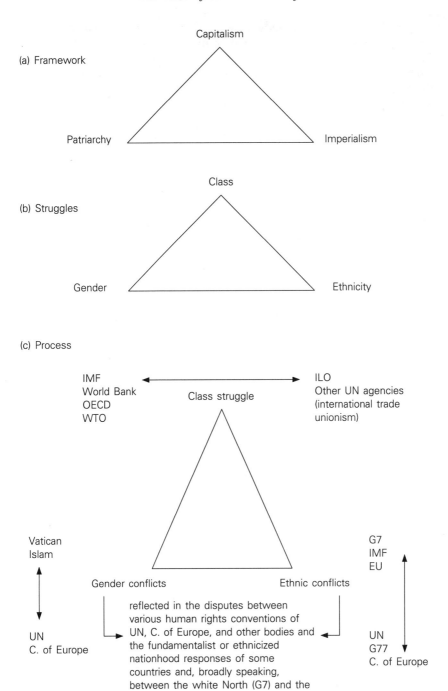

Figure 2.1   *Global interconnectedness*

adopted by the various representatives of the interests of global capital, and the complex global agenda setting of the UN, the EU, the Council of Europe and other agencies on issues of equal gender opportunities and ethnic diversity and equality. These theoretical concerns will be revisited in the final chapter.

3

The Social Policy of Global Agencies

In Chapter 1 it was argued that questions of social policy – the ways in which governments and non-governmental actors seek to shape economic and other policies so that they contribute to social objectives – are increasingly the business of supranational and global actors. Organizations such as the International Monetary Fund, the World Bank, and the International Labour Organization as well as a host of non-governmental international organizations are involved in (1) influencing the shaping of national social policy, (2) engaging in transnational redistribution and regulation, and (3) occasionally providing for citizens or at least empowering citizens when states fail them.

In this chapter an attempt is made to catalogue the explicit and implicit social policies of the major supranational and global actors and institutions. Some caveats are necessary at this point to explain what is and what is not attempted. The chapter is not a detailed history of any of the organizations, neither does it do full justice to the range of policy areas that many of the organizations are involved in. Some international organizations such as the World Health Organization and the United Nations Educational, Scientific and Cultural Organization (UNESCO) are excluded. A study of the health policies of international organizations by Koivusalo and Ollilah (1997) has, however, been undertaken in parallel to this one. The focus is on (1) the broad orientation to economic and social policy and (2) the specific policies on income transfer and related social security measures promulgated by these organizations. In terms of the attempts made below to classify and categorize the policy of the organizations the starting point will be the diverse worlds or strategies for welfare that were identified in Chapter 2.

There is a vast literature in both development studies and political economy that also addresses the role of the World Bank and the IMF, for example in terms of their impact on the social development of poorer countries. No attempt is made here to systematically review this vast literature. Rather what is attempted is to look afresh at these global actors in terms of where their pronouncements and policy advice fit into the emerging global discourse on the future for social policy in developed countries. The focus is not their history, not their organization culture (although this will be mentioned), not the impact and effectiveness of their interventions in individual countries (the subject of Chapter 4), but their *voice* in this increasingly important global inter- and intra-agency dialogue.

It is as members of epistemic communities (Haas, 1992) that we are interested in the pronouncements of professionals within these organizations. Our interest is in how these organizations wield power not only through tangible mechanisms such as economic conditionality but also through shaping the terms of the discourse about social welfare.

One area of related literature that we do explore in order to contextualize this work is that on international organizations, within the discipline of international relations. This is discussed more fully below where we assert that the research undertaken for this book leads us to support the tendency that argues international organizations have independent lives of their own as policy making and agenda setting bodies and are not merely the tools of the intergovernmental politics that formally underpin them.

For the purposes of this chapter our method has been to review the official pronouncements of the organizations in the field of social policy and to interview key professionals in the human resources, social policy and social security sections of the body concerned. By doing this and not focusing also on what is being said by the economists in the organizations on economic management, there is already an in-built bias that probably leads to our presentation of some of these organizations as more sympathetic to the social purposes of economic activity than they actually are. The justification, however, is clear. The conflict between the profit maximization goal of capitalist economic activity and the demands for social benefits to accrue to workers and others in the process is endemic. The usual conflict between a ministry of finance and a ministry of labour is a reflection of this. Our interest is in the range of possible social policy responses to the economic 'imperative' articulated by the social policy and human resources specialists of these organizations. Do they defer to the economic imperative and fashion a workfare social policy in response, or do they contend and argue for a modification of economic activity in the interests of redistribution, regulation and provision within and between states?

In this chapter we focus on policy pronouncements and the mechanisms that organizations have for influencing a country's social policy. In the next chapter we focus down on the specific policy recommendations these organizations have articulated for our sample of post-communist transition economies. It will be shown in the next chapter that the social policy and practice of some of these international organizations has shifted as a result of their encounter with the social policy history and popular social policy expectations of the post-communist countries. The present chapter could not have been written without noting this recent development. The reader will have to wait until Chapter 4, however, before seeing the detailed evidence upon which the case is made that there is a fluidity in the social policy of some international organizations in the face of the encounter with 'communism'.

The chapter, following an initial discussion of the 'supranational actors versus servants of government' debate, continues through each of the major international organizations beginning with the IMF and ending with several UN agencies such as UNICEF and UNDP. Key subglobal regional supranational organizations such as the EU and NAFTA are reviewed in the same way. Through a focus on recent UN summits and an examination of North–South conflicts in the social policy arena the chapter concludes with a dialogue with development studies and with some implications spelled out for the emerging debate on the reform of global governance. These points are taken up more fully in the concluding chapter.

Supranational actors or servants of government?

The focus of this and the subsequent chapter is on the major international organizations and their influence on social policy making in transition societies. A key issue, therefore, is whether these organizations have lives of their own above and beyond the reach of the national governments that fund and support them. Are they the tools of the most powerful states that fund them, or do they have the autonomy to develop and fashion policy relevant to the global issues they address? Does the World Bank speak for the USA and the United Nations social agencies for the South, thus perpetuating stalemate, or is there scope within the Bank and the UN agencies for a class of international civil servants, in dialogue with inter-national non-governmental organizations, to fashion the elements of a global social policy that speaks to the interests of all? This question is obviously addressed at the most general level within the political science literature in the arguments about the tension between national sovereignty (Camillieri and Falk, 1992) and an emergent cosmopolitan governance (Held, 1995). More specifically relevant to this chapter is the literature that addresses the role of international organizations. Boardman has suggested that there are three views on this issue. International organizations can be seen (1) as a means of transforming international society, (2) as instruments of state policy or (3) as reflecting a pluralistic world community. There has however, within the political science literature, been relatively little atten-tion given to particular international organizations (IOs) and their links. De Senarclens (1993: 453) concluded, in an article written for a special issue of the *International Social Science Journal* which focused on theoretical perspectives and current trends in international organizations studies that 'the study of IOs has made scarcely any progress over the past few decades'. This, it is argued, has resulted from the dominance of the 'realist' approach to the study of international relations which sees them as servants of government. The lack of detailed sociological or political scientific analysis of these organizations could also be attributed to the way many of them are written off as tools of the capitalist North by dependency theorists who have been interested only in their impact on development possibilities.

One curious trend in the literature has been to demonstrate how major government actors, particularly the USA have politicized organizations like

the World Bank. Here Brown (1991) has argued that the non-political
technical role of the World Bank has been subverted by the USA when it
has explicitly attempted to intervene in the Bank's business in relation to
regimes the USA is unhappy with (Allende's Socialist Chile in the 1970s,
for example). This intervention, according to Brown, breaks the Bank's
charter, Article VI, which states that political activity is prohibited: 'the
Bank and its officers shall not interfere in the political affairs of any
members.' The curiosity value of this approach is that it then has to do an
intellectual somersault to justify, as Brown does, the taking into consideration by the Bank in its lending policy the environmental (we would add the
social) impact of its policy on a country. Brown argues that 'there is a
difference between injecting totally extraneous political matters into Bank
lending decisions and considering the human rights or environmental
implications of lending projects themselves. To continue to ignore the
possible negative impact of Bank funded projects upon human rights . . .
would [not] serve the interests of international cooperation' (1991: 239).

The approach adopted in this study of international organizations is
precisely to pull out for explicit critical examination the *political content* of
the advice of the Bank, the IMF, the OECD, the ILO, etc. in the social
sphere. The approach is to regard these organizations, in the words of de
Senarclens (1993: 460) as 'depositories of principles and norms which
confer on their secretariats a degree of political autonomy . . . they are
involved in their own right in conflicts of interest and power struggles
between actors on the international stage'. More precisely this study is
located within an approach which looks for the transnational networks that
operate within and between governmental and non-governmental international organizations and that in effect, establish a transnational or global
discourse that is the backcloth against which global decisions are made.
Jonsson has suggested that 'transnational networks may have an impact on
national policy making in various direct and indirect ways' (1993: 471).
This study will demonstrate the usefulness of this approach in the sphere of
social policy. To the extent that the transnational network that is the
subject of this study is an epistemic community of human resource and
social policy scholars, there might also be support for Haas's claim that
epistemic communities 'called upon for advice under conditions of uncertainty . . . have often proved to be significant actors in shaping patterns of
international policy co-ordination' (1992: 35).

This is not to argue entirely against those who, to the contrary, see the
policy of international organizations as derived from major state interests.
It is hard, for example, to dispute Anne-Marie Burley's conclusion that 'the
similarity in substance and scope between the domestic law of the *liberal*
welfare state and the international law of co-operation in the post-war
world has long been recognised . . . the roots of contemporary multilateralism lie in one particular liberal state's vision of the world as a
domestic policy, economy or society writ large' (1993: 146) or for that
matter Goldstein's assertion that 'Gatt's creation stemmed from American

power' (1993: 222). The contribution of this study is to suggest that, while it is true that the social policy of official international organizations is shaped in part by the policies of the most powerful state actors under-pinning them, nonetheless the IOs themselves and particularly their human resource specialists have a degree of autonomy within this framework which has increasingly been used to fashion an implicit global political dialogue with international NGOs about the social policies of the future that go beyond the political thinking or political capacity of the under-pinning states. They become, in other words, the forum within which the transnational global politics of the imminent future is fashioned. They do this in substitution for the explicit political democratic forums that do not yet exist effectively at a global level. To return to Brown, our concern is precisely not that the Bank, for example, is drifting from its technical path and in danger of being politicized by government but that the Bank is, quite properly, making continually political decisions and is, in the absence of a global politics, (along with other IOs) *the* locus of global social policy making.

The International Monetary Fund: unrepentant liberalism?

Whereas the explicit involvement of the World Bank in the global debate concerning the best way to alleviate poverty is evident even to those with only a cursory knowledge of the social development literature, the role of the IMF in this global discourse is at first, and second, glance relatively muted by comparison. As Susan George and Fabrizio Sabelli's (1994) book on the Bank testifies, the World Bank is an increasingly open institution welcoming a dialogue with its detractors. The same can hardly be said about the IMF. An interview with an official in the Bank is an Open Sesame to all the Bank phone numbers, corridors, and many reports. An interview with an official in the IMF, across the street, is a more or less chaperoned event with no side avenues open to be explored. That having been said there is finally emerging through the work of Kopits (1994), Tanzi (1992; 1993), Ahmad (1993), Chand and Shome (1995), Bruno (1992), Hardy (1991) and others some attempt at public accountability to professional colleagues by the fiscal affairs and human resource technical specialities inside the IMF. At the World Summit on Social Development the Fund even produced a glossy brochure on the social dimensions of its policy dialogue (IMF, 1995a).

The impact of the IMF and World Bank structural adjustment pro-grammes in developing countries has of course generated a vast and critical development studies literature. The requirement that to access loans governments should open their countries to free trade, reduce their public expenditures, and ensure a non-inflationary monetary policy has been argued by many to be the cause of impoverishment, the further indebted-ness of many countries, and the political exhaustion of potential opposition forces (Ghai, 1991; Haggard and Kaufman, 1992; Rodrigeuz and Griffith-Jones, 1992). The policies of the Bretton Woods institutions have generated calls for the end of the tyranny of the Bank and the Fund over developing and transition countries. In the section on the World Bank below we will examine whether the call to replace structural adjustment by adjustment with a human face (Jolly, 1991) has been listened to. We will examine the new priority given to poverty alleviation by the Bank and assess the meaning of this in the light of the emerging global discourse on social policy. But what of the more immune IMF? Does it still articulate a policy of unrepentant free market liberalism? Does it feel it has any responsibility towards the social casualties of austerity structural adjustment packages?

Killick and Malik (1991) usefully summarized the social impact of IMF inspired structural adjustment policies in the developing world as:

1   having an appreciable effect on the distribution of incomes, although these are apt to be complex and vary from one situation to another
2   meaning that groups of the poor can indeed be among the losers, with the urban working class particularly at risk
3   ensuring that governments adopting Fund programmes are nonetheless free to adopt measures to protect vulnerable groups, although there may be hard negotiations with the Fund over measures which are liable to create large claims on public revenues.

As early as 1992 the Fund did acknowledge the shortcomings of some of the structural adjustment programmes it had influenced: 'Mistakes have been made . . . One of the results, as is well known, is a greater emphasis on social aspects of adjustment and the explicit incorporation of affordable safety nets in an increasing number of instances' (IMF, 1992). However the underpinning defence made by the IMF of its structural adjustment policies, which are acknowledged to have a negative impact in the short term on some citizens, is that 'social development requires a strategy of high quality economic growth' (IMF, 1995a: 1). Such a strategy requires macroeconomic stability, a marked based environment for trade and investment, good governance through accountable institutions and a transparent legal framework, and participatory development through active involvement of all groups in society' and, most relevant to this chapter, 'sound social policies, including social safety nets to protect the poor during the period of economic reform, cost effective social expenditures, and employment generating labour market policies' (IMF, 1995a: 1). Its role in social policy advice is acknowledged to be limited. The Fund often works in tandem with the Bank and the latter takes responsibility for social policy. Unlike the Bank – and this was reaffirmed at an IMF board meeting in 1988 – the Fund does not establish conditions on the use of its loans related to income distribution. Nonetheless it claims that while supporting 'labour market policies aimed at ensuring high employment through competitive and flexible wages and at removing other rigidities it adheres to ILO principles' (1995a: 7).

The thrust of publicly stated IMF social policy in the short term is the safety net. These can 'comprise targeted subsidies, cash compensation in lieu of subsidies, improved distribution of essentials such as medicine, temporary price controls for essential commodities, severance pay and retraining for retrenched public sector employees, employment through public works, and adaption of permanent social security arrangements to protect the poorest' (1995a: 15). In the longer term the stated aim is 'to achieve significant real growth in social expenditures including primary education and health . . . [while in some cases] . . . shifting resources away from university education or advanced medical care' (1995a: 18–22).

If the IMF and the Bank tend towards the same safety net social policy strategy what, if anything, distinguishes them in their recommendations to and dealings with government? The Bank, as we shall see, attaches social conditions to its loans; the IMF does not. The Bank, eventually, publishes its country specific advice; the IMF, in general, does not. Over and above this, based on published works and interviews with Fund officials in their Fiscal Affairs Division, it is reasonable to conclude that the IMF tends to avoid means tested social assistance schemes as they are difficult to implement in egalitarian and partially monetized economies, whereas the Bank has supported them. The IMF is sceptical of indexing benefits to prices in an inflationary economy, or to wages, as this would allow pensioners to share in new economic growth; the Bank often supports indexing minimum pensions. The Fund defends work tested food for work programmes as a non-discriminatory self-targeting policy (Chu and Gupta, 1993); the Bank is less clear about this. In other words the flavour of IMF social policy thinking is one that might be relevant to the impoverishment of the South. The concerns of those interested in the debate between pay-as-you-go or fully funded wage related social security systems are not often addressed in IMF thinking on social policy. Etisham Ahmad, now working in the Fiscal Affairs Division of the IMF wrote, while at the Bank, the chapter on social policy of the OECD/IMF/EBRD/Bank joint study of the Soviet economy. He concluded that:

1   There are a number of measures available to protect the vulnerable including 'cash transfers, the provision of specified quantities of certain essential goods at given price, or food stamps' (OECD, 1991f: 137).
2   'The danger to be avoided is to construct an elaborate and expensive social security edifice that provides benefits to a privileged subset of the target population, in the presence of poverty and need' (OECD, 1991f: 192).

Kopits (1993) however, when head of the Fiscal Affairs Division of the IMF, did address explicitly the issue of a longer term strategy for social security, as distinct from safety net short-termism. The perceived crisis of the typical European Bismarckian social security system, he suggests, is seen to result from 'generous eligibility for benefits granted for political expediency rather than on the basis of either past contributions or genuine need' (1993: 103), together with 'excessive claims for sick pay, partial disability pensions, early retirement pensions, length of service pensions, and health care benefits' (1993: 105). Reform is required which is cost effective. 'Social security can no longer be viewed simply in terms of magnitude and coverage of benefits, but must be assessed also in terms of fiscal and allocative costs' (1993: 108).

The IMF has since 1989 provided assistance to more than a dozen countries in the design of new social security schemes. These include Algeria, Bolivia, Brazil, Greece, Hungary, Indonesia and most former Soviet republics. In proposing reforms Kopits suggests the following considerations. Firstly, there is the cultural and historical context. In some societies the extended family or village structure 'operates relatively well as an informal social security scheme obviating the need for the urgent introduction of large scale public pensions' (1993: 108). At the other end of the spectrum, where 'households have been atomized . . . there is an immediate need for provision of an extended safety net, as in much of the former Soviet Union'. Secondly, social security schemes should not 'interfere with the efficient allocation of resources and not act as a disincentive to save or to work'. Thirdly, the link between benefits and contributions should be strengthened but also contributions should be kept relatively low. Fourthly, they should discourage waste by, for example, introducing user fees in health and education provision. Fifthly, a clear distinction should be drawn institutionally between elements of the scheme such as pensions, sick pay, etc. Lastly, the schemes should be 'financially self sustaining over a long period of time'.

The proposals stressed by Kopits point in the direction of greater individual investment funds with individually earned benefits. They create the possibility for a greater role for Chilean-style mandated private pension funds. They suggest an overall retrenchment in contributions and benefits levels in the public sector of the scheme. In terms of public poverty relief of the pensioners in some countries they suggest a greater role for means tested assistance. In a manner which we will find recurring in the World Bank work on pensions, Australia and New Zealand crop up in a footnote as the only countries that have 'faced up to' the limits of the Bismarckian strategy by means testing all benefits (1993: 105).

The IMF, in sum, continues its normative role of 'fostering economic policies that have traditionally been labelled liberal internationalist' (Pauly, 1994: 120), but it has, in common as we shall see with the Bank, come to acknowledge the social impact on the vulnerable of some of its structural adjustment programmes. The *Annual Report* of the IMF in 1994 noted that 'the Board reaffirmed its recognition that some policy measures may have important distributional implications, that such distributional effects can undermine public support for the reforms, and that the design of Fund supported reform programmes should evaluate and seek to mitigate the short term adverse effects of policy measures on vulnerable groups' (IMF,

1994: 120). It is to the role of the Bank in this task of poverty alleviation in the context of structural adjustment that we now turn.

The World Bank: a safety net for the poor?

As a development bank the World Bank is far less cautious than the IMF about proclaiming in public its mission to foster social development to eradicate poverty.

> It is intolerable that, as the world approaches the twenty-first century, hundreds of millions of people still lack minimally acceptable levels of education, health and nutrition. Investing in people must therefore be the highest priority for developing countries – until human capital limitations no longer restrain growth or keep people in absolute poverty. Investing in people is the core of the World Bank's work

asserts Armeane Choksi, its Vice President for Human Resources (World Bank, 1995d: v).

The World Bank has clearly responded to the earlier criticisms of its policy and practice in developing countries by adopting an anti-poverty strategy (de Vries, 1996). The *World Development Report* by the Bank in 1990 focused on poverty. In 1991 the policy paper *Assistance Strategies to Reduce Poverty* was published. This was followed by the 1992 *Poverty Reduction* handbook. This focus of the World Bank on poverty in developing countries had already led to some softening of the earlier structural adjustment policies in Africa and Latin America. More socially sensitive adjustment policies were being conceived and implemented. The criticism of, for example, UNICEF in its report *Adjustment with a Human Face* (Cornia et al., 1987) had already begun to tell a little. By 1993 the Bank was able to claim that the 'share of adjustment lending that addresses social issues climbed from five per cent in Fiscal 1984–86 to 50 per cent in 1990–92. In Fiscal 1992, eighteen out of thirty-two adjustment loans included an explicit poverty focus, and fourteen of these adjustment loans had tranche release conditions' (World Bank, 1993, xi).

Interestingly, and this is a point we shall return to at length in the next chapter, the events in Eastern Europe of 1989 overtook this new 1992 anti-poverty initiative and, in a development that had not been foreseen, led to a major focus of the Bank's work on poverty alleviation being the countries of the CIS and Eastern Europe. This meant that the Bank was having to deal with and make recommendations for developed industrial economies on the mainland of continental Europe. It was ill equipped to do this and, in order to undertake the task, it needed to recruit a significant number of new officials and engage a new tranche of consultants more familiar with the income maintenance systems of developed economics and more sensitive to the social guarantees of the earlier regimes. The Human Resources Sector of the Europe and Central Asia Division of the Bank expanded rapidly.

Whereas the dominant tradition and practice in the human resources sectors of the Bank had been influenced by US liberalism at home and South American models of private welfare development abroad, combined with anti-poverty thinking appropriate to developing countries, the new influx of talent was engaged in a different discourse. These people brought an understanding of and commitment to the 'European' tradition of wage related social security systems and a sensitivity to the guarantees of 'communism'. Within this context it can be argued that it is not simply that the World Bank is an important actor (as we shall see in Chapter 4) in shaping post-communist social policy but that the pre-existing social guarantees of 'communism' have and continue to influence the Bank and reshape its understanding and thinking about appropriate social policy. Of course the factors leading to what has become a significant internal Bank dispute are more complex than this. Also shaping Bank thinking are the 'little miracles' of South East Asia that have demonstrated the case for state infrastructural expenditure on education and health, thus denting the case of the liberal fundamentalists (World Bank, 1993d).

Susan George claims that the Bank treats heretics badly: 'The research staff it recruits and the consultants that it hires are overwhelmingly trained in the same macroeconomics curriculum . . . to think in the same ways. They are trapped inside the glass walls of their own world view and led to believe theirs is a monopoly of the truth' (George and Sabelli, 1994: 199). Stern (forthcoming), in a draft of a chapter on the World Bank as intellectual actor for the second volume of the Bank's official history, claims that 'opposition can be regarded as misguided, uneducated or malevolent'. The ultimate heresy would be the position of Daly (in Cavanagh et al., 1994) who, in leaving the Bank, argued that there should be a 'move away from the ideology of global economic integration by free trade and export led growth and towards a more nationalist orientation that seeks to develop national production for internal markets as the first option, having recourse to international trade only when clearly much more efficient'. The Bank as a defender of GATT, argue George and Sabelli, could never accept this view. This argument is probably sound, for now, when it comes to the broader global and macroeconomic strategies supported by the Bank (but even here there is debate between fundamentalist liberal and state led infrastructure investment approaches), but it is not clear that the argument can be pressed to include the Bank's views on how, within the logic of capitalist development, to combat poverty or construct appropriate social policies. Commenting on the Bank's intent articulated in its 1993 *Annual Report* (World Bank, 1993a) that it intends to apply its research capacity to the priority areas of poverty, equity and social welfare issues, George suggests that the Bank's culture will thwart its ambitions to intellectual excellence in this field also. To suggest however that there is one Bank view on poverty and social policy is, the evidence of this study suggests, not true. There may, as we shall argue, be a dominant view but there is intense internal controversy among human resource specialists on the topic. In organizational terms also there are divisions inside the Bank, each with its distinctive approach.

Around 1993 the Bank reorganized and located most of its technical support staff in new departments of the Environment, of Education and Social Policy and of Development Economics. These sell their skills to the country specific operations. Even this is made more complicated by the fact that there are small specialist human resource support teams inside the operations departments advising the human resource operations specialists! The Vice Presidency in charge of Education and Social Policy owns the public face of Bank anti-poverty policy but this is not necessarily the same as that articulated by the human resource operations people. Further complication is provided by the fact that the Environment Department has located within it a Social Policy Thematic Team. Additionally there is a separate Policy Research Department which is distinct from the operations evaluation units in the country operations divisions. Our case study of the work of the Bank in Eastern Europe in the next chapter will illustrate in detail the conflicts that have emerged within and between these depart-ments with regard to policy advice in that region. In general terms the discordant voices of the Bank on the topics of poverty and social policy can be grouped as follows.

The dominant public face view of the Education and Social Policy Department combines labour intensive growth with investment in health and education backed up by an ill-defined safety net for the poor. This embraces a number of ideas through food for work programmes (although the Bank favours this less than the IMF), partial subsidy of goods and services and unresolved ideas on cash based social assistance. A technical head count of the poor combined with some mechanisms of income transfer, if informal systems are not working, characterizes this approach. Where this department addresses public social security schemes it tends to talk in terms of flat rate and means tested provision. The heretics in the Social Policy Thematic Team of the Environment Department prefer a more anthropologic and social assessment of the social relations involved in the generation of poverty. In a further contrast within the human resource operations division in Eastern Europe, and between these operations people and their small team of specialist advisers, controversy exists about the desirability of wage related pay-as-you-go state social security systems versus fully funded and privately managed individual accounting schemes. Proponents of the former are also to be found in the Policy Research Department. Proponents of the latter are concentrated in the Education and Social Policy Department and the Development Economics Depart-ment. The next chapter will document this story in more detail. In brief the following discordant publications from the Bank reflect this internal debate.

On pensions policy the Bank is, as a consequence of these internal divisions, in the unusual position of seeing published at the same time, by staff and consultants working in different parts of the Bank, two differently orientated texts. One of these, published by the Development Economics

Vice Presidency (World Bank, 1994b), edited by Estelle James and the focus of much controversy with the ILO and ISSA, proposes for transition economics severely reducing public pension provision to either a mere subsistence level universal flat rate or even a means tested flat rate system funded by payroll tax or general revenue. There should be a wage related pension scheme ideally individually accounted and privately managed as a second tier. In addition a third voluntary private pillar is proposed. The other publication produced from within the operations division for Eastern Europe (Barr, 1994) sets out policy options much more in keeping with existing practice in mainstream European systems. The common ground with the first position is the need to raise pension age, and the protection of minimum benefits. The differences are in the scope for state wage related pensions and their private alternatives and the degree of solidaritic redistribution embodied in the scheme.

The separate Education and Social Policy arm of the Bank responsible for the poverty strategy was recently commissioned to produce a paper for the Joint Development Committee of the World Bank and IMF on social security reforms and safety nets (World Bank, 1993f). It argues that 'Chile made a dramatic break with the past when it switched to a [pension system] operated by the private sector', but continues 'reforms of pension systems along the Chilean lines may be an unrealistic goal for . . . countries of Eastern Europe and the FSU. An intermediate approach might be a two or three tiered system, including a public scheme providing only the minimum subsistence pension' (1993f: 71). This approach is endorsed by the paper of the chair of the particular Joint Development Committee meeting at which the issue was discussed (27 September 1993). Thus, despite the continued dispute, Bank policy on pensions might be in danger of hardening in the direction of a residual minimum state pension plus private individual accounts. This story is taken up again in Chapter 4 where the impact of the encounter with Eastern Europe on Bank policy is considered in more detail.

Policy on means tested safety nets, however, remains unresolved and experimental even at the official level of the Joint Development Committee. The chair concluded that 'there is no general consensus on the correct approach to these [safety net] problems or the detailed solutions appropriate in each case' (1993f: 6). The joint paper does, however, in its discussion of the administrative obstacles to means tested safety nets, comment that 'Public works programmes paying low wages may provide a cost effective, if more limited, alternative with admin costs reduced through self selection' (1993f: 79). This clearly reflects the influence of IMF thinking mentioned earlier. The Education and Social Policy Department of the Bank has been commissioned to produce a report on the effectiveness of social safety nets which will focus on best practice. Similar research is to be undertaken by the Operations Evaluation Unit and the Policy Research Department!

While internal Bank discussion is evident it is nonetheless possible to discern a dominant approach which is powerful in its logic and derived

ideologically from the broader Bank consensus on the need for free trade
and deregulation. This is the social safety net approach, or as I will coin it,
social liberalism – liberalism with a human face. Nelson (1992: 232–44)
captures the political logic of this dominant approach sharply when
addressing the twin equity issues that exist in the structural adjustment
process. One issue is what to do with the very, often rural, poor who 'can
be helped without jeopardizing the economic requirements and constraints
of adjustment'; and the other is how to buffer the 'urban formal sector
workers and middle strata from the social costs of adjustment without
undercutting the adjustment effort itself'. Faced with these twin problems,
'the World Bank, the IMF and other external donors encourage governments to protect the poor [but] often urge them to stand firm against the
demands of labour unions and urban popular classes.' Carol Graham, a
one-time visiting fellow in the Vice Presidency for Human Resources at the
World Bank, describes with clarity the political logic of the dominant Bank
policy on the dust-jacket of her volume on *Safety Nets, Politics and the
Poor 1994*. It is worth reproducing in full:

> Countries worldwide are attempting difficult transitions from state-planned to
> market economies. Most of these countries have fragile democratic regimes that
> are threatened by the high social and political costs of reform. Governments –
> and ultimately societies – have to make hard choices about allocating scarce
> public resources as they undergo these transitions. A central, often controversial,
> and poignant question is how to protect vulnerable groups and the poor. What
> compensation, what safety net, will be provided for them?
>
> In this book, Carol Graham argues that safety nets can provide an environ-
> ment in which economic reform is more politically sustainable and poverty can
> be permanently reduced. However, these two objectives frequently involve trade-
> offs, as vocal and organized opponents to reform often concern governments far
> more than the poor do. These organized and less vulnerable groups tend to place
> heavy demands on the scarce resources available to governments at times of
> economic crisis. Governments that fail to address the social costs of reform,
> meanwhile, often face popular opposition that jeopardizes or even derails the
> entire market transition.
>
> The author examines these trade-offs in detail, with particular focus on how
> political and institutional contexts affect the kinds of safety nets that are
> implemented. For example, reaching the poor and vulnerable with safety nets
> tends to be more difficult in closed-party systems where entrenched interest
> groups have a monopoly on state benefits. In contrast, dramatic political change
> or rapid implementation of economic reform undermines the influence of such
> groups and therefore can provide unique political opportunities to redirect
> resources to the poor.
>
> Rather than focus their efforts on organized interest groups – such as public
> sector unions – which have a great deal to lose in the process of reform,
> governments might better concentrate their efforts on poor groups that have
> rarely, if ever, received benefits from the state. The poor, meanwhile, may gain a
> new stake in the ongoing process of economic and public sector reform through
> organizing to solicit the state for safety net benefits.

Against organized labour, against European corporatist social security
structures, and for the very poor: that is the political strategy of the
dominant anti-poverty thinking in the Bank. The new alliance the World

Bank is making with NGOs in order to more effectively reach the poorest (Cleary, 1996) is part of this strategy. By being seen as defenders of the poor in the South (the World Bank and Oxfam interestingly recently joined forces to lobby the US Congress to continue to release funds to the Bank) and co-opting a section of the international NGOs into this project the Bank's strategy is to out-manoeuvre the attempts by the ILO (see later) and the EU (also later) to maintain patterns of state wage related social security systems that serve the narrow interests of the regularly employed in the globalized economy. The dispute between the Bank and the ILO for example on good governance is an echo of this. While, as we shall see, the ILO believes the best defence for social security is tripartism (Cichon and Samuel, 1995), the Bank believes this excludes the poor from effective participation in poverty policy making.

The Organization for Economic Co-operation and Development: from welfare as a burden to welfare as investment?

Whereas since the founding Bretton Woods Conference of 1944 the IMF has the self-appointed role of making the world safe for free trade with minimum impediments to the 'allocative efficiencies' of the market, and the World Bank has increasingly assumed unto itself the enormous task of facilitating economic development globally while protecting the poor and the environment, the OECD founded in 1961 has the relatively modest aim of helping to achieve the highest sustainable economic growth and employment and rising living standards among its member countries. Nonetheless it does have a secondary aim of contributing to economic expansion in non-member countries and to the expansion of world trade (Article 1 of Convention of OECD). Unlike the IMF and the World Bank it does not provide loans on economic or social or political conditions. Its influence is limited to sharing the experience of member states among others and, through its string-free technical assistance, encouraging societal learning of best practice.

As with the IMF and the Bank its social policy concerns are reactive to or otherwise largely bound up with the prime economic growth orientation of the organization as a whole. Social considerations enter if they are regarded as a help or a hindrance to economic growth. It is not possible however to ascribe a meta-policy on economic and social matters to the OECD. Rather there is the Economic Directorate, which is 'IMF flavoured', on top and the less powerful Directorate of Education, Employment, Labour and Social Affairs which pursues its own agenda. Apart from the Centre for Co-operation with Economies in Transition which will be focused on in the next chapter, there is also an independent research centre on development which has fashioned an orientation of its own on social and economic development issues. Unlike the IMF and the Bank the OECD is situated in Europe and staffed by many more Europeans, and has a board voting policy which does not privilege the USA. One highly placed OECD official reported to me that the USA really did not take any notice of what the OECD did or said.

The Directorate of Education, Employment, Labour and Social Affairs was established in 1974 and achieved a high profile for the topic of social policy by the conference it convened in 1980 on the welfare state in crisis in OECD countries. While bringing the matter of social welfare higher up the agenda it concluded that 'Social policy in many countries creates obstacles to growth' (OECD, 1981). The association of the OECD with the 'welfare as burden' approach stems from that publication. Further work on social expenditures in OECD countries followed from this initiative. The interest in this and the enthusiasm of Ron Gass as Director of the Social Affairs Directorate led to the first meeting of social affairs ministers in 1988. OECD work in this field continued and became widely used among scholars. Publications followed on pensions (OECD, 1988a; 1993a), on health expenditure and policy (OECD, 1990b) and on unemployment (OECD, 1993f). The Council of the OECD in 1991, concerned about the burden of taxes on employment to sustain welfare expenditure, gave rise to further work on social policy by the Directorate, under the new Director, Tom Alexander. Concerned not simply to repeat the 'welfare as burden', liturgy and learning perhaps from parallel work of the OECD Development Centre which, in its review of the dynamic South East Asian economies concluded that 'limited but effective action by the state . . . [has led to] . . . rapid return to growth' (OECD, 1993b: 41), the social affairs official responsible for the draft of the impending ministerial conference fashioned the *New Orientations for Social Policy* document that asserted 'Non inflationary growth of output and jobs, and political and social stability, are enhanced by the role of social expenditures as investments in society' (OECD, 1994a: 12). This and other sentiments such as 'restrictions on social expenditure could be counter productive if the objectives of social policy are sacrificed. Jeopardising the quality of life . . . may be the most costly route of all' (1994a: 13), were adopted with minimal change as they progressed from the office in the Social Affairs Directorate, through middle and high rank meetings of government ministers, to the 1992 ministerial conference itself.

It is worth reproducing the five new orientations in full:

Contributing to social and economic welfare Non-inflationary growth of output and jobs, and political and social stability are enhanced by the role of social expenditures as investments in society.

Reconciling social policy objectives and budget limitations There is a need to reconcile social programme costs with overall limits on public budgets, but at the same time to ensure that economic measures are consistent with programme effectiveness and social objectives.

Managing the mix of public and private responsibilities The optimal balance should be sought between public and private sector responsibility in providing for the variety of needs of society, and in light of the comparative advantage of each sector.

Encouraging and facilitating the development of human potential High priority should be given to active measures which relate to employment, rather than to reliance on income maintenance alone; in general, the emphasis should be on the encouragement of human potential as an end in itself, as well as a contribution to market efficiency. Consistent with this objective, income transfer programmes should be structured to foster self-sufficiency through earnings, without sacrificing the goals of system social protection.

Achieving greater policy coherence Greater policy coherence should be achieved by a renewed focus on the means by which the strands of policy – setting goals, formulating policies, implementing them and thereafter administering programmes – may be pulled together across social, labour market education and economic policies and across levels of government.

Taken together these orientations reflect that, in contrast to the US influenced IMF and World Bank, the economic and social policy of the OECD represents a much more balanced set of economic and social considerations typical of mainstream European social and economic policy. The head of the social affairs section of the Directorate of Education, Employment, Labour and Social Affairs explained that the OECD preferred to work from the political realities of countries and attempt to balance economic and social considerations and work out the budgetary implications, whereas the IMF approached this as a top-down budget balancing exercise.

The *Annual Report* of the OECD for 1992 in its report of this work goes even further and articulates that 'The role of social policy . . . is to provide a framework which enables the fullest participation in all aspects of society for its citizens . . . to achieve this goal social expenditure should be regarded as underpinning the quality of life for all citizens' (OECD, 1992a: 174). This comes close to privileging social over economic policy, and comes close to a vision of social development being reflected in the work of some of the UN agencies we examine below. The distinctiveness of this approach will also be apparent when we examine in the next chapter some of the work undertaken by the OECD jointly with the ILO in relation to Eastern Europe.

Subsequent to the *New Orientations* conference work is proceeding in the Social Affairs Directorate on country social policy assessments with a limited number of volunteer countries. Hungary is one of these, and we will examine that country in the next chapter. While therefore we might conclude that social concerns and a supportive approach to social expenditure are higher on the OECD agenda than on that of the IMF or the Bank, a cautionary footnote is necessary. As part of the concern to balance and reconcile economic and social pressures it is significant that the OECD has commissioned studies recently on the various means tested social assistance programmes operated by member states. Publications resulting from this (Gough, 1995) are likely to profile the manner in which certain OECD countries, namely Australia and New Zealand, combine an extensive welfare state with a selective policy of targeting out potential beneficiaries via means tests. The likelihood is that this will chime with the anti-European, anti-state wage related social security approach of some in the Bank and will further challenge those European countries, and the EU as a whole, who might prefer to maintain the Bismarckian policies of universal social support.

The International Labour Organization: the setting and keeping of global labour and social standards

In refreshing contrast to the neo-liberal preoccupations and orientation of the IMF and the World Bank and to a lesser extent the OECD, the International Labour Organization derives its brief to set and keep common international labour and social standards from the social democratic climate of the period after the First World War. In the context of the Bolshevik unrest sweeping Europe the Treaty of Versailles, which settled the terms of the peace, included an important reference to labour conditions. In a phrase which has resonance today in the context of the drive to free trade and the consequent perceived danger of the race to the welfare bottom, the Treaty noted that 'the failure of any nation to adopt human conditions of labour is an obstacle in the way of other nations which desire to improve the conditions in their own countries' (quoted in Woolcock, 1995). Part XIII of the Treaty was concerned with international effort to establish common provision for: the right of association, wages for a reasonable standard of living, an eight hour day and a 48 hour week, no child labour, equal remuneration for men and women, and equal rights for migrant workers. These provisions were not, however, linked to any sanction or linked to trade law. The attempt, as we shall see in the next section, to link increased trade with common labour and social standards continues today. The strategy, via the adoption of ILO conventions, the first of which dates from its founding year in 1919, was to persuade governments by peer and moral pressure to sign up and ratify conventions of good practice. Only when governments ratify conventions has the ILO any power to seek an enforcement of them.

Initially the ILO conventions were concerned strictly with labour standards, although by 1934 convention 44 required that those states ratifying the convention maintain a system of unemployment benefits or allowances. Just as the political climate of 1918–20 established the ILO, so did the next phase of social optimism in the wake of the Second World War provide greater scope for the work of the ILO. The Keynesian climate encouraged the ILO at its Philadelphia meeting in 1944 to declare the convention on freedom of association and the protection of the right to organize. The declaration also asserted that lasting peace was only possible on the basis of social justice and that this embodied the right of human beings to economic security and equal opportunity. As a consequence the ILO was to be responsible for 'examining and considering all international economic and financial policies and measures in the light of this fundamental objective' (Plant, 1994: 158). At the same time the ILO was instrumental in enabling the UN to convert its 1948 Declaration of Human Rights into the 1966 Covenant on Economic, Social and Cultural Rights. Articles 6–10, for which the ILO was responsible, covered the rights to work, to decent conditions and to strike, and importantly (Article 9) to social security and (Article 10) the right of families to social protection and social assistance.

Throughout the 1950s, 1960s and 1970s, therefore the ILO established a large number of conventions which, if, ratified, provided for a well functioning system of social insurance, social support and social assistance. The conventions, nearly 200 cover employment policy, human resource development, social security, social policy, wage fixing machinery, conditions of work, industrial relations, labour administration, and the protection of women, children and indigenous peoples. An important emphasis in the internal workings of the ILO and in its policy prescriptions is tripartism, that good governance to secure social security requires the consensus of industry, workers and government.

The ILO can claim some success over the years of its existence. The ratification of its conventions is by no means universal. However by 1994 the average number of ratifications per country had reached 41 (ILO, 1995c: 115). More conventions are ratified by developed countries (average of 52 in Europe, 42 in the Americas, 27 in Africa and 21 in Asia) although this does not mean ILO influence in developing countries is minimal (Strang and Chang, 1993). However, Strang concluded that 'the ILO's most concrete contributions to policy are seen in the laggard welfare states of the industrialised world'. Here 'where welfare is politically viable but contested international standards most usefully amplify, legitimate and depoliticalize policy options.' In such cases reform elites use external standard setting ('our international obligations') to further labour and social reform. The ILO, then, 'celebrates the enlightened social and labour policy of Western Europe' and is involved in 'a difficult bootstrapping operation, using the existing prestige of the Western welfare model to promote its further realisation' (1993: 259).

It comes as no surprise that this European welfare policy orientation of the ILO should have come under challenge in the 1980s with the ascendancy of neo-liberal thinking and the increased influence of the IMF and the World Bank in shaping structural adjustment policies in many developing countries. How has the ILO held up to this challenge? What are the prospects for the continued influence of the ILO? We shall address these questions briefly below, amplify the points in Chapter 4 where we examine concrete examples in the context of structural adjustment in post-communist countries, and return to them in the concluding chapter. The specific issue of whether and how to build labour and social standards into free trade agreements will be picked up in the next section on the World Trade Organization.

Reviewing the impact of the 'decade of structural adjustment' (the 1980s) on ILO policy and practice and the maintenance of standards, Plant concluded that as more flexible forms of working contract were being encouraged in more developing countries in the context of the globalization of production there was a real danger that 'the relevance of the ILO's standard setting framework will be necessarily limited as a reference point for addressing practical problems experienced by a growing proportion of the workforce in most developing countries' (1994: 194). The Director General of the ILO asked in 1991 at a conference on the informal sector: 'Have we been too ambitious and unrealistic in our standard setting activities, and thus contributed to the widening gap between the protected workers of the modern sector and the large number of people in the informal sector deprived of any form of social protection?' (1994: 193–8). He answered that standards should not be lowered in this context but an appropriate strategic response might be 'to concentrate in the first instance on the promotion of core standards'. These would cover the basic human rights of association, equality of opportunity, and abolition of child labour. However, as Plant comments the real issues in structural adjustment are not these but 'how adjustment can take place without undue sacrifice for employment and social protection and how enough of the state budget can be set aside for unemployment compensation, retraining of redeployed workers etc.'.

In the context of the globalized restructuring of work, and the particular struggle between international agencies (Chapter 4) to influence post-communist social policy, the following shifts in thinking, internal debates, and dilemmas appear to exist for the ILO. First, can it hold the line in favour of state social security against a mixed state/private system? Here the new dominant tendency articulated by Cichon (1994a; 1994b) and others is to accommodate some mix of provision in order to defend the basic Bismarckian structure. The ILO has, however, fought long and hard to expose the flaws in the dominant World Bank thinking on pensions (World Bank, 1994b) by arguing that there is no demographic imperative leading to privatization, that the European-type schemes are sustainable, and that the privatization strategy is merely a cover to increase the share of private capital savings. Moreover it is argued that the strategy is risky and imposes a heavy burden on current workers who have to finance the existing pay-as-you-go system as well as funding their own schemes (Beattie and McGillivray, 1995; Cichon, 1996). Secondly, can it hold the line for wage related social security when such policy increasingly reflects the interests of a reducing number of citizens? As we shall see in Chapter 4 Standing (1992) has articulated from inside the ILO the case for a basic citizen's income policy. It is interesting to note that, in an exchange of fax communications with me in 1995, while ILO defenders of the Bismarckian tradition assert that 'citizen's income . . . is nowhere seriously considered for implementation . . . the untested and simplistic concept has never been promoted in any national ILO social protection project' (Cichon), the protagonists of a citizen's income strategy insist that while the conservatives have the field at the moment . . . we [the ILO] have published articles and books on this, held ILO seminars on it, and behind the scenes, some very senior officials support the idea' (Standing). Thirdly, in the face of the power of the Bretton Woods institutions to force at best a social liberal agenda, how can the ILO maintain a broader commitment to social security and social protection? Here two kinds of response are forthcoming. One is to work to create the political and social conditions to enable citizens to resist the fiscalization of welfare. Cichon and Samuel (1995) argue, as we shall see in Chapter 4, that to make social protection work there is a paramount need for forms of governance, including tripartism, that bring the views and interests of those to be socially secured into the decision making process. Cichon in a personal communication elaborated as follows: 'We [the ILO] try to promote the empowerment of citizens (or better, residents) by fostering multi-party or tripartite governance of social protection schemes. Pluralistic governance of social protection should help entrench redistributive structures within a society that are adequate countervailing powers against the fiscalisation of social policy.' The other response is to attempt to secure a greater role at the international level for the ILO when structural adjustment is on the agenda. Plant (1994) has proposed, following a 1993 ILO conference resolution to this effect, that procedural guarantees should exist that ensure that no proposal for labour law reform, in the context of World Bank facilitated structural adjustment, should be submitted to governments without prior ILO consultation. The other way in which the ILO might secure a greater role for itself in the emerging global governance reform agenda is in relation to inserting a labour or social clause into trade agreements policed by the World Trade Organization. The prospects for this are discussed in the next section. Finally it should be noted that the ILO has been concerned by the thrust of the Bank strategy and argument that the protection of the poor in the context of structural adjustment (secured by a safety net) is quite a separate matter from the social security of established workers (secured by 'unaffordable and inflexible' social insurance schemes). In its contribution to the World Summit on Social Development the ILO stressed that its labour standards strategy was not incompatible with policy to eradicate poverty in developing countries. It noted the importance of 'alliance building, involving in particular a search for the common interests of the trade unions, the employers and other groups in civil society. New groups entering the labour market need to be organised and represented, dialogue needs to be established with the associations, action groups, and local communities which often represent substantial segments of the poor' (Rodgers, 1995: 177). However it also seemed to recognize the writing on the wall in terms of the threat of flexible employment and globalism to labour standards by concluding that 'It is imperative to promote universal coverage of at least a minimum set of protections, such as those ILO conventions that relate to primary legislation in the areas of child labour, discrimination, and occupational safety. In the context of poverty eradication a clear focus must emerge on what and how to regulate' (1995: 174). This leads to the link between standards and free trade discussed in the next section.

The World Trade Organization: can social and labour standards and free trade coexist?

Nowhere is the historic role of the ILO to prevent competitive free trade undercutting labour and social standards put more sharply to the test than in the context of the ongoing global debate about whether and how to insert a social clause (guarding against social cost cutting) into free trade agreements. A compelling historic counterpoint to the contemporary global irresolution on this issue is the view taken by President Roosevelt in the context of the 1937 New Deal legislation. He asserted then that 'Goods produced under conditions which do not meet rudimentary standards of decency should be regarded as contraband and ought not to be allowed to pollute the channels of interstate commerce' (quoted in Collingworth et al., 1994: 10).

The completion of the GATT negotiations in 1994 ushering in an era of greater free trade has prompted the concerns that this will undermine those social protection measures and labour and social regulations and standards that have been secured at least in parts of the developed capitalist world. We have reached the bizarre moment in history when calls to conserve social protection measures in Europe by exporting them to other countries via, for example, social clauses in trade agreements are labelled by an alliance of free market fundamentalism and some Southern governments as protectionism.

The following series of press reports at the time of the final GATT negotiations are instructive and relevant 'The charge that developing countries are engaged in social dumping – competing unfairly by denying their workers basic rights and decent conditions – is potent' (*The Economist*, 9 April 1994). However, 'Developing countries were intensifying their opposition to the inclusion of social clauses into the final [GATT] agreement, fearing that attempts to set minimum global standards . . . were an attempt by the west to indulge in back door protectionism . . . The French kept up the pressure . . . saying that the World Trade Organization would be a better forum than the ILO for setting and policing labour market standards' (*Guardian*, 13 April 1994). But nonetheless, 'No preparatory work had been completed towards inserting social clauses into the GATT agreement' (P. Sutherland, Director General GATT, *Guardian*, 14 April 1994), and indeed the World Trade Organization was established without such work being done.

The opinion of developing and middle income countries was almost universally opposed to the insertion of social clauses. The strongest defender of the idea of inclusion apart from France was, interestingly, the USA (Woolcock, 1995). Historically it has operated a kind of social clause unilaterally in the context of its 1984 Trade and Tariff Act. In determining with whom it trades preferentially the USA excludes those countries that do not recognize its interpretation of workers' rights. This includes the right of association, the right to organize, the prohibition of forced labour, a minimum age for child labour, and acceptable conditions of work. These are not the same as and are generally weaker than ILO conventions that the USA does not ratify. Peer pressure plus loss of preferential trade terms has, over the years, led to changes in labour standards of some countries with which the USA trades. The European Union has very recently introduced a bilateral clause, which offers additional trade preferences for countries which meet the ILO convention on forced labour, freedom of association, collective bargaining and minimum age of employment. Only the forced labour part is currently operational. The remainder takes effect from 1998 (Woolcock, 1995: 17).

The GATT and now WTO rules would outlaw this kind of preferential trade based on a unilateral social clause. In 1953, for example, Belgium attempted to trade preferentially with those countries that had a universal family allowance scheme (Esty, 1994). This was outlawed under the GATT because it does not cover the general economic, labour and social context within which manufacturing takes place. However, Woolcock asks whether the WTO is 'up to rulings which go against the interests of its two most important members' (1995: 22). The prospect is that unilateral social clauses might emerge, he suggests, which are less demanding than ILO sponsored social clauses. Progress on this issue has not been easy inside the ILO also. The ILO for example agreed in 1994 at its seventy-fifth conference to establish a working party on the implications of free trade for social standards. The ILO competence in this field was, after all, challenged by the idea that the WTO might regulate global labour standards. However, such is the politically charged nature of the issue, and such is the potential for a North/South split, that the ILO governing body would only agree that the working party to consider the issue should be the entire 56 person governing body itself. Woolcock (1995) reports that 'The main proponents of a social clause (the US administration, the French government and the trade unions) faced the main opponents (India, China, Brazil and the employers).' By its second meeting in April 1995 it became clear that little progress was possible and it was agreed that the issue of a sanction based social clause should be set aside for the time being. At the World Trade Organization's meeting of ministers in December 1996 the debate was pursued with vigour. A compromise emerged in the final declaration. On the one hand the conference committed itself to the 'observance of internationally recognised core labour standards' and noted that the ILO is the competent body to set and deal with labour standards. On the other it was resolved that 'the use of labour standards for protectionist purposes is rejected' and that 'the comparative advantage of countries, particularly low-wage developing countries, must in no way be put into question'. The WTO and the ILO will continue to collaborate. The meaning of this declaration is to open the different interpretations: the International Confederation of Free Trade Unions applauded the commitment to core labour standards by the WTO, and the Malaysian Trade Minister concluded that 'there will be no more talk of labour standards in the WTO' (Khor, 1997).

The impasse on this issue illustrates sharply the complexity of the contending interests converging to shape a post cold war global social policy that might be concerned to achieve at one and the same time the increased prosperity of the South (via free trade), the greater redistribution of resources from North to South, and the regulation of the global economy in sustainable ways that preserve and enhance the social achievements of developed welfare states. This issue will be returned to in the final chapter when the current global governance reform agenda is reviewed.

Subglobal regional actors:

The EU and NAFTA compared: social regulation versus liberal capitalism?

In the foreword to the book by Grinspin and Cameron examining the political economy of North American free trade, it is asserted that

> Accelerating globalisation during the 1980s undercut the domestic social contract in the advanced industrialised countries. What was required, and absent, was a social contract on a global scale . . . There was no global labour ministry, there could be no floor to buttress global labour standards, let alone a global minimum wage. *Laissez-faire* had returned, via the back door of trade and corporate investment, with the inequalities and instabilities that it implies . . . In North America regional economic integration has proceeded under entirely conservative auspices, rejecting high wages and continental regulation. Free trade undermines what is left of the mixed economy, which is seen as archaic and protectionist.

The argument continues that

> NAFTA lacks even the embryonic safeguards of the EC: no regional development fund, no common regulation to prevent a 'race to the bottom', in labour and environmental standards and no movement towards democratic political and governmental institutions on a continental scale. (1993: xiv)

Four futures are envisaged. Either the world gives in to *laissez-faire* and the decline in standards and the political chaos this gives rise to; or there is a return to post Second World War national regulation with high trade tariffs; or there is a sustained attempt to create mixed economy instruments on a global scale. Fourthly, and most likely, is the creation of standards and redistributive and regulatory policies on a regional scale.

NAFTA and the EU, then, represent contrasting approaches to tackling at a subglobal regional level the problems posed to national welfare states by increased globalization and pressures to free trade. In Europe, developing from the earlier initiatives of the Council of Europe which are described in the next section, the Single European Act of 1987 already embodied a social dimension. This provided for free movement of workers and social security for migrant workers (Article 51), equal pay for men and women (Article 119), health and safety standards (Article 118a), conditions of work (Article 118) and the requirement to establish a social dialogue with employers and employees (Article 118b). While the Delors vision, articulated in 1988, for a Community Charter on Fundamental Social Rights was not accepted in its entirety the Social Chapter of the Maastricht Treaty of 1992 embodied and strengthened the idea that a common market in goods and services required common and compatible approaches, if not entirely convergence, among member country social policies. These together with the redistributive Structural Fund established in 1979 and strengthened in 1992, and the work on poverty and social exclusion, represent in comparative global terms a bold approach to building a regional social policy. A level of European legal, political and social citizenship has already been achieved (Meehan, 1993). States have lost sovereignty to supranational authority in the sphere of social policy in Europe (Leibfried, 1994).

Having said this, of course, these achievements and plans for their further development have come under pressure from a number of sources in recent years that reflect the constraints upon the EU as a whole operating in a global competitive arena. Internally the UK has resisted the policy drift, preferring instead a less regulatory NAFTA approach while advancing the interests of Atlantic capital against Rhine capital (Hodges and Woolcock, 1993). Certainly jobs have been created more readily in the North American context and this led the EU to focus sharply in a White Paper on how to combine economic competitiveness with social protection (European Commission, 1993a). More recently the report by Padraig Flynn, European Commissioner for Employment and Social Affairs on *Social Protection in Europe* (European Commission, 1995b) returns to this theme. A number of social policy initiatives are scattered around these recent EU documents which try to balance the requirement of firms to lower their overhead costs with the desire to maintain modified forms of social protection. Among these are suggestions for:

1   reducing employers' social security costs
2   maintaining levels of social protection for those who work shorter hours
3   allowing income from work to be topped up with income from social security (or vice versa)
4   allowing the self-employed to access benefits
5   recognizing in the benefit system the work of carers.

The working out, then, of a European level social policy has led to frustration for those who would have liked to see a fully fledged social democratic approach. The balance of political forces across Europe together with the absence of European level corporatist structures involving close government and homogeneous trade union movement collaboration suggest that high taxation, highly redistributive policies are not on (Huber and Stephens, 1993). However the dominant Christian democratic orientation of the major European players is likely to continue to marginalize the neo-liberals. This social consensual centre will, nonetheless, have to find acceptable social policy solutions that maintain the EU's competitiveness while, at the same time, working on a global level to establish comparable global policy approaches. One interesting contribution to the rethinking of supranational social policy in the context of the global restructuring of employment has been made by Albert Weale (1994). While also suggesting that the extremes of market liberalism and fully institutional social policy are not on the European agenda, he argues the case for a progressive liberalism. This progressive liberalism has much in common with the social liberalism approach of some in the World Bank that was described earlier. One element would be that the EU not only involves itself in the business of supranational social *redistribution* (the structural fund) and the business of supranational social *regulation* (the articles on workers' rights, for example) but also enters the business of supranational social *provision*. A minimum European social assistance payment either of the Atkinson (Atkinson and Morgensen, 1993) participation income kind or of the van Parijs (1995) citizen's income kind could be paid for out of a carbon tax and provide a European-wide minimum safety net against the threat of welfare tourism and migration.

In sharp contrast is the almost complete absence of anything recognizable as a social dimension to the North American Free Trade Association. There are no significant redistributive mechanisms to bridge the gap between countries of different levels of development. There is no attempt to deepen the participatory democratic institutions at a supranational level. There are no substantial mechanisms in place to promote the upward harmonization of social, labour and environmental standards (Grinspin and Cameron, 1993). Under pressure from the labour movement and the environmental movement in the USA and Canada, amendments to the agreement in the form of the North American Agreement on Labour Co-operation (NAALC) were negotiated at the last stages, but in practice they seem to have provided little scope for labour and social standard harmonization as they concentrate on reinforcing existing domestic legislation. There is now a Labour Secretariat of NAFTA and by the middle of 1995 four labour disputes had been brought before it by US unions, accusing the Mexican government of not enforcing its own ILO standard labour laws. No findings against Mexico have been made, leading the unions to claim that the labour side-accord of NAFTA is a 'grand fiasco' (*The Economist*, 18 February 1995: 48).

Clearly the emergence of global social policy will be paralleled by the emergence of diverse regional social policies. A key issue for the future is whether arguments about subsidiarity, currently played out in Europe to justify the delegation of key policy decisions from European level to national level, will be replicated globally to justify the delegation from global to regional level of key regulatory decisions. Subglobal regional regulations would only be a stopgap measure. In the context of cross-regional free trade they would always be in danger of being subverted by those regions adopting a very weak regulatory framework. The tension between the EU and NAFTA in this regard is a case in point. Clearly some in the EU see the resolution of this problem lying in the adoption of EU-type regulations at a global level and will continue to pursue this argument at the World Trade Organization and in G7 summits. As Hirst and Thompson conclude: 'The EU will be most successful if it acts to promote international economic governance rather than introduce inward-looking and territorially bounded policy measures' (1996: 200).

The Council of Europe: would-be champion of a Social Charter?

Unlike the EU and NAFTA the Council of Europe is not an economic free trade zone. Established in the wake of the Second World War to symbolize the human rights concerns of free market capitalism in contradiction to the socialist orientation of the Eastern bloc, it has now developed into an intergovernmental organization that embraces West and East: almost 40 countries are members. The council, through its European Court of Human Rights, has established supranational authority over member states in the field of human rights. In the sphere of social rights the Council had established by 1961 a European Social Charter that embodied 19 fundamental rights. Four more were added in 1988. In all they cover the areas of employment protection, social protection, and rights for categories of people like children and migrant workers. A further revision of the Charter was completed in 1996 and has received its first country signatories. This has generated a list of 31 rights and adds rights such as the right of protection against poverty and the right to housing. Some of the rights in the sphere of employment were strongly influenced by ILO Policy; some go beyond ILO standards. The Council also has established a European Code of Social Security. Whereas adherence to the European Convention on Human Rights is obligatory on members, signing up for the Social Charter is optional. If signing and ratifying, member states must sign up for 10 clauses of which six must be of a specified nine. This menu basis does allow, therefore for countries to, for example, avoid a commitment to the right to organize or the right to social security. Somewhat similarly to the situation of the ILO the Council of Europe can be accused of establishing a large number of worthy goals in the social sphere to which those who are not interested need not pay attention.

While in the cold war years the Council's Social Charter was rather like a sleeping beauty (Hulse, 1995), with the rush of post-communist governments to embrace, at least initially, extreme neo-liberal and antisocial economic policies the Social Charter has assumed a greater importance, especially in post-communist countries. Supporters of social protection, as we shall see in Chapter 4, point to the need to subscribe to European standards as a reason for resisting the most extreme cost cutting initiatives of their ministers of finance. In this context it is not without significance that the enforcement mechanisms of the Charter are about to be strengthened. A protocol for collective complaints against a country's failure to live up to what it has ratified was adopted by the Committee of Ministers in 1995. This will allow labour and social movements to use the monitoring procedures of the Council to pressure laggard governments. Previously the monitoring was relatively hidden from view in a Committee of Experts report.

The Directorate of Social and Economic Affairs of the Council does not regard the Social Charter as the most significant aspect of the Council's social policy (it has actually been managed by the Directorate of Human Rights). It prefers instead to point to its Social Development Fund, used to help member states solve problems resulting from migration, its work on social exclusion, and its attempts to further the implementation of the UN Convention on the Rights of Children. It has steered a working party on the social and economic consequences of the restructuring of the economies of Europe which reported to a summit of Heads of Council of Europe states in October 1997. Emerging from this working party are recommendations that the Council of Europe should play a role *vis-à-vis* the World Bank as was recommended by Plant (see earlier) for the ILO. When the Bank proposes labour and social reforms for member countries the Council should approve them in terms of any threat they might pose to the maintenance of the Social Charter standards. Of equal importance in the recommendations under discussion is the idea that social protection policy, in the context of the restructuring of work, should increasingly shift from employment based to citizen based entitlements (Council of Europe, 1995a). The Health and Welfare Committee of the Parliament of the Council has recently called for a report on social policy and this could lead to the Directorate codifying further guidelines for social policy for member countries in the near future.

The Council represents a unique supranational body which, for nearly the whole of one very large continent, is attempting to set the rules of the game on human rights and social and labour rights for the operation of capitalism. It embraces developed and developing nations. It embodies within it the tension between the desire to protect the social achievements of western welfare states and the wish to let currently excluded countries into a fair share of world trade to facilitate their development. It represents a mini UN system for a region of the globe although it is not the UN's representative in the region. In this sense it competes with the UN Economic Commission for Europe which is one of the UN bodies, as we shall see, which is under threat in the desire on the part of 'leading' northern states to streamline the UN. Equally it represents a form of intergovernmental association alternative to that of the projected monetary union of the EU. For some it could serve as an alternative model to the EU for the social regulation of the economies of the pan-European region. The Council of Europe should not be ignored by policy analysts.

The UN agencies UNICEF, UNDP, UNRISD: the global social reformists?

Returning from the regional to the global and casting around for opposition to the free market fundamentalism of the IMF and the 'at best' safety net social liberalism of the World Bank we encounter, along with the ILO, other elements of the UN system. The United Nations is a complex and divided organization. Even its work in the social sphere is divided among a number of agencies. In overall charge of these activities is the Economic and Social Council of the UN. As we shall see in Chapter 6, this is one of the bodies that some reformist elements in the North would like to see strengthened and streamlined. This committee, through its Social Development Commission, was responsible for the UN Summit on Social Development that took place in 1995 and upon which we report in the next section. This, however, is not the place to describe systematically the diverse agencies of the UN or to track policy proposals and resolutions through the labyrinth committee structure. Other books do the former (Luard, 1990; Roberts and Kingsbury, 1989) and much more work on the latter is required. Rather, what is important for our purposes here is to pick out for particular attention those elements of the UN system which, largely through the entrepreneurial and visionary drive of its key professional cadre, have stood out as the counterweight to the otherwise *laissez-faire*, free trade antisocial orientation of the Bank and the Fund. As we shall describe in more detail in the final chapter, there has emerged a global intra- and inter-agency discourse on the future for social policy and social development and certain UN agencies have been very active in this discourse.

It's as key voices in this discourse that we are interested in the UN agencies at this point. The WHO and UNESCO are not so prominent here. Rather the agencies that spring to mind, that advertise their publications in the same places that the World Bank sells its *World Development Reports*, are UNICEF, the UNDP (United Nations Development Programme) or more particularly the section that publishes the UNDP's annual *Human Development Report*, and the semi-autonomous research institute UNRISD (United Nations Research Institute for Social Development).

Long before the Bank invented its poverty programme, in the decades of unreformed fundamentalist structural adjustment that did so much to further indebt the South to the North, it was dedicated professionals such as James Grant, Head of UNICEF until his recent death, Richard Jolly, Frances Stewart and Giovanni, Andrea Cornia, UNICEF economists, and others inside UNICEF who did so much to (1) monitor the impact on children of the global economic conditions of the 1980s, (2) articulate an alternative strategy of adjustment with a human face (Cornia et al., 1987) and (3) engage not only in public polemic but directly with the Bank and Fund professionals to attempt to shift thinking. Jolly (1991) reports that as early as 1982 James Grant was in discussion with leading Bank and Fund personnel on the impact of adjustment policy. As a consequence a joint Bank/UNICEF meeting took place in 1994 at which the UNICEF paper entitled 'IMF Adjustment Policies and Approaches and the Needs of Children' was presented. To cut a long story short (detailed in Jolly, 1991) the influence that began then and continued through, for example, the annual UNICEF publication on *The State of the World's Children* led to the reform of World Bank policy and the adoption by it of lending strategies that aimed to protect the poorest as we described earlier. By 1995 UNICEF was able to make the following claim: 'In 1990 the World Summit for Children set goals for reducing deaths, malnutrition, disease and disability among the children of the developing world. Four years later, a majority of nations are on track to achieve a majority of these goals' (UNICEF, 1995a). The impact of UNICEF on Bank thinking and strategy continues as will be described in the next chapter. Practical arrangements are now in place for concrete collaboration between the two agencies in their parallel work in Eastern Europe.

Towards the end of this period the work of UNICEF was reinforced by the work of the report office of the UNDP. In 1990 it began its series of annual publications entitled the *Human Development Report* (UNDP, 1990; 1991; 1992; 1993a; 1994; 1995a; 1996). It fashioned, out of the earlier debate among development analysts, a new measure of social progress, the human development index. As we saw in Chapter 2, this combines longevity with educational attainment and a modified measure of income to rank countries on a scale somewhat differently from the rank order that would pertain if GNP alone were used. This would further reinforce the paradigm shift from fundamentalist liberalism towards some kind of socially orientated adjustment and development policies that would increasingly be articulated by even IMF and World Bank economists.

The 1992 *Human Development Report* joined the emerging debate on the reform of global governance (which will be examined in more detail in Chapter 6) and argued that 'Human society is increasingly taking on a global dimension. Sooner or later it will have to develop global institutions to match . . . a system of progressive income tax (from rich to poor nations) . . . a strengthened UN' (UNDP, 1992: 74). Interestingly Richard Jolly of UNICEF fame has moved to author the 1996 UNDP report and, in characteristic style, has drawn the world's attention to the widening economic inequality that is developing both within and between countries as we noted in Chapter 2. Working rather more in the background but coming to prominence in the context of the global debate at the World Summit on Social Development, the UNRISD had been commissioning a series of working papers from leading scholars on the impact of global-ization on societies. Its publication *States of Disarray: The Social Effects of Globalization* (UNRISD, 1995b), after analysing the array of social disintegrative effects of globalization such as those of identity crisis, war and conflict, the internationalization of crime, the uncertainties of changing work and changing family life, makes an imaginative call for the concept of citizenship to be reformulated above the level of the state, not only at a regional (e.g. EU) level, but on the global terrain.

The report reminds us that citizenship has three central propositions: individual and human rights, political participation, and socio-economic welfare.

> In practice, these three propositions of citizenship developed in sequence: accept-ance of individual and human rights led to social mobilization for political participation, which then implied progression to socio-economic welfare . . . Many of the issues that were central to the long debate on national citizenship are at the forefront of current attempts to channel global forces of socio-economic development, in a more constructive direction. Perhaps the time has come, therefore, to focus attention explicitly on global citizenship. (1995b: 168)

The concrete institutional reforms that might follow from the adoption of this global social reformist perspective are discussed in Chapter 6.

The UN summits: social policy and the social development dialogue

It was argued in Chapter 1 that a dialogue was needed between the academic disciplines of social policy and development studies.

The former's preoccupation with the developed world and the latter's with the developing were becoming an obstacle to creative thinking and appropriate policy development in a shrinking globalized world. The South was developing models of welfare development different from the estab-lished welfare states of the North. The continued global inequities required new thinking about social redistributive mechanisms between North and South. The futures for welfare everywhere were likely to be different from the past and involve a greater degree of shared understanding and policy prescription between analysts who had traditionally focused on separate parts of the globe. The events in post-communist societies discussed in the next chapter add a further strength to this point.

The need for this shared understanding between development studies and social policy was reflected recently in new thinking emerging from the social development professional team inside the Overseas Development Admin-istration of the UK government. At a seminar in 1995 a definition was sought of social policy relevant to the needs of social development advisers. The following was agreed upon: 'Social policy is any policy developed at supranational, state, local, or community level which is underpinned by a social vision of society and which, when operationalised, affects the rights or abilities of citizens to meet their livelihood needs' (ODA, 1995b: 26). This approach to social policy, which is usable by analysts of developing and developed societies confirms that students of social policy every bit as much as students of development studies must take a detailed interest in the recent work of the UN Economic and Social Committee and its mobilization of the several recent UN summits on aspects of development.

The Social Summit of the UN held in Copenhagen in 1995 was only the latest, but was the most significant, in a line of recent summits. In 1990 there had been the World Conference on Education for All, and the World Summit for Children. In 1992 there was the Rio Summit on Development. In 1993 in Vienna there was the World Conference on Human Rights and in 1994 the International Conference on Population and Development. The all-encompassing theme, however, of the 1995 Social Summit represented the most significant global accord on the need to tackle issues of poverty, social exclusion and social development, North and South.

All the diverse agencies already described in this chapter together with a host of NGOs contributed through the preparatory committee sessions of 1994 and 1995 to the draft declaration and programme of action tabled at Copenhagen. Some of the most far reaching and radical proposals embodied in the draft were in the event, lost as the diverse national, regional and agency political interests lobbied at the conference. The proposal supported, for example, by the UNDP report office (UNDP, 1994) for a new global tax on financial transactions to fund social development was lost. The idea for a 20/20 accord, defended determinedly by for example UNICEF (1995c), whereby the North would commit 20 per cent of its aid to social issues in return for the South committing 20 per cent of its public expenditure to social development, was equally shelved. Moves to set firm commitments on debt relief floundered. Progress was achieved, however, in getting the summit to re-endorse ILO standards as ones that should be aimed at and in getting an acknowledgement that issues of poverty and exclusion within one country were not just the sovereign concern of that country but were a globally shared responsibility (see UNRISD, 1995b, for a larger review of the summit and its follow-up). Of significance, and a point to be returned to in Chapter 6 is the fact that some of the radical proposals were lost not solely because of the resistance of the more liberally inclined northern countries but also because of the opposition of some of the G77 southern group of countries. Leaders of many such developing countries did not want, for example, to be committed to the 20/20 accord. The struggle for social reformist ideas has to be won in the South as well as the North.

The summit concluded with the following commitments:

Commitment 1   We commit ourselves to creating an economic, political, social, cultural and legal, environment that will enable people to achieve social development.

Commitment 2   We commit ourselves to the goal of eradicating poverty in the world, through decisive national actions and international co-operation, as an ethical, social, political and economic imperative of humankind.

Commitment 3 We commit ourselves to promoting the goal of full employment as a basic priority to our economic and social policies, and to enabling all men and women to attain secure and sustainable livelihoods through freely chosen productive employment and work.

Commitment 4 We commit ourselves to promoting social integration by fostering societies that are stable, safe and just and that are based on the promotion and protection of all human rights, as well as on non-discrimination, tolerance, respect for diversity, equality of opportunity, solidarity, security and participation of all people, including disadvantaged and vulnerable groups and persons.

Commitment 5 We commit ourselves to promoting full respect for human dignity and to achieving equality and equity between women and men, and to recognizing and enhancing the participation and leadership roles of women in political, civil, economic, social and cultural life and development.

Commitment 6 We commit ourselves to promoting and attaining the goals of universal and equitable access to quality education, the highest attainable standard of physical and mental health and the access of all to primary health care, making particular efforts to rectify inequalities relating to social conditions and without distinction as to race, national origin, gender, age or disability; respecting and promoting our common and particular cultures; striving to strengthen the role of culture in development; preserving the essential bases of people-centred sustainable development and contributing to the full development of human resources and to social development. The purpose of these activities is to eradicate poverty, promote full and productive employment and foster social integration.

Commitment 7 We commit ourselves to accelerating the economic, social and human resource development in Africa and the least developed countries.

Commitment 8 We commit ourselves to ensuring that when structural adjustment programmes are agreed to they include social development goals, in particular eradicating poverty, promoting full and productive employment and enhancing social integration.

Commitment 9 We commit ourselves to increasing significantly and/or utilizing more efficiently the resources allocated to social development in order to achieve the goals of the summit through national action and regional and international co-operation.

Commitment 10 We commit ourselves to an improved and strengthened framework for international, regional and subregional co-operation for social development, in a spirit of partnership, through the United Nations and other multilateral institutions.

Assessments in the immediate aftermath of the summit range from those who believe it did nothing for the poor (Eve-Ann Prentice, *The Times*, 13 March 1995) to those who believe

[The summit] will be remembered as the place where the monetarist juggernaut began to lose momentum . . . it has succeeded in checking attempts on the part of some to define social development purely in terms of economic growth . . . the programme of action . . . may ensure that the performance of the World Bank and IMF will no longer solely be judged in narrow economic terms, but also in terms of their impact on the basic rights of the world's poor, whose interest they claim to serve. (Patricia Feeney, Oxfam, *Guardian*, 13 March 1995)

The following interim conclusion can be drawn and will be developed further in Chapter 6. First, the summit was where the global debate on how to reform and regulate the Bank and Fund in the light of social concerns was really joined. The debate will be long and hard fought. UN insiders will want to strengthen the Economic and Social Committee. Reformist northern and some southern governments will want to reconstitute this as a UN Economic and Security Council with greater credibility in the eyes of the Bank and Fund. The Bank will continue to claim that by adopting a social development and anti-poverty policy it can be the global ministry for welfare. Secondly the summit was where the role of global NGOs as a surrogate for UN democratic accountability was endorsed. In Chapter 5 we examine the positive and negative aspects of this development. Thirdly, the global power struggle for alternative strategies for economic and social development was established as being between Europe and an alliance of some southern countries who are less interested in social regulation. The work of the new South Centre in seeking a paradigm shift on this issue among many developing countries could be a crucial element in future global politics (see Chapter 6). Finally, the summit was where the political strategy of the Bank and IMF became clear. Having responded to the call of the 1980s to take poverty seriously they are now able to claim, correctly, that they have a social policy and that in effect they will use this South (and East) orientated safety net social policy to challenge the conservatism of some northern welfare states. 'Why should the North not learn from the South and East?' responded the Bank's Vice President for Human Resources Armeane Choksi when challenged on this point in Copenhagen.

Conclusion: discordant voices in the global arena?

In this chapter we have seen that the debate about how to secure social welfare for all at global, regional and national level has now taken on a global dimension. This chapter has focused on the diverse views about the best future for welfare that have emerged from the leading global and regional supranational and intergovernmental organizations. Consensus does not exist, despite the superficial accord of the UN summit that social development issues are important. Rather what is emerging from this analysis is an intra- and inter-agency discourse about the direction economic and social policy should take in the context of globalism. In the next two chapters this discourse will be examined more concretely in relation to the more specific advice offered to a sample of East European and former

Soviet Union countries as they engage in the transition from 'communism' to a version of capitalism. The views of these agencies in specific areas of income maintenance policy will be charted together with an analysis of the instruments the organizations have at their command to shape national policy. Chapter 5 will continue this study, extending the canvas to international NGO in the context of the former Yugoslavia. The global social policy discourse and the possible global institutional and policy reforms implied by it will be returned to in the final chapter.

4

International Organizations and the Making of Post-Communist Social Policy

The policy making vacuum filled by international organizations

After the collapse of the 'communist' regimes across Eastern Europe in 1989 the key question of interest to social policy analysts was what kind of social welfare system would replace the state bureaucratic collectivist system. This had been characterized by universal work based entitlement to a system of welfare payments and services which combined a proletarianized egalitarianism alongside a wage related system whereby privileged workers obtained privileged pensions and other benefits. The *nomenklatura* continued to enjoy special access to better services (Deacon, 1992). As was suggested in Chapter 2, the characteristics of the state bureaucratic collectivist system had much in common with the European conservative corporatist tradition. The workplace and a contract between government and trade unions dominated the entitlement system. The benefits reflected acknowledged status differentials between workers, although often the reverse of those in operation in capitalist welfare systems. There would be a certain logic in converting this system, certainly as far as income maintenance policy was concerned, into an insurance based Bismarckian (European conservative) wage related benefits system backed up with universal benefits for categories such as children and a small social assistance system for uninsured categories. Indeed some of the countries in the region, notably Czechoslovakia and Hungary, had developed such systems in common with Central Europe between the world wars. Equally however, a priori, it could be deduced that most of the countries which were heavily indebted to the West would be under strong pressure to cut their state welfare budgets and adopt a much more liberal or residual approach to social welfare. The likelihood of the ex-communist countries passing smoothly over to social democratic forms of welfare policy could have been dismissed as unlikely at the outset. Such high taxation and highly redistributive policies would be unlikely to find favour with the new entrepreneurial capital that was about to be born. A future social welfare regime different from those in the West was also suggested as an outcome of the reform process. A post-communist conservatism whereby the *nomenklatura*, factory manager and workforce tried to conserve the existing set of social relations of workplace welfare in the face of pressures for marketization was suggested (Deacon, 1992).

What became immediately evident in the first flush of political and economic reform was that debates of any kind about social policy became relegated to almost last place in the priority of many of the new governments (Kziespolski, 1993a; Potucek, 1993). A myth that the market place would solve all the problems grew up alongside a clear rejection of all things social as being essentially socialist and part of the past to be forgotten. In 1989 the high point of neo-liberal economic thinking in the USA and Britain conspired with the anti-socialist sentiment of post-revolutionary Eastern Europe to knock the careful consideration of alternative social policies almost off the agenda. Governments were, in general, concerned with economic, legal and political institutional reform and not social institutional reform. Matters of national identity and property privatization took precedence. At the same time there was, for the most part, a low level of active civil society and pressure group engagement with social policy issues. The social structures were to become, or so it seemed, fluid. One's future position in the emerging diversity of fortune and misfortune was not clear. New sets of social interests had not yet coalesced to underpin an active and contested politics of welfare. This was to come later. By 1995 most countries in the region had re-elected ex-communist parties precisely because they spoke to the concerns of those who were to see, between 1989 and 1995, their existential security undermined on all fronts (lower incomes, unemployment, rise of mortality rates, increased homicide, falling school attendances, rocketing rents and transport costs, closures of crèches, erosion of pension and other benefit levels: see UNICEF, 1993a; 1994; 1995b for a detailed monitoring of these changes). The pensioner lobby, for example, would become a powerful one by 1995.

Into the vacuum of national social policy making in the wake of the 1989 events stepped the international organizations. The scramble for the future direction of Eastern European, and later the former Soviet Union, economic and social policy was on. Everybody acting at the supranational and global level – the World Bank, the EU, the ILO in particular – could see that the future of the nature of global capitalism, not only East European capitalism, was going to be fought out in the region. The titanic struggle between idealized capitalism and demonized socialism and communism was over (at least for the foreseeable political future). The stagnation of the cold war years was broken. The UN and other actors who had become neutered by the politics of the cold war were to take on a new lease of life. Now at last the aspirations of the post Second World War days whereby the international organizations would be entrusted to manage the world safely would be given a new lease of life. Whether Eastern Europe was to become a women friendly, redistributive, socially just and well regulated kind of capitalism like Sweden; a cut-throat, devil-take-the-hindmost kind of unsafe casino capitalism like the USA, or worse Brazil; or perhaps a socially managed if unequal kind of capitalism like France and Germany, was to be, at least in part, in the hands of the army of human resources specialists from international organizations about to descend on the region. This chapter tells how this story was to unfold in three countries in the region: Bulgaria, Hungary and Ukraine.

Making Eastern Europe safe for capital: the logic of international organization intervention

Despite differing emphases, the actual justification given for involvement with social policy in CEE countries by the international agencies follows a similar pattern. According to the COE:

> It is imperative to incorporate these countries into an effective system for the protection and promotion of fundamental social rights . . . in order to prevent social upheavals which may be painful for the people and dangerous for their still vulnerable democracies. (Mros, 1993: 41)

The Centre for Cooperation with the Economies in Transition of the OECD, in exploring its co-ordination with the ILO in its work programme, stated:

> in the absence of a quick and effective policy response to the emergence of major social and labour market problems at the beginning of the transition, there is a risk that the ongoing reform process may be impeded, delayed or some steps even reversed. (OECD, 1993c: 271)

According to the Commission of the EU:

> Co-operation between the Union and the CEE countries on the social dimension of transition is essential to reduce the risk of the population rejecting democracy and the market economy because the social and human costs are too high. (European Commission, 1993b: 70)

Concern to stabilize the process of market reform and prevent its slowing down, with appropriate attention to the social costs of transition, thus characterized the motivation for intervention by all of these agencies.

How to intervene and with what policies in the social sphere was to become, however, a matter of debate and disagreement between the organizations. Indicative of the tensions that were to emerge is the contrast to be found, for example, between the interim conclusions of the joint study of the Soviet economy undertaken by the IMF, World Bank, OECD and European Bank for Reconstruction and Development (OECD, 1991f) and the parallel articulation by the Director of the ILO in May 1991 of its motivations and policies (ILO, 1991a). The chapter on 'Labour Market, Social Safety Net, Education and Training' of the joint report, written by Etisham Ahmad, then of the Bank and now of the IMF, concluded, as we noted in Chapter 3, that 'the danger to be avoided is to construct an elaborate and expensive social security edifice that provides benefits to a privileged subset of the target population, in the presence of poverty and need' (OECD, 1991f: 191–2). Prefiguring what was to become the safety net strategy of many in the Bank and IMF, the chapter continues: 'if the state can actually ensure minimum standards of living for the entire population, it will have achieved a major objective of any social security system.' By contrast the ILO was talking of setting up a specialist outpost in Budapest which would address the nine areas of concern that the ILO had. Among these were the 'encouragement of social dialogue and tripartism' and 'helping formulate social security legislation including policy on health, pensions, sick pay, family and unemployment benefits' (ILO, 1991a).

Among the other tensions that were to emerge at an early stage were between those who in effect argued that nothing short of a major social redistributive effort, i.e. a new Marshall Plan for Eastern Europe and the former Soviet Union, would stabilize the new market economies, and those who favoured traditional structural adjustment loans on commercial terms aimed at enabling the new economies to grow their way out of impoverishment. The UN's Economic Commission for Europe commissioned a study of the lessons to be drawn from the post-war experience of US aid to Europe in which the point was well made that 'US aid was provided in a [particular] form – grants rather than loans – [and] the US did not interfere when these countries pursued economic and social policies which often differed significantly from those enjoying popular support on the other side of the Atlantic' (Panic, 1992: 32). However, this was not to be the post-1989 experience. As Koves (1992) reported, 'Financial assistance is explicitly subordinated to IMF conditionality, and the issue is no longer aid but a very hard bargain.' This was despite the negative experiences of structural adjustment elsewhere and the reports of not unimportant study groups that were cautioning against a strict conditionality approach. Raymond Barre, who had been Prime Minister of France, was among a team of experts commissioned by the Institute for East–West Studies to evaluate and recommend on aid strategy. It concluded, in relation to Hungary, Poland and the Czech and Slovak Republics, that 'In view of their size and scope, the impact made by international organisations on assistance to transition is very great. This makes their philosophy concerning assistance particularly significant . . . Thus conditionality, in particular IMF conditionality, could be more flexibly applied to the three countries' (Barre et al., 1992: 56). One aspect of the concern reflected in this report was the feeling among a number of politicians [that] the Bretton Woods institutions lacked the requisite European perspective to respond to the needs of the region' (Hughes, 1993: 597). The European Bank for Reconstruction and Development (EBRD) was developed on French initiative to compensate for this. However, the USA succeeded in limiting the role of the ERBD in anything other than the private sector and the ERBD did not, for example, develop any systematic work on human resources or social policy. For the purposes of this study it became an unimportant actor. A further aspect of the emerging debate and of the strategy of those who called for a Marshall Plan was that of *co-ordination* between organizations and actors. This point will be returned to after a discussion in the next section of the instruments available to organizations to influence policy.

The motivations for interventions were clear. The goal to make the East safe for capitalism was evident. The significance of the social dimension – that some protection was needed against impoverishment if the political support for reform was to continue – was widely understood. To see the West as unified in its approach, however, as some have suggested (Gowan, 1992; 1993; 1996), is mistaken. Disagreements between fractions of capital and the organizations that most reflected their interests (IMF for the USA, EU for Germany) and within and between the teams that made up the human resources specialists in these organizations was to become all too evident, as the case studies below illustrate. The West may, as Gowan suggests, be intervening to win the East for capital; this is not in doubt. The important point is: for what kind of capitalism, with what measure of social policy?

The instruments and institutional infrastructure used by international organizations to shape policy

The instruments available to agencies to influence a government's social policy are several and varied. The main forms are shown in Table 4.1. All of these instruments operate within institutional structures that have been developed to enable the agencies to address more effectively the needs of a region.

Thus the Council of Europe (COE) has established the Demosthenes programme, whose official objective is the 'securing of democracy in countries in transition'. The method by which this goal is pursued in Demosthenes is by 'making available the expertise of existing member countries through workshops, seminars, courses, study visits and scholarships'. The focus is on the constitutional, legislative and administrative aspects of establishing 'western-style' democracies and, it is assumed, market-style economies with their accompanying social problems.

Thus a small but significant part of the Demosthenes programme (12.4 per cent) covers 'social affairs' – assistance sought by the Eastern and Central European countries in dealing with western-style problems such as rising unemployment and mechanisms for dealing with wage bargaining. The Demosthenes programme is administered by the Directorate of Political Affairs, but draws upon the expertise of members of the Directorate of Social and Economic Affairs in the delivery of the programme. The latter have outlined their contribution as being:

1   to provide information on standard setting and co-ordinating instruments of the Council of Europe
2   to give legal assistance on draft legislation
3   to draft model provisions to cover the branches of social protection as they appear in the Code on Social Security, to enable countries to draft their own legislation with reference to the model provisions.

Table 4.1 *Social policy instruments used by supranational bodies*

Instrument	Application
Loans with social conditionality	World Bank lending on condition of social policy change
Loans with economic conditionality	IMF lending on condition of economic policy change (with social policy implication)
Additionality incentive	EU provision of grant matched to local resources
Legal regulation	COE powers to report shortcomings in member country social policy where party to COE Social Charter; similarly re ILO where countries have ratified ILO policy
Technical assistance training	ILO, EU, World Bank, OECD, UNICEF, UNDP etc. Provision of technical advice and training sessions
Political agreement	EU agreements with associated states
Resource redistribution (not on loan basis)	EU Structural fund (if extended to CEE); COE Social Development Fund; UNICEF/UNDP grant aided projects
Co-ordination conferences and associated publications	Open to all to be used to influence climate of opinion among organizations
Hosting and underpinning	UNDP, while not directly engaged, might house and/or finance the work of say the ILO

The Council does not through this programme consider it part of its remit to make country specific recommendations. Instead, it invites countries' ministers, or 'other significant players', to training sessions where a range of Western European model welfare states are presented, seemingly to allow observers to 'mix and match'.

The history of the OECD's involvement with Eastern and Central Europe since 1989 mirrors, to a certain extent, the original official concerns of the OECD as it was when set up for the administration of Marshall Aid in 1949. The OECD's Centre for Co-operation with Economies in Transition (CCET) was founded in 1990 on US monies, apparently to secure an American foothold in the West's rush to influence policy development in the East. The importance attached to the work of the Centre was apparent in the appointment of Salvatore Zecchini of the IMF to head the Centre, at the level of Deputy to the General Secretary of the OECD.

The Centre's main role has been to design and oversee annual work programmes, the content of which – policy advice, technical assistance and training – has a familiar ring, putting the expertise of the Secretariat and member countries at the disposal of countries engaged in economic reform. One of the four key themes in the General Work Programme is 'social problems related to restructuring'. The decision of the Directorate for Social Affairs, Manpower and Education to collaborate with the ILO on the delivery of part of this programme is interesting and suggests that the US influence might not permeate down to the actual social policy analysis and advice tabled at conferences of the Centre. In 1993 was held a joint

ILO/OECD Conference on Labour Market and Social Policy Implications, introduced by Guy Standing of the ILO and Georg Fischer then of the Directorate of Social Affairs, which simply concluded that more detailed work was needed on designing social protection schemes for the newly marketized economies. The timing of this collaboration with the ILO coincided with evidence of a move by the OECD as a whole, as discussed in Chapter 3, away from condoning the retrenchments made in several Western European welfare states on the grounds of 'economic efficiency' (OECD, 1994b).

The bulk of the Centre's work has focused on the states that are 'most advanced in the reform process', defined by the Centre as 'partners in transition' (PIT). A smaller section of the Centre's work has targeted the four largest of the 'new independent states of the Soviet Union' (NIS) with a similar remit. The pattern of work established so far has been demand led from the PIT and NIS countries themselves. This form of organization means that influence and direction remain rather *ad hoc*, the content of programmes being decided, in part, by the orientations of individual applicants. For instance, while requests from the Polish government came via the Ministry of Labour for a specifically labour review, the Hungarians applied through their Ministry of Welfare for a labour, social security and social assistance review. This review and the associated report (OECD, 1995b), which is the first detailed evaluation of the social policy of a country since the *New Orientations in Social Policy* document (OECD, 1994a), is of particular interest and is discussed in the Hungarian case study later.

The special role afforded to the Commission of the EU in assisting the transition process in CEE derives from the G24 group of countries allocating the EU this co-ordinating responsibility at the outset. The PHARE and later TACIS programmes have become the biggest source of direct transfer of funds from West to East. A huge infrastructure of local offices has been established in all PHARE and TACIS recipient countries. The PHARE (*Pologne/Hongrie: assistance à la réstructuration economique*), administered by the DGI (External Relations Directorate), is, as its name suggests, a technical assistance programme designed to facilitate the economic transition in neighbour states. For PHARE this means a focus on financial reconstruction and encouragement of the private sector, especially small and medium sized enterprises. However, one of the core areas specified for targeting has been 'social', though this is delineated in the official literature as being 'social [only] in the sense often used in the Community that relates to questions of employment: labour market agencies and policies, including particularly training, and social security arrangements'. The TACIS programme was established on similar lines a little later to channel aid to countries of the former Soviet Union. Country studies incorporating an 'identification of problems' are drawn up largely by personnel contracted to the PHARE and TACIS programmes on a short term basis. From there the EU audits bids for monies from countries, which are then assessed in the light of the data built up on an applicant country and the relevance of the project to the perceived social needs of the country.

The specific EU priorities in the social sphere within the PHARE and TACIS programmes are hard to identify as the stated goals are so general and the projects approved so diverse. Within the TACIS programme the emphasis in the social sphere has been on the social consequences of enterprise divestiture of social assets and the means of establishing alternative provision. This situation of policy incoherence was mulled over by personnel in the DGV (Social Affairs Directorate), who had argued that they would achieve a more directed and less fragmented input in the social policy sphere if the responsibility for part of the programme was delegated to them. They did attempt to establish a DGV European Social Security Team that would win DGI PHARE contracts and steer Eastern Europe towards a more consistent set of 'European' social security policies. This initiative floundered on the rocks of UK resistance. The UK has been unilaterally very active via the 'know-how' fund and has promulgated policy not in keeping with the EU Social Chapter. However, in 1996 under the Consensus Programme of PHARE a new approach to assistance in the social protection sphere was developed. This required social sector policy reviews to be undertaken for each country and outline policy recommendations to be made with a view to pre-accession negotiations. A conference organized in late 1996 compared the reviews of about 10 country studies and drew general lessons for countries wishing to emulate best practice in European social security and allied social protection schemes.

This new initiative may bring a little more coherence into the situation. At present PHARE and TACIS projects, being subcontracted out to consultants and other 'experts', are necessarily prone to a certain 'randomness' with respect to the type of policy advice being delivered. Inconsistencies which arise as a result of the differing perspectives of consultants are compounded by the tensions reflecting the battle within the EU as a whole between the Euroliberals and the Eurocorporatists. An interesting difference is to be noted between the work in Poland on social assistance where the EU contract was given to the World Bank who then subcontracted the task to the British Council, and that done for the Czech Republic, where the contract was won by the ILO who subcontracted a highly thought-of Fabian British expert on social assistance. Again, in the case of the Baltic states, the desk officer at PHARE in Brussels felt it more appropriate to draw on best practice within Eastern Europe, and awarded a contract on social assistance to a Czech social security expert. Further details of this kind will be reviewed in the case studies below.

The intervention of the EU in the social policy affairs of Eastern Europe has not, however, been restricted to the variable technical assistance under the PHARE or TACIS programmes. The EU has negotiated political agreements with all of the countries in our study which make reference to the need for countries to amend their social protection schemes in line with Union expectations. A White Paper on the relationship with Eastern Europe generated a subsequent document on the accession process (European Commission, 1995b). Many of the concerns of this paper are with the need of social policy to reflect the European social dimension. A meeting of the European Parliament on 17 April 1996 (DOCPE, 198: 354) stressed the need for modern social security and health schemes in the region, and for any social welfare privatization in the region to focus on the not-for-profit sector. While DGI PHARE and TACIS intervention may have had a certain randomness about it, the political thrust of the Parliament has been more consistently encouraging towards a European model for the social policies of the region. As reported earlier (Deacon, 1994) this was first articulated clearly by the Economic and Social Committee of the Parliament in 1991 in a lengthy opinion critical of East European countries which felt they could develop a market economy without the adjective 'social'.

The World Bank and the IMF did not need to establish any new departments of institutions to operate in Eastern Europe. The Bank already had an operations section for the countries of the region. However, the Europe and Central Asia region was divided into three for the purposes of human resource operations work. Department 1/2 covered, under the leadership of Ralph Harbinson, most Central and Eastern European countries. Department 3 covered most of the former Soviet Union, under Robert Liebenthal. Department 4 covered the Baltics, the Ukraine and western former Soviet Union under James Harrison. Because of this expansion the Bank did however, as was reported in Chapter 3, need to actively recruit a large number of new staff, often Europeans, to work in the region. This, as we show later, contributed to a shift in Bank social policy thinking. The Bank also has resident representatives and technical teams in most of the countries. The scale of the Bank's work in the region outstrips everything else.

Similarly UNICEF did not establish any new policies or procedures or institutional substructures to handle the region but it has worked to secure adoption by several governments in the region of its national programme for action approach. Most evident in the work of UNICEF in the region has been the monitoring reports produced under the direction of Giovanni Andrea Cornia of the Child Development Centre in Florence (UNICEF, 1993a; 1994; 1995b) which have given high global profile to their findings concerning the impoverishment generated by the transition in the region. This point will be developed in the next chapter.

Finally, in contrast, the ILO did establish a new institutional arm in order to give a high local public profile to its work in the region, which it saw as increasingly becoming that of challenging the unsocial structural adjustment policies of the Bretton Woods institutions. The Central and East European Team (CEET) based in Budapest was established in 1992 under the Directorship of Guy Standing who used the position not only to undertake with enormous energy a large number of country surveys and reports but also sometimes to articulate the case for a citizen's income approach to income maintenance rather than the conservative Bismarckian approach. Other colleagues in the team such as Michael Cichon were defenders of the more traditional Bismarckian approach.

In Table 4.2 a mapping is provided of the degrees of intervention of these organizations in the region for the sample of three countries to be discussed in detail below. It is evident that most organizations have been highly active in most places. How they interacted within each country and how they sought competitive advantage or opportunities for co-operation will be detailed later.

Finally, in this review of the institutional structures established by these major players to shape social policy in the region there is a need for a brief mention of the matter of co-ordination and collaboration. There are a number of aspects to this: first, the formal attempts to co-ordinate activity at global level; secondly, the competition for co-ordination at global/ regional level; thirdly, the opportunities taken by several less powerful actors – independent research institutions for example – to bring disparate actors together; and fourthly, the issue of desk officer co-ordination for specific countries.

At the outset the World Economic Summit 1989 decided that aid to Eastern Europe from the Group of 24 nations should be co-ordinated through the then EC PHARE programme. There is an aid co-ordination office of G24 alongside the Brussels PHARE and TACIS centres. It is little more than a data base. Within each country there are EC/EU PHARE or EC/EU TACIS offices which attempt the task of aid co-ordination on the ground in collaboration with the aid co-ordination offices of the ministry of foreign affairs of the government concerned. The speed of intervention and the conflict of interests involved have been such that except in a few well known cases the co-ordination has been at best partial. Ministries of labour and social affairs (and indeed other ministries not part of this study) have often been overrun with advice. This process, coupled with the competitive tendering policy of the PHARE and TACIS offices, has led to an element of randomness in the determination of which major actors get to intervene in the social security and social assistance sphere.

The other point of note regarding G24 broad policy co-ordination (as distinct from operational co-ordination) is that the ILO, a major contender for influence with a different perspective, is excluded, unlike the IMF, World Bank, OECD and ERBD, from formal participation in G24 policy meetings (Lipow, 1994: 12) although it has been 'increasingly associated with the coordination activities of the G24' (ILO, 1995c). The ILO has also sought to exercise its own co-ordination strategy. A significant event in this regard was the joint ILO/OECD Conference on Labour Market and Social Policy Implications of Structural Change in Central and Eastern Europe in 1991. The key actors here had been Guy Standing of the ILO (later to head the East European team) and Georg Fischer of the OECD. In other ways the ILO has sought to counter its marginalization at the G24 level. It

Table 4.2 *International organization intervention in the case studies, 1989–96*

	IMF	World Bank	EU PHARE or TACIS	Council of Europe	OECD	ILO	UNICEF
Hungary	Continuing story of standby loans periodically offered but tranches held back because budget conditions not met; crisis in 1995 re insurance fund deficit	Structural adjustment loan with social conditions (1990); social sector loans	PHARE assistance with social work and NGOs (1991–2); association agreement	Member (1990); signed Social Charter; seminars	Detailed social policy study; PIT	Little role and influence; report on labour market (1994)	National programme of action in preparation
Bulgaria	As above; crisis in 1996 re enterprise closures	Structural adjustment loan with social conditions (1991); social sector loans; assistance with enterprise lay offs (1996)	PHARE assistance with civil society development (1994); association agreement	Member; signed Social Charter	PIT	EU UNDP funded continuing major intervention	National programme of action in preparation
Ukraine	As above; crises in 1995 and 1996 re budget deficit and unpaid wages	Social sector study (1993); possibility of social sector rehabilitation loan	TACIS social consequences of restructuring project (1994); partnership agreement	Member (1996); joint ILO advice on social security	NIS	UNDP funded continuing major intervention	National programme of action in preparation

organizes its own information and exchange meeting three times a year for G24 nations. It has, as we shall see in the case studies, collaborated closely on the ground with the UNDP, EU and Council of Europe but has, in general, been marginalized by the Bank and the Fund. It has since 1990 organized 15 information and co-ordination meetings in the labour and social fields with participation by the donor and recipient countries and other international organizations concerned (ILO, 1995c).

A number of semi-independent institutions have been active in the process of policy debate within and between international organizations. Among these have been the International Social Security Association (ISSA), the European Centre for Social Welfare Policy and Research, the National Agency for Welfare and Health of Finland, the European Institute of Social Security and, already mentioned, the Institute for East–West Studies. The ISSA, which shares offices with the ILO in Geneva, holds annual research conferences and in 1994 focused on the theme of the perceived challenges to social security arising from changes in the global economy and from post-communist developments. The occasion was used to permit a controversial dialogue between a spokesperson for the World Bank's liberal pension reform agenda, Estelle James, who advocates a smaller role for state wage related benefits and a larger role for the market with associated means testing, and staunch defenders of the European Bismarckian tradition. Sheila Kamerman, summing up, refuted the Bank strategy by asserting: 'it would be absurd to propose – or even consider – turning a universal system or mixed system into a completely means tested or means tested and voluntary system when what is now in place is working' (1995: 17). The ISSA also contributed significantly to furthering the cause of sustaining European social security systems in post-communist countries through the publication of their compendium of developments in the region (ISSA, 1994a). Within this, Cichon of the ILO and Kopits of the IMF articulated their rather different concerns about social security policy in the region: Cichon warned against the 'minimum safety net – minimum protection' approach 'which will ultimately lead to a long term reduction of the level of the social protection of the population' (1994a: 55), and Kopits equally warned against the transplanting of the Chilean private pension system into former socialist economies 'in the absence of financial markets' (1994: 69). Support for a mixed state and private system is evident in both accounts but with rather different degrees of emphasis.

The European Institute of Social Security (EISS), equally concerned to export the positive experience of the European tradition eastwards, held a seminar in 1992 on the theme of social security reform in the region. Significantly the international organizations represented included the EC (DGV), the Council of Europe, the ILO and the ISSA. The Bank and the Fund in general don't spend (waste?) their time engaging in these attempts at cross-organization dialogue. They were invited to but were absent from an early initiative by the National Agency for Welfare and Health of Finland at which a Conference on Competitive Society in CEE – the Social

Dimensions, attended by the ILO (Standing again), the OECD (Duskin), the ERBD (Gass) and the UN Social Development and Humanitarian Affairs office, Vienna (Sokalski) concluded, perhaps rather vaguely, that '[social policy] must be an integral part of the transition strategy dealing with short term problems while promoting long term concerns of distributive justice and social protection' (National Agency for Welfare and Health, 1992: 24). One of the co-sponsors of this conference had been the UN affiliated European Centre for Social Welfare Policy and Research. They too, under the leadership of Bernd Marin, had been very active in lobbying for sound social policy in the region. A Conference of European Ministers Responsible for Social Affairs in the UN European Region held in Bratislava in 1993 concluded, though the endorsement of a thoroughly documented policy analysis of the region (European Centre Vienna, 1993), the same social policy principles that had been tabled in Finland a year earlier. The conference went further and supported the idea of 'trans-national social policy programmes designed to prevent mass unemployment and absolute pauperization' (1993: 227) and called for the UN at the European regional level to be involved in this work. This conference was very much about engaging in preparation for the World Summit on Social Development in 1995 (see Chapter 3) and about the struggle to secure, on the pan-European continent, a role for the UN in contradistinction to the EU or the Bank.

Not so much co-ordination, rather jockeying and lobbying for positions of influence and authority, is how to characterize the complexity of the parallel interventions by the plethora of international (not to mention national) organizations active in Eastern Europe and the former Soviet Union between 1989 and 1996. It was left to desk officers of each of these bodies in each of the countries to try to minimize the mess and maximize the opportunities for constructive collaboration on the ground. The three case studies that follow demonstrate some examples of this (ILO and UNDP collaboration; IMF and World Bank collaboration; even EU DGI and World Bank collaboration) but also demonstrate that the major ideological and institutional divide between the human resource epistemic communities of the Bank and Fund on the one hand and the ILO, COE, EU DGV and UNDP on the other are rarely bridged in practice.

The economic, political, social and demographic characteristics of the three selected countries are diverse. They range from Hungary, our first example, which had already begun economic reforms before 1989 and which has been seen by many commentators to be most ready to join Europe, to the Ukraine where newly elected President Kuchma is still trying to convince a very reluctant Parliament to change economic course. Bulgaria lies between these extremes. All are indebted to the West. All are carrying a budget deficit higher than that acceptable to the IMF. The worst of the inflation and fall in living standards is probably over for all three countries although Bulgaria in 1996 was facing a new economic crisis. Unemployment rates are set to continue to rise in the Ukraine. Only

Hungary has escaped the decline in male life expectancy. A common feature is that in the mid 1990s all the countries re-elected ex-communist parties to power largely in response to the failure in the short term of market reforms to improve living standards, initiated with varying degrees of enthusiasm by the first post-communist governments.

Hungary: IMF and World Bank call the shots?

In sum the story that unfolds for Hungary is one in which the IMF and the World Bank have been the major international actors seeking to shape the income maintenance and other social policies of successive Hungarian governments, but they have had to wait until the re-election of the former Communist Party in 1994 to find a government, or at least a Ministry of Finance, eager to co-operate with the Bretton Woods institutions against public and constitutional court opposition. The ILO role has been negligible, as has that of the PHARE programme of the EU. The EU association agreement has provided some reference point for the Ministry of Welfare as has the Council of Europe's Social Charter which the government has signed. The OECD has put Hungary at the top of its list of transition countries to undergo its new extensive social policy assessments in the light of its *New Orientations for Social Policy* document. The OECD struggles to offer advice as to how the government might reconcile the cost cutting and structural adjustment requirements of the IMF with the concerns of equity and social cohesion. It has offered advice on the least painful ways of balancing the books, which has not always been heeded.

IMF involvement with Hungary reaches back to before the transition. Hungary became a member of the IMF and the Bank in 1982 and detailed attempts at structural adjustment were experimented with in the days of market reform under the old regime (Andor, 1995). However, 'the consociational system's reliance upon compensation-based consensus-building frustrated IMF pressure for rapid adjustment' (Henderson, 1992: 251).

Ironically the initial position of the Hungarian Democratic Forum that won the elections in 1989 was to lobby for debt forgiveness, quite against IMF strategy. The financial crisis of 1990, however, ensured that agreement was reached with the IMF and the Bank on a strategy to manage the economy. The IMF had previously undertaken a mission in 1989 at the request of the outgoing government to offer advice on reform of the social security system. It had already concluded that the social insurance fund would be in deficit and would reach 10 per cent in due course. It recommended a package of measures including 'partial indexation of pensions, tightening eligibility and screening for disability benefits, the shift of responsibility of sick pay to employers . . . taxation of family allowances' (Plant, 1994: 12). Standby credit was agreed with the IMF in association with the 1990 budgets that cut subsidies on fuel, food, alcohol and other items and raised personal taxes. The bulk of the budget cut was achieved despite strikes by taxi drivers and other opposition groups.

Two structural adjustment loans (SALs) were agreed with the Bank. SAL 1, worth $200 million in 1990, had social conditionality built into it. Eligibility conditions for social security were to be tightened, subsidies reduced, and unemployment insurance introduced. It was further stressed that a system of social assistance (a minimum safety net) was to be introduced. Bank reports on the degree to which the government met these conditions have varied. For public consumption the Operation Evaluation Division summary concluded that 'The SAL conditions were satisfied on time . . . A social safety net that provides unemployment benefits and social assistance is now in place, but much more needs to be done to rationalize social expenditure in general to target them to the needy' (World Bank, 1993e). However, in an interview the head of the resident mission in Budapest noted that three bank concerns regarding the planned Social Assistance Act had not been satisfied. These were the establishment of a nation-wide standard, a budget mechanism to balance need and cost between regions, and the ending of the use of a non-household family means test. Weaknesses in social assistance policy and practice were to be drawn attention to later by the OECD. SAL 2 nonetheless went ahead in 1992, again with social conditions connected to the release of tranches of money. A requirement that the pension age be raised was not met but funds were nonetheless released because of action in the macroeconomic sphere. A condition that sick pay responsibility be shifted to employers was only met in part, i.e. for a shorter period of 10 days. No 'progress' had been made at this stage either in other policy areas identified by the Bank in its 1992 study as needing attention (World Bank, 1992b). These included the desirability of differentiating the family allowance payment by the number of children. Less controversial, however, was the Bank funding ($138 million) of the infrastructure for the newly independent pensions and health insurance body. At this point (May 1994) the Bank resident representative in Budapest was forced to the conclusion that in the sphere of social security and income maintenance the Bank 'has been completely uninfluential . . . a humbling experience'. An interview was concluded at that point with the suggestion we come back in four years' time to see if the Bank had achieved more with the then predicted new ex-communist government. A report on social policy reform was being prepared for the new government (World Bank, 1994c).

The second bite at the cherry was indeed to come with the election of the Socialists (ex-communists) and Liberals in 1994 under the Prime Minister Gyula Horn. Almost their first step was to call in the IMF. A public dance of disavowal ensued in which the government put blame on the IMF for forcing it to introduce stringent budget cuts, and the IMF, in the person of its President Michel Camdessus visiting Budapest in October 1994, argued that the economic conditions necessitated that the government should act. An austerity budget was introduced and, despite much protest and some concessions, was passed in May 1995. It provided for the end of universal family allowances (means tested except for fourth and subsequent child or children with special needs), universal child care grants for working mothers, free higher education, and free health care. Charges and means tests were to cut the costs in these and other areas. Employer responsibility for sick pay was to extend beyond 10 days. The background was the high cost of social expenditures in Hungary as a percentage of GDP (25.3 per cent in 1993 compared with the EU average of 21.8 per cent) and the limited capacity of government to raise more revenue given that, for example, the payroll taxes for social security were already very high at 49 per cent, far larger than normal in Western Europe and being evaded (World Bank, 1995b). The constitutional court ruled many of these changes as illegal, contradicting constitutional guarantees to social support. The government has, however, found legal and technical ways round the decision and by modifying regulations is reintroducing the bulk of these measures (Vince, 1996). It is interesting to note that in some aspects of the above reform the World Bank's views have been adhered to and in others not. The compromise regarding family allowances – the original intention had been to means test all allowances for all children – was in line with Bank thinking (World Bank, 1992b). The retention of even means tested child care support – the universal system had hitherto won international acclaim for its support of working mothers – is opposed by the Bank as an unnecessary interference in the labour market (World Bank, 1995b).

The government is not, however, out of the wood as far as the IMF and Bank are concerned. A new standby loan was agreed with the IMF after the May 1995 austerity package except that a precondition for signing has not been met. This relates to the agreement, which doesn't yet exist, between the government and the pension and health insurance funds to cut their budgets and their continued reliance, despite their formal independence, on the state budget. Both the IMF and the Ministry of Finance are on the same side against the reluctant insurance funds, who are backed up by public opinion and opposition parties. The policy issues behind this continuing dispute relate, however, in part to the long standing controversy over pensions policy. All international organizations are agreed that the pension system needs reform. Pension age entitlement needs to be raised and greater clarity in the relationship between contributions and benefits is needed. Early retirement should no longer hide unemployment. Although agreement exists that a three tier pension system should be put in place – basic earnings related mandatory, and voluntary top-up – the disagreements are about the relative size of the basic, and the extent to which the pooled risks pay-as-you-go system is to be replaced by individual accounts in fully funded schemes. The Bank on this occasion seems to be supporting the liberal version of a minimum flat rate state pension and a fully funded privately managed individual accounting for the second tier (World Bank, 1995b). This is despite the alternative view, also expressed by other Bank human resources specialists, that the choice between the US inspired liberal strategy and the more mixed European tradition is up to governments (Barr, 1994). In the event and in the hope of satisfying conditions for the standby loan agreed with the IMF, the government in May 1996 submitted to Parliament proposals to reform the pension policy in line with the liberal wing of the World Bank. The proposal is for a three tier scheme. Thirty per cent of the pension would be a pay-as-you-go scheme but this would provide for a basic pension set as low as 60 per cent of minimum wage. A further 60 per cent would be a fully funded, individually accounted, scheme with investment of funds privately. A top-up voluntary scheme would exist for wealthy individuals. The scheme is opposed by the leaders of the existing pension funds who argue that the private scheme will put pensions at risk. They favour a wage related state managed second tier. At the same time parliament has approved the stepwise rise in pension age entitlement to 62 for both men and women (from 55 for women and 60 for men). This was decided upon also to reduce the budget deficit in the funds as part of the strategy of meeting IMF conditions.

In this relatively charged atmosphere the OECD launched its first detailed review of the social policy of a country since its *New Orientations* strategy was adopted by OECD ministers in 1992. The report on *Social and Labour Market Policies in Hungary* (OECD, 1995b) was discussed in Budapest in late 1994 and was in response to the Hungarian authorities' request that the OECD examine the effects of the transition process on disadvantaged groups. The thoroughly expert and considered report is not shot through with the economic fundamentalism of equivalent Bank accounts. It acknowledges the real fiscal constraints upon existing welfare policy but goes on to try to find the least socially painful way of reforming policy. In some areas of course, such as the raising of retirement age, it is in agreement with the others; but in the matter for example of family benefits it steers, perhaps under the influence of Bettina Cass, its consultants for this chapter, a unique course. On pensions the report doesn't come out so sharply in favour of a private funded second tier. Rather it cautions: 'experience has shown that these options are not without risk to individuals or without cost to the public purse' (1995b: 127). On family allowances the report states that 'allowances account for far too great a proportion of family incomes for recipients – particularly those with several children – to be able to deal easily with their sudden withdrawal' (1995b: 155). The package of ideas suggested to balance fiscal constraints with family need includes taxation of benefits, merging the child benefit and the child care allowances, subsidized child care for working mothers (means tested), but not means testing the basic allowance.

Significant about the OECD report is also its focus on the shortcomings of the Hungarian social assistance system, a point already noted earlier. In the chapter devoted to this it addresses the concern that the present Social Act 'suggests no minimum level of support for a nuclear family dependent upon social assistance' (1995b: 71). It argues how such a minimum could be established and paid for and organized with appropriate cost sharing by block grants with appeals procedures built in. The concern is returned to in the concluding chapter where it is stated:

> if reductions in unemployment benefits, pensions outlays, and subsidies to families with children are to be accomplished without unacceptable disruption of people's lives, an appropriate safety net must be functioning as quickly as possible. The outlays on the safety net are the necessary precondition for the expenditure reductions in other programmes . . . The other condition for a national standard would be the establishment of procedures to encourage those receiving such payments to participate in economic life. Such policies would facilitate entry into the labour market for those receiving assistance by ensuring the availability of child care and also by providing opportunities for active participation for all recipients of support.
>   The object of this admittedly far reaching reform would be to ensure all Hungarians *as citizens* a minimum level of support to enable them to survive the hard times their country is now experiencing. (1995b: 184)

With these words the OECD's Education, Employment, Labour and Social Affairs Directorate certainly appears to be at least putting itself firmly behind the social liberal safety net approach to income maintenance, but could also be interpreted as setting out a case for serious consideration to be given to a citizen's income policy in post-communist countries. What influence this report will have in the context of the bigger players such as the Bank is not evident at this stage. Perhaps it will have indirect impact via the emerging professional social policy lobby.

Alongside the work and influence of the IMF, World Bank and OECD, that of the other international organizations pales into insignificance in the field of income maintenance in the Hungarian context. Significant by its absence is the ILO, which given the location of the Central and East European Team in Budapest is ironic. It was variously explained to us as due to the weakness of the tripartite system in Hungary, the personal chemistry between ILO and ministry staff, and by Plant as being for 'linguistic reasons . . . in that the ILO's Conventions and Recommendations have not been translated on a systematic basis into the Hungarian language' (1994: 24). A largely descriptive report on the labour market was undertaken in 1994 (Nesporova and Simonyi, 1994) but nothing approaching the major contributions to policy debate that we will describe for the Bulgarian and Ukrainian cases below.

The PHARE programme devoted few of its resources to the income maintenance field except for some work in 1992 on reform of local authority social programmes prior to the passing of the new inadequate Social Act dealing with social assistance. The European agreement did provide the justification for a seminar in 1993, funded by PHARE and undertaken by Bernard Brunhes consultants on Social Protection: Co-operation and Convergence in the Period of Transition (V/5643/93-EN). Conclusions did stress the need for building social consent, and, interestingly, the need to intensify the work of the Council of Europe (paragraph 23.6). In its turn the Council of Europe has conducted seminars in the country. UNICEF, quite early in the transition, published its volume on the needs of children (Cornia and Sipos, 1991); this included a chapter on Hungary which once again stressed the argument against means testing child benefits and for establishing a sound social assistance scheme. Interestingly Sandor Sipos moved on shortly afterwards from UNICEF to the human resources team in the East European Operations Division of the World Bank. He was to join the European as distinct from the liberal faction there and to be appealed to in the context of the conflict about means testing child benefits by Hungarian social policy lobbyists to make it clear that the Bank did not necessarily support full blown means testing of benefits.

An attempt has been made in Table 4.3 to capture the main points of the advice offered by the main international organizations in the field of income maintenance during the recent reform debates in Hungary. Where certain actors have had a limited role, e.g. UNICEF and UNDP, their general policy orientation on these questions is summarized for all countries later in the chapter. This table should be read in conjunction with the opening paragraph of this Hungarian case study where the relative weight to be attached to the role of each organization was reviewed. Although organizations have been active in the field and clearly influential in supporting some kind of social policy reform it is evident, when one compares what has been advised against what has been achieved, that many of the specifics of social policy advice have not been readily adopted. All organizations have been concerned about the need for an underpinning universal social assistance safety net but nothing of the sort has been achieved. Most organizations counselled against means testing child benefits but this has gone ahead, albeit in a form favoured by the World Bank. Perhaps the call to reduce unemployment entitlement has been heeded. Pension age entitlement has now been raised and the stalemate on pension reform has been finally broken in favour of a World Bank influenced policy proposal. The presence of most of the ideas of these international organizations and the very real power of some of them is a backcloth against which national policy continues to be made.

Bulgaria: tripartism creates a level playing field between Bank and ILO?

In contrast to the Hungarian story the major feature of the Bulgarians' encounter with international organizations in the sphere of income maintenance has been that of fairly continual dogged resistance to the requirements of the IMF and the wish of the Bank to lend money to support reform in this area. This resistance has been heavily influenced by the continuing power of the trade union movement which has used the tripartite structure of decision making and consultation to object not only to the thrust of Bank policy but also to the details of which Bank funded consultants are to be used by the government in particular cases. This

Table 4.3 Advice of international organizations to Hungarian governments on aspects of income maintenance policy, 1989–96

	World Bank	IMF	ILO	EU	OECD	COE
Safety net	Define nation-wide benefit level and means tested eligibility criteria	Well targeted, short term benefit necessary to mitigate negative aspects of reform on vulnerable groups	Social assistance net was necessary as an immediate response to marketization	PHARE advice to local social services offers	Citizenship entitlement to minimum support a priority	Minimum standards of social assistance encouraged in compliance with Social Charter
Child Benefit	Retention of universal family benefit in some form, but this should be taxed; proportion to be means tested, but only for smaller families	Means testing required	–	–	Tax child benefits; merge with child care allowance	Family benefits should be generally available and by implication state funded
Unemployment	Unemployment benefit should be flat rate and lower than the minimum wage; length of benefit reduced; disincentive features are important	High employment should be assured through competitive and flexible wages and removing rigidities; where unemployment occurs, public works schemes are favoured	Long term unemployment may be helped by public work schemes and subsidized jobs, reducing working hours, job share and retraining programmes; benefits set too high could act as a disincentive to work	Local initiatives in job creation favoured; retraining schemes a priority	Active unemployment measures should be targeted on the long term unemployed	Standards and duration of benefits set in Social Charter and code of Social Security

Pensions	Pension age must be raised and programmes reformed; three tier with second tier fully funded and not redistributive; tighten disability eligibility	Need restructuring and eligibility tightened; insurance fund deficit to be ended	Special programmes recommended for older workers; early retirement schemes too costly but gradual retirement favoured; little detailed advice	Advice given on setting up contributory schemes; raise age	Raise pension age; alternative options for implementation of the tiered system	Minimum pension levels encouraged in compliance with Social Charter; development of supplementary insurance scheme supported
Sickness	Differentiation according to occupational group should be discontinued; downsize and move cost to employers	Downsizing, alongside other health cutbacks	Should be insurance based; level linked to minimum wage as ILO convention	—	—	Minimum standards encouraged in compliance with Social Charter, but supplementary insurance schemes supported

resistance has continued throughout the years of the reforming coalitions under the UDF and looked likely to continue under the new government of the ex-communists elected at the end of 1994. By 1996, however, in the eye of a further economic crisis the new government appeared initially to be conceding to IMF wishes but later felt unable to carry this through, resulting in the opposition call for early elections which were set for 1997. The failure of the ex-communists to grapple with the reform issues lead to their defeat in these elections. The Bank even before 1996 has nonetheless played a part in the social protection reform debate by laying down social conditions as part of its structural adjustment lending where it could get a toe-hold. The ILO has, by virtue of the greater importance attached to tripartism, been a more significant player in Bulgaria than in Hungary and has been equally doggedly determined not to let the country drift from the path of building a solid system of insurance based social security, coupled with tax based social support backed up by a social assistance minimum. Minor but significant roles have been played by the EU in the sphere of collective bargaining, by the Council of Europe in the spheres of the Social Charter, and by other international organizations all of which are described below.

Bulgaria, unlike Hungary, was always much more closely identified with the Soviet Union. It owed its independence from the Turkish yoke to Russia. Neither had there been in the 1970s and 1980s any significant growth of an intellectual opposition to the Zhikov regime (Deacon and Vidinova, 1992). It came as no surprise that the first democratic elections after the 1989 events voted the ex-communists renamed as the Bulgarian Socialist Party (BSP), back into power. Although they were subsequently voted out of office in 1991 when the Union of Democratic Forces (UDF) won a slim majority, the instability of the political situation meant they were never far from power. The UDF was dependent upon the Turkish Minority Rights and Freedom (MRF) party to hold power but the MRF withdrew its support in 1992 because of policy differences for rural areas. There followed a period of government by experts and then a period of caretaker government which handed in the towel in late 1994 to clear the road for fresh elections which gave the BSP a clear absolute majority in Parliament again. The BSP had always been for a gradual transition to a market economy, and the UDF for shock therapy. The real differences between the periods of office are however small as the tripartite system within which both the Confederation of Independent Trade Unions (a reformation of the old trade union movement) and Podkrepa (the new trade union movement) wielded significant power assured continual attention by all governments to compensation policies that were designed to protect the working class from the social costs of transition.

Thus the social security system was modified during the 1990 round table discussions to cope with the impact of anticipated price rises by fixing a 70 per cent level of compensation against rising prices for all salaries and benefits. At the same time a very generous system of wage related unemployment benefits was introduced with benefit set at 100 per cent of previous salary for the first month, decreasing to 50 per cent in the sixth month. This policy of high levels of benefits and compensation, coupled with the collapse in trade with the Soviet Union as a result of the failure of Comecon and the subsequent financial impact of the war in Yugoslavia led to periods of massive inflation and a real drop in living standards of about 30 per cent. Naturally the IMF has continuously been reluctant to establish credit agreements and urges a more rapid pace of reform on successive governments. The relationship with the IMF got off on a bad footing when the BSP in 1990 stopped paying any of its foreign hard currency debts. An IMF loan was sought in 1991 which would be conditional on the removal of price controls on food and other services. In January 1992 the IMF expressed concern about the high level of compensatory social agreements. Further credit from the IMF was suspended in 1992. Matters between the government and the trade union movement came to a head in 1993 after a strike to maintain compensation for price hikes. At this point the Labour Minister Matinchev proposed only a 28 per cent compensation policy which was unacceptable. Round table discussions ended and were not renewed until the BSP obtained power again in 1995. This period of seeing off the trade union threat gave a window of opportunity for a new deal to be struck with the IMF in April 1994. A new loan of $421 million was agreed and tranched, with the conditions for its full release that the budget deficit be reduced to 6.2 per cent of GDP and structural reforms be speeded up.

While the IMF conditionality shapes the budget constraints within which Bulgarian social policy has to operate, it is World Bank advice and conditional structural adjustment lending that engages more directly with the details of particular income maintenance policies. The World Bank has however been up against the same reluctance to do business as the IMF. The trade union presence has been felt here also, as is described below. Perhaps the relationship with the World Bank in the field of social security got off to a bad start because the labour market and social security expert accompanying the World Bank's first ever mission to Bulgaria in June 1990 (World Bank, 1991c) was Louise Fox, who was then and has subsequently been identified with the more orthodox liberal free market wing of thinking among the Central European human resource specialists. Before some common ground was later to be established between this liberal wing and the 'European' wing associated with Nic Barr (1994) and others, Louise Fox argued that

> The Bulgarian system of [social insurance and social welfare] is far from the goal
> . . . of transparency in the way funds are collected and distributed . . . account-
> ability is weak, the opportunities for abuse are widespread.

More concretely in relation to the compensation policies agreed between the BSP and the trade unions she wrote

> the government will have to hold the line on current entitlements, effecting real
> reductions where possible. Options for short-run benefit reduction include leaving

family benefit at the current nominal rates, reducing unemployment benefits to a flat rate, and making workers responsible for the first day of sick leave. (World Bank, 1991c: 126–8)

Elsewhere (Fox, 1994a, 1994b) she argued for raising the pension age, to 'lessen the dependence population on the public pension programme', and developing a private pension alternative.

A structural adjustment loan was agreed with the Bank in 1991 and the release of the second tranche of $100 million in 1992 was made dependent upon a number of conditions including action in the social policy sphere. The eleventh condition specified that:

> By mid-March [1992] the following action ought to be taken: to use technical assistance to update pensions and social benefits; to co-ordinate a draft social net safety law with the Bank and to reduce early retirements. Foreign advisers would also help draw up a law on sick pay provisions and determine procedures for establishing a minimal poverty line. (Alexandrova, 1992)

This concern of the Bank to speed reform of the state social security system, to establish funded pension and sick pay schemes, and to prioritize a safety net law began the White Paper debacle. The attempt by the Bank to urge the Ministry of Labour and Social Affairs to develop a co-ordinated review of all income maintenance policies using foreign consultants stumbled upon the rocks of a divided ministry which had within it strong vice ministers separately responsible for employment, pensions, social assistance etc., and of the implacable opposition of Krastyo Petkov, President of the Confederation of Independent Trade Unions (CIUB). A meeting between Fox and Petkov produced a compromise whereby the proposed Harvard consultants would be replaced by a team of Bulgarian experts including Douhomir Minev who had been in the CIUB's Institute of Social Security and was to become briefly an employee of the ministry. As described later, Minev's (1993) report on pensions turned out to support much of the Bank's thinking against that of the ILO, even praising the Chilean solution, but for now the foreign consultants had been seen off. Galina Sotirova, of the resident World Bank mission in Bulgaria, acknowledged in an interview in March 1995 the sidelining of the Bank's efforts and concluded that 'we can only do what governments want'.

The Bank also offered sectoral loans to different sections of the ministry but all refused to take them up except for Marianna Manalova, Vice Minister for Social Care and Social Assistance. The logic of this acceptance was obvious in that cutting across all the Bank's concerns was the view that the safety net for the poor needed to have more money spent on it. This section of the ministry stood to gain in importance. Even here the final agreement to the deal by the Minister of Labour (Matinchev) was only brokered when Sandor Sipos, one of the 'European wing' of the human resources section of the Bank, replaced Louise Fox as the person responsible for Bulgaria and met personally with him.

The Ministry used the Bank loan to ensure that the advice it received on the further development of social assistance came from the European tradition. The three short-listed bids acceptable to the ministry were from the British Council, the UN Vienna Centre, and the Lahti University of Finland. The last won the contract and during 1994 and 1995 offered advice on the strengthening of the social assistance system. This team was led by a Finn who is also actively involved as a Council of Europe expert on the Social Charter.

In an interesting development, the generally thwarted World Bank was to keep an eye on the European social assistance team and the work of the Bulgarian authors of the social security White Paper through the separate engagement by the Bank of Igor Tomes as a senior policy adviser to the Ministry of Labour and Social Affairs. He wrote progress reports in December 1994 and February 1995 and used these to continue to fly the flag for Bank policy and comment favourably where, under the continued drip of IMF and WB pressure coupled with the realization of its own Bulgarian consultants that changes were needed, the ministry was beginning to move in the 'right' direction. Thus in the second report the 'plan to remove categories of work as preferential groups in the mandatory social insurance [scheme] from the general system and to offer private funded supplementary pension funds instead is basically a very good idea' (Tomes, 1995: 8). Where, however, it was felt that the Finnish social assistance team were straying from the preferred path this was firmly pointed out. Thus Tomes notes 'that a recommendation to make social assistance a personal, not a family right . . . has proved to be dangerous in many of the transition countries' (1995: 10). He was equally critical of a proposal to maintain universal child benefits and to extend entitlement to unemployment insurance benefit.

While the Bank struggled to get a foot in the door the ILO was welcomed with open arms when the government in 1993 asked the ILO to review the first draft of the White Paper on social security which, by then, had been drafted by the Bulgarian expert advisers. The ILO responded to this invitation by sending a high level team representative of both the Geneva Social Security Department and the ILO CEET in Budapest. Michael Cichon represented the latter. The ILO obtained UNDP funding for this mission. In its report it was able to draw heavily on the substantial work it had already undertaken for the country review of the Bulgarian situation. Its report *The Bulgarian Challenge: Reforming Labour Market and Social Policy* had been recently completed and had already concluded, in opposition to the Bank's views, that 'social security is a means of fostering social solidarity, by ensuring collective security against personal risks [and that therefore] its development should be governed by a tripartite board' (ILO, 1994e: 212–13).

It is instructive to compare and contrast the ILO's (1994b) commentary on the White Paper and the development of Bulgarian social security with that of the World Bank (1994a) made at about the same time. They are sharply different both in the extent to which they perceive there to be a funding fiscal crisis to be faced by the government and in their detailed policy recommendations, although there is also common ground. Both reports generate two scenarios over a future period. For the Bank the first scenario is to assume a steady state with no change in income transfer policy, no change in retirement age, continued replacement rates but with a steady fall in formal employment and hence a reduction in the tax base. The second assumes significant cuts in benefits in a way that most protects the poor, such as raising the retirement age to 65, cutting child benefits for 50 per cent of population, reducing all benefit replacement rates by 25 per cent, but doubling the amount available for social assistance. The first scenario 'will take the economy towards fiscal disaster. Payroll taxes of the order of 50 per cent of wages are bad . . . and the system is likely to move heavily into deficit . . . [requiring] 15 per cent of GDP' (World Bank, 1994a: 70–1). The second scenario would lower this to 8.7 per cent of GDP.

For the ILO, in scenario A the population of pension age increases by five per cent unemployment increases by 47 per cent, the population below working age decreases by 25 per cent, while replacement rates stay constant. Scenario B is one in which the same applies but replacement rates for pensions, unemployment benefits and social assistance and take-up for the latter two all *increase* by 50 per cent. In the case of the no-change scenario, in stark contrast to the Bank, it is concluded that 'the cost of the present social security scheme remains bearable for the economy' (ILO, 1994b: 43). The percentage of GDP estimated (excluding health care as per the Bank) is about 16 per cent. In the case of the radical improvement policy it is concluded that 'the total relative benefit cost would still not exceed today's EC average.' The GDP estimate is approximately 21 per cent. It is none-theless conceded that a high payroll tax would be required to sustain this and this would be possible because the share of the GDP going to wages is low in Bulgaria. In common with the Bank the ILO concludes that 'the creation of undue incentives for informalisation of the labour market must be avoided . . . this prompts a careful analysis of the way in which social security is financed.'

While there may be economic assumption differences built into the two futures sketched for the Bank and the ILO, the real difference between them is ideological. What the Bank regards as fiscal disaster – 15 per cent of GDP spent on income transfers – the ILO regards as bearable. Where the Bank sees only scope for cuts, the ILO sees scope for improvement. The comparative scenarios are summarized in Table 4.4.

There is common agreement between the bank and the ILO on the scope of the then White Paper – both seeing it focus too narrowly on insurance benefits – and on the pension age – both agreeing that a raise in pension age is inevitable. There is a sharp difference on whether priority support should be given to the minimum pension or all pensions, or whether family benefits should be means tested or not.

Compared with the major efforts at influence made by the Bank and the ILO, the contribution of the other international organizations in this policy

Table 4.4   *World Bank and ILO futures for Bulgarian social security*
(% GDP)

	World Bank		ILO	
	Current policies (1992)	Radical reforms (cuts) (1997)	Current policies (1992)	Radical reforms (improvement) (2010)
Unemployed	0.7	0.5	1.30	2.94
Children	2.1	0.8	1.12	1.12
Old pensioners	8.3	5.0	} 8.83	13.27
Other pensioners	1.3	0.9		
Sick and maternity	1.7	0.5	0.63	0.67
Social assistance	0.5	1.0	1.19	2.16
Total	14.6	8.7	13.06	20.16

Sources: ILO, 1994b; World Bank, 1994a

area has been limited. The PHARE programme focused on the building of NGO capacity in this period. Some small sums were diverted to paying for the computerization of the social assistance system. The Council of Europe has advised. A seminar on the Council's Social Charter was held in June 1995 and this reinforced the decision of the ministry to sign up for the Charter. The UNDP underpinned the ILO effort in a way which we will see again in the Ukraine. The OECD was not a major player compared with the situation in Hungary. Table 4.5 attempts to capture the main aspects of policy advice in Bulgaria of the limited number of major international players. The policy advice of the Council of Europe, not shown in the table, is similar as for Hungary (Table 4.3).

Where has all of this activity left Bulgarian income maintenance policy and what impact have the organizations had? Little movement was made in the direction of radical reform of the pension and sick pay schemes. There was latterly in the 1993 White Paper an acknowledgement of the need to raise the pension age, to move towards the setting up of a separate pension fund but funded on a pay-as-you-go system, and to tighten up eligibility for maternity and sick pay. At the same time the continuation of a wage related state scheme was confirmed as was the continuation of the universal payment of family benefits. A national social assistance scheme has been developed and will be codified in a new law on social welfare. The first published policy document of the government, the *White Book* of early 1995, suggests that the BSP was not, unlike its Hungarian counterpart, about to embrace IMF or World Bank thinking more enthusiastically than its predecessors. Rather the flavour of future Ministry of Labour policy was captured by a statement made by the new BSP minister in response to a question about the role of external actors: 'When the World Bank comes I have to tell them it is not East European social policy we are discussing but European social policy of the past 100 years.'

Table 4.5 *Advice of international organizations to Bulgarian governments on aspects of income maintenance policy, 1989–96*

	World Bank	IMF	ILO
Safety net	Universal social assistance must be introduced concentrating on the poorest; provision in kind or food coupons as an alternative at local level	Well targeted, short term net necessary to mitigate negative aspects of reform on vulnerable groups	The second 'safety net' is accessible as a last resort temporary measure only; need to strengthen legal eligibility criteria
Child benefit	Need based family allowance recommended; reduce the universal coverage; introduce means tests	–	Universal family benefits paid out of national taxation favoured
Unemployment	Flat rate benefit with strengthened monitoring to maintain incentive to return to work; supplements payable for retraining participation	High employment would be assured through competitive and flexible wages and removing rigidities; where unemployment occurs, public works schemes are favoured	In the long term the link should be phased in between benefit and previous earnings, and length of entitlement extended
Pensions	Low retirement age makes system unsuitable; private pensions addition suggested; maintain state as minimum pension	Need restructuring and eligibility tightened	The raising and equalizing of pension age is endorsed; link to previous earnings should be improved; no maximum ceiling on state pension
Sickness	Employer to be responsible for initial sick days; reduce replacement rate	–	Replace variable entitlements with standard replacement rate; employers to be responsible for sick pay; tax the benefit

However, by 1996 the Bulgarian economy was facing a severe crisis with 100 per cent inflation predicted for that year. In this context the ex-communist government presented to Parliament and the IMF a policy for closing about 70 loss making enterprises which would be accompanied by a $150 million World Bank loan agreed in June 1996 to pay the equivalent of six months' salary to redundant workers. The Bank felt that it was able to do this because it was 'pleased with the enhancement of the safety net' (*New European*, 18 May 1996). Further progress in the direction of Bank thinking (albeit the European wing) was the decision in November 1995 of the Parliament to approve a new social security law that would establish a separate fund disconnected from the state budget. The initial thinking seemed to eschew a privatization policy in favour of a state pay-as-you-go scheme with employer and employee contributions. Given even this level of policy change the Bank and government agreed, at last, a loan in this area of Ministry of Labour policy. A loan of $24.5 million over 20 years focused on social security reform was agreed in June 1996.

The ILO, according to an interview with Michael Cichon, is 'not going to let Bulgaria go . . . it's a question of the best time for the next intervention'. Whether the minister, working with the ILO, can secure a viable European social security system depends, of course, on whether the Bank's economic prognosis is more accurate than the ILO's. There is a real danger that by seeking to maintain and improve the social protection system of the past the government will lose the opportunity of moulding a less generous system appropriate to the new impoverished circumstances. Outside the remit of the state an untaxable and unregulated private goods and labour market is flourishing in Bulgaria. The fears of the Bank that the fiscal base of the government is eroding seems well grounded. The future for Bulgarian social policy could well become not the tension described for Hungary between a desirable European conservatism and a more affordable social liberalism, but one between a possibly unviable post-communist conservatism and an antisocial liberalism waiting in the wings. The collapse of the government and the consequential early elections called for 1997 which resulted in the defeat of the ex-communists do not bode well for the future of Bulgarian social policy.

Ukraine: the Bank searches for a counterpart while the ILO and UNDP talk with the old guard?

Of the countries in our small sample the Ukraine represents the extreme end of the spectrum between those post-communist countries well on the way to market liberalism and those best characterized as post-communist conservative. The story that unfolds below is therefore one in which the IMF is continually having to hold back on its credits when repeatedly promised budgetary reforms are not implemented, and in which the World Bank was still in 1995 trying to find a reliable counterpart in the government who would be willing to borrow money to effect changes in Ukraine's social protection system. In this relatively stagnant situation the ILO, supported by an unusually dynamic country based UNDP presence, has secured a high profile in Parliament and the Ministry of Labour for its analysis of and prescriptions for reform. While working co-operatively with the existing Ministry of Labour and Ministry of Social Protection and the Parliamentary Commission for Social Policy and Labour Affairs, both the ILO and the UNDP have nonetheless called for more sustained reform than the President can persuade his government to deliver. Bit parts have also been played by the EU, Council of Europe and UNICEF. The OECD seems to have had little presence.

Consecutive headlines in *The Economist* grasp the sense of frustration that western capitalist interests have felt when observing the small progress being made towards reforming the Ukraine economy in the direction of the free market. 'Independent, but not yet free' (13 June 1992), 'Dead again' (2 October 1993), 'Ukraine on the brink' (of economic disaster) (27 November 1993), 'Better late than never maybe' (22 July 1995), 'Reformer anonymous' (2 September 1995) and finally 'Slipping back? (25 November 1995) are headlines that skim the surface of a story of stalled attempts at economic reform. In a nutshell very little progress towards market reform was made under the first President of Independent Ukraine, Leonid Krauchuk. The then Prime Minister Leonid Kuchma who had tried to initiate some reform steps was forced to step down in September 1993 when a huge strike wave spread across the Eastern Russian orientated oblasts. Presidential elections followed and in July 1994 by the slimmest of majorities Kuchma won. Parliamentary elections earlier had secured an ex-communist majority in the Rada. From 1994, therefore, the scene was set for a struggle between ex-communist Kuchma as President who favoured economic reform while redeveloping ties with Russia and the communist, socialist and peasant dominated Parliament (or former Supreme Soviet) which continually resisted the social and labour market consequences of such reforms. The power struggle between the President and the Parliament, within which Kuchma has slowly secured for himself control over the Cabinet of Ministers and its programme, continued into 1995. By June 1995 Kuchma 'had succeeded in establishing Presidential control of the central government, thereby taking it out of the hands of the central Rada' (Bojcun, 1995: 82). As Bojcun notes

> the struggle over the division of state powers is by no means just a struggle for power. The functional division between the arms of the state masks . . . a complex ideological division between the Rada's left wing block and the President's team and his supporters in the Rada. It is no longer a division between capitalism and socialism/communism as the long term goal of the transition period that is under way. It is more a choice between different paths for Ukraine to the capitalist society and the world market, with still widespread disagreement about the relative benefits of ties to the East as opposed to the West, the welfare state versus neo-liberal austerity in welfare, and so on. (1995: 83)

The stop-go policy of the IMF towards Ukraine has reflected this power and ideology struggle. When the IMF could see a chance of furthering reform it would lend, or not, credits as it felt appropriate. In 1994 a \$700 million loan was agreed but disbursements were withheld later that year. Again in 1995 'after months of tortuous negotiations' (*EIU Country Reports*, second quarter 1995: 16) a \$2 billion credit was agreed. The condition, of course, was that Parliament agree a budget that cut the deficit from 8.6 per cent of GDP in 1994 to 3.5 per cent in 1995. This implied a cut in subsidies including those on rents. The Parliament, while approving the budget, voted for compensation mechanisms to be set up to protect the poorest. The battle continued throughout 1995. After the IMF agreed to release three of the four tranches of the loan, the last payments were put on hold. In late October a large workers' protest across Ukraine demanded an end to short-time working. In December, Ukraine was accused of not paying its gas debt to Russia. By January 1996 it was reported that 'A year into Ukraine's ambitious market reform effort initiated by Kuchma over a year ago, the battle to implement a serious market programme is slowly being lost . . . As a result the IMF put off a scheduled vote on the remaining standby programme . . . hoping to force country officials back on track by March' (*New Europe*, 21–7 January 1996: 10). Later in 1996 the story continued with new IMF loans negotiated to give back-pay to miners and many other workers. In summary the economy is still largely state managed; about one-third of the workforce is on short time or laid off with no pay and no benefits (because they are not officially unemployed); and powerful vested interests in the state sector of the economy still block marketization.

In terms of specific opinions about the social policy reforms that are necessary, the IMF devoted a section of its published *Economic Review of the Ukraine* (IMF, 1995c: 30–1) to the matter of poverty and the social safety net. It observed that 'old age pensioners living alone, or those deprived of land or housing, are increasingly vulnerable in the current environment. The pension fund has, thus, become unable to achieve financial balance and provide a satisfactory level of minimum benefits at the same time.' In contrast the employment fund was in surplus and 'served as a reserve against future claims on unemployment compensation, in the event that large scale open unemployment should emerge'. Overall 'the system of social protection will need to be reformed . . . [as it] reflects years of . . . trying to support the incomes of large sections of the population.' Rather optimistically (in its own terms) the report goes on to note that 'the government has recently begun to reform its social protection policies and envisages the introduction of a safety net.' Finally it inevitably concludes that

As a government curtails budgetary expenditures and cuts the budget deficit, it is inevitable that the present social services will be streamlined. This will involve dismantling the system of subsidized housing and utilities, and increasing cost recovery for communal services; rationalizing and simplifying the existing system of benefits; and reducing distribution costs in order to improve the cost-effectiveness of the system. The Government intends to ensure that spending, in real terms, is targeted towards the most needy, in particular child benefits and supplements for low-income pensioners. The Government also plans to reform the Pension Fund. Low retirement ages (60 for men and 55 for women), preferential treatment for many categories of workers, and a large number of invalids and war veterans, combined with an aging population, make the present system unsustainable. Among the reforms envisaged by the Government are later retirement ages, tightening of eligibility criteria, removal of exemptions to age limits, and further flattening of the pension structure.

One of the indicators that has emerged as a measure of the willingness of the Ukrainian government to reform and one that has featured in both IMF and, as we shall see later, World Bank conditionality has been rent levels. The IMF has insisted that subsidy on housing gradually be removed. A consequential decree of government in 1994 stated that subsidy on housing and heating and other service costs should be reduced so that the amount consumers pay should be progressively raised to reach 60 per cent of actual cost in 1996. At the same time, however, it was agreed that rents should not exceed 15 per cent of a 'family income'. A system of means tested housing allowances was to be established to protect the poorest. USAID was recruited to the task in 1995 of setting up a new pool of 10,000 personnel to implement the policy and raise rents. The likely success of this was reviewed with some scepticism by the Ministry of Social Protection when interviewed in 1995.

The World Bank entered the Ukrainian battleground quite early in 1993 with all guns blazing and diagnosed dire problems in its Social Sector report (World Bank, 1993a). Locating itself in the abandoned offices of the Central Committee of the Communist Party it offered dramatic and instant solutions in line with its historically derived liberal policy, but has made very slow progress, searching still for government partners sympathetic to Kuchma's reform approach. In the process it has had to work alongside, if not actually with, the ILO and soften some of its zeal. The Bank reported that 'in 1992, the overall cost of social protection (pensions, allowances, subsidies, and social services) was budgeted at more than 40 per cent of GDP. Virtually no other government in the world bears such a burden' (1993a: 1). It concluded that 'the burden of providing benefits or wages to nearly two thirds of the population, while one third works in directly productive activities, has grown to exceed any possibility of being financed by the economy and government' (1993a: 1–2). Classically, therefore, the review of the social sector concluded that three principles must inform the necessary reforms: first, those who are poor, or made poor, must be protected fully; secondly, 'all benefits above the poverty line should be continued only to the extent that resources permit' (1993a: 2); and thirdly, the efficiency of social spending must be increased. Its instant solution, which in 1993 fell largely on deaf ears, is encapsulated in Table 4.6.

In the context of the greater optimism for reform in 1994 the World Bank did manage to negotiate a $500 million loan. The release of the second tranche of this loan was made conditional on social sector reform. In specific detail the conditions included the measures in Table 4.7.

The problem for the bank, however, in steering these conditions through, and in its attempt to negotiate (as it was doing in 1995) a new $300 million social sector rehabilitation loan, was to find reliable government counterparts. At that point it had identified Pynzenyk as First Vice Premier for Economic Reform, a sympathetic Deputy Minister of Social Protection, and individuals elsewhere in government. No minister either of labour or of social protection could, however, be counted as a friend. At the same time

Table 4.6 *Past, current, suggested and sustainable policy for public social spending: World Bank's views on Ukrainian social policy, 1993*

Spending category	% of GDP under alternative approaches				Policy actions required
	Actual experience in 1989–90	Budget 1992	Suggested programme for 1993	Sustainable programme beyond 1993	
Employment and labour market policies	–	0.8	2.4	3.7	Expand active policies by strengthening employment service; all cash benefits at single rate near minimum wage
Pensions	8.0	13.9	11.3	7.7	Flat rate pension for 1993 near minimum wage; introduce personal saving accounts in 1994; gradually raise retirement age beginning in 1993
Family allowances	1.0	8.8	6.2	3.4	Target on single parents and families with three or more children and elderly living alone
Consumer subsidies	8.0	5.1	3.0	0.0	Reduce in 1993 then eliminate all untargeted subsidies after 1993
Education	5.0	7.8	7.0	6.0	Reduce unnecessary staff by attrition; eliminate stipends for foreign students; reform vocational training to support active labour policies
Health	3.0	7.7	7.0	6.0	Reduce hospitalizations and staff with out-patient care; cut numbers of new medical students; expand imports and production of selected essential drugs
Total	25.0	44.1	36.9	26.8	Introduce budgeting by objective in selected ministries

Source: World Bank, 1993a

because many welfare functions continued to be undertaken by enterprises this meant that some 70 sectors of government, according to the World Bank's programme development officer for the Ukraine, were implicitly involved in welfare reform. Of the fact that the ILO and UNDP talked to the existing ministries, the Bank's resident development officer would only comment: 'Do they live in the same world?' She saw the work of the ILO and UNDP, which is described in more detail below, as giving succour to

Table 4.7   *World Bank Ukraine loan release conditions, November 1994*
(extract)

Policy area	Measures before 28 November 1994	Measures between 29 November 1994 and end 1995
Safety net	Initiate two strategic policy papers, one on social assistance and the other on pensions and unemployment compensation	Completion of policy by 15 March 1995; implementation of comprehensive policy
Pension fund	Pension expenditure adjusted so as to maintain pension fund in balance in 1994; pension supplements to low income pensioners indexed to inflation; other pension benefits will be correspondingly reduced in real terms to ensure the fund is in balance	Continue to protect low income pensioners; initiate measures to strengthen the pension system over the long term, e.g. by gradually raising the normal retirement age for both genders and by discouraging granting of pensions to active workers
Employment fund	Extension of credits from employment fund to enterprises for job creation discontinued; explore mechanisms for strengthening benefits for the unemployed, including replacing severance pay in part with unemployment compensation	Initiate implementation of comprehensive reforms of unemployment compensation scheme

Source: World Bank

the communists and socialists in the Parliament by its focus on the social and health costs of the transition.

In pursuit of dynamic counterparts the Bank noted in a memo to the government in 1995 that 'if an effective counterpart arrangement is established, a project preparation unit for the social protection project . . . might accelerate project preparation. The unit would need to be headed by a strong executive with the delegated authority of, for example, a Vice Premier.' Recognizing that the existing ministers were more sympathetic to the ILO than the Bank, the note continued that 'it might be possible to broaden the scope of the project preparation unit to include social protection projects offered by the international community generally. A general project preparation unit for social protection projects has in fact been proposed by the ILO. The World Bank would consider this initiative very seriously, provided it has the support of the Ukrainian Government.' This story is taken up again after the background to the work of the ILO in the Ukraine is described below.

The Bank and ILO public competition for influence, which in 1995 appeared to be giving way to at least covert co-operation, was reflected in a number of ways, not least the timing of seminars and missions. One such competition took place in April 1995. The World Bank had planned to hold a seminar with the government from 27 February to 2 March 1995, but had to postpone this until 25–9 April. This let the ILO slip in first with a high level mission on 10–12 April to address the several ministers and appropriate vice presidents. Perhaps as a consequence, the ministerial staff would have been better prepared to respond critically to one of the papers scheduled to be tabled at the World Bank seminar. This was on the topic of targeting and drew lessons from the experience of Latin America (Grosh, 1995).

The interventions of the ILO and the UNDP in the Ukraine are so intertwined that they are best described and analysed together. The UN presence in the Ukraine is a model of how things should be. In 1992 Boutros Boutros-Ghali determined that there should be unified UN offices in the countries of the former Soviet Union and some East European countries. Located in the same place in Kiev are the WHO, UNDP and UNHCR, with UNICEF to follow. The ILO had separately developed its regional outpost in Budapest but sends representatives frequently to Kiev. Guy Standing of the ILO CEET proposed to the UNDP in November 1992 that the ILO and UNDP collaborate in the country. This took the form initially of the UNDP underpinning the major review of the labour market and social policy undertaken by the ILO CEET (ILO, 1994a). In typical ILO mode the report develops from the government's own conception of social protection reform. In 1993 it was expressed in the form of the Ministry of Labour's concept of social security of the population in Ukraine, which encompassed the four branches of social security (unemployment benefits, health care benefit, employment related disease benefits, pensions), safeguards against the loss of income due to inflation, providing social assistance to the poor and disabled, and providing benefits for victims of technological, environmental and natural disasters. The ILO noted that 'with respect to the complementary roles of social insurance and social assistance, the overall structure of the suggested social protection system strongly resembled those operating in Central and Western Europe, notably the one in the Federal Republic of Germany' (1994a: 264). The chapter on 'The Challenge of Social Protection' from which the above quotes are drawn was written by Michael Cichon who we identified earlier (Chapter 3) as on the wing of the ILO CEET concerned to defend traditional Bismarckian schemes of social insurance. His recommendations in the chapter are broadly sympathetic to the ministry of labour conception but he points out that there are several budgetary problems that need to be addressed. Sharing some of the Bank's concerns, the view is expressed that priority needs should be given to the establishment of a social assistance scheme, as 'deficiencies of the present social assistance system make this urgent' (1994a: 271) and that cash benefits in the social insurance and social support system need to be adjusted at two speeds: 'the basic layer [to combat poverty] should follow inflation or average wages and the second layer could be adjusted in line with general economic development' (1994a: 270). The need for tripartite forms of governance is also stressed.

This report was presented to a tripartite Conference on Reforming Labour Markets and Social Policy in Ukraine in September 1994 organized by the Ministry of Labour, the ILO and the UNDP. It was this conference that the programme development officer for the World Bank regarded as being against the IMF and the World Bank. It certainly laid the foundation upon which the ILO was to build in making sure it would be included in any detailed technical assistance work in this sphere that might be initiated by the Bank. One of the recommendations put to and endorsed by the conference was that a 'technical conference of pension specialists be convened in Kiev, under the auspices of the Government and with the involvement of international technical and financial agencies, including the ISSA, the ILO, the IMF, the World Bank and the EU. This conference should clarify the advantages and disadvantages of alternative pension systems, including the mix of public and private pension provision' (1994a: 796).

This conference was to be followed by another significant event to strengthen the arm of those wishing to protect the social welfare system against IMF inspired budget cuts. The UNDP offices had in 1993 launched, in association with the Ukrainian Academies of Sciences, a programme of research to apply the methodology of the UNDP's *Human Development Report* to the Ukrainian situation. This resulted in February 1995 in the publication of the very impressive *Ukraine Human Development Report 1995* (UNDP, 1995b). It argued for a human development strategy for the Ukraine based on the four Es of empowerment, equity, employment and the environment. It charted the human costs of the transition in terms of falling population, worsening life expectancy, rising morbidity, increasing poverty and widening inequality. It recommended political reforms to empower citizens, to employ citizens, and to protect the environment. In terms of the E for equity it discussed in detail the need for reforms in the social protection system. Specifically (UNDP, 1995b: 46–7) it called for:

Basic income guarantee With a minimum wage above subsistence, a social assistance system, and family benefits linked to average wages.
Pensions Minimum pensions to reflect consumer prices and wage related pensions to follow economic growth. Pension age to be raised.
Sickness and maternity benefits Initial sick days to be covered by the employer. Maternity benefits to stay at 100 per cent of earnings.
Unemployment benefit Payable for 12 months, decreasing to a minimum income.
Child and family benefits The right to receive child benefits up to the age of 16 without income test to be extended to cover all families with three or more children. When financial situation allows, this right to be further extended.

With the politics inside the Ukraine balanced between the economic reformers and the economic conservatives, and the politics of the highly visible international actors balanced equally between a more economic liberal inclined World Bank and a more social protection orientated ILO

They cooperate because they are ideologically on two extremes

and UNDP, it was not surprising that both the Bank and the ILO should find themselves needing to collaborate in order to establish the agency of change, an executor of reform with whom both of them would have to do business in order to nurture their particular variants of capitalism.

Following the September 1994 conference the ILO with UNDP finance undertook a further mission to Kiev which resulted in a further review of social protection reform which was made available to the government in early 1995. The contents of this reflect the earlier work. Compared with the World Bank's dire projections about the economic burden of social security the executive summary of this ILO (1995a) report argues: 'there is no hard and fast rule as to how much a society should spend on social protection. Much depends on societal priorities and on value judgements . . . A minimum level of social protection in the context of Ukraine is estimated to cost at least 22 to 23 per cent of GDP. The country has already reached, or even fallen below, that minimum level. Rather than allowing any further erosion of benefits, there should be urgent efforts to improve revenue collection.' The report goes on to propose the establishment of a national project management unit to be set up immediately to co-ordinate assistance and implement policy in this field. Events later in 1995 and 1996 which followed the end of our fieldwork in the Ukraine will prove whether the twin approach of the Bank and the ILO to force the pace of reasoned social reform in the Ukraine will prevail against post-communist conservative forces.

Compared with the above, the parts played by the other international organizations in the Ukraine have been relatively minor. The EU has at certain points responded to the Ukraine in terms of its being an impoverished country needing conventional aid. In April 1994 the Commission developed plans to spend ECU 100 million in emergency food aid in the wake of a farming crisis. In addition to signing a partnership agreement in June 1994 the EU has included the Ukraine among one of the first former Soviet Union countries to receive funds under the TACIS system which are earmarked for consultancy work on the social implications of economic restructuring. The TACIS field officer in Kiev saw this work, aimed in part at enabling major industries to shift from concealed unemployment to open unemployment and in part at enabling enterprises to shed their social welfare functions, as complementing the work of UNDP which was also calling for the establishment of a conventional unemployment benefit system in lieu of continued hidden industrial subsidy. The ECU four million project begun in 1994–5 is designed to set up pilot studies of how state enterprises might divest themselves of their social protection responsibilities in the process of privatization. The project is geared to exploring NGO, local authority, and private alternatives to the large range of child care, nursing, housing, invalidity and other social benefits currently associated with state employment. Advice will clearly depend on the particular predilections of the private consulting firms selected for the work, in this case PdS of the Netherlands. This unpredictability of advice led Cichon of the ILO to comment that the TACIS system for the former Soviet Union was a 'multi-million pound disaster'.

Membership of the Council of Europe for the Ukraine was a contentious issue but it was finally agreed in 1996. Policy advice work has hardly got under way. Finally, UNICEF is preparing a national programme of action but details are not yet available.

The diverse attempts by the different international organizations to influence Ukraine income maintenance policy are summarized in Table 4.8. There is, in fact, considerable unanimity about the need for unemployment benefits in lieu of hidden unemployment, for social assistance, and for raising the pension age. There are some differences with regard to child benefits and wage related pensions. As has been suggested above, however, there has been little progress in any aspect of these policies. Pensioners still retire early and no new pension and insurance fund has been established. Unemployment remains hidden. Many subsidies remain in place. No significant restructuring of the earlier state socialist system of social protection has happened. The only real difference between now and 1993 when the World Bank predicted disaster is that inflation has enabled the government to erode the real value of benefits so that they now count for a smaller proportion of GDP, with the consequence that more of the population is poorer and the poorest remain unprotected.

The role of the major international organizations in Eastern Europe compared

The three case studies analysed reveal some important points of similarity and difference. The IMF and the World Bank are always there. The Fund is the constant reminder to government that the transition to capitalism requires a reduction in the public sector borrowing requirement and, where raising revenue is difficult, this normally implies expenditure reduction in the social protection sector. Specific recommendations to government as to how to do this and still provide a safety net are generally secret although the Fund is beginning to explicate its thinking as we summarize below.

The World Bank, despite very different situations, is everywhere doggedly persistent in its search for a counterpart, in its attempt to lend money in the income maintenance sector, and in its predictions of economic crisis if a policy shift isn't embarked upon. This shift is typically from attempts to sustain the inherited pensions and other social insurance benefits to a targeted policy of developing a social assistance system, conserving only flat rate pensions and limiting entitlement to other benefits, while creating an individually accounted, fully funded, privately managed second tier of pensions. As discussed below, however, Bank policy between countries is more variable than this and internal divisions exist as to what constitutes best policy.

Table 4.8 *Advice of international organizations to Ukraine government on aspects of income maintenance policy, 1991–6*

	World Bank	IMF	ILO	UNDP
Safety net	Adequacy of net an expressed aspect of concern for the Bank	Increased targeting necessary; large scale social redistribution no longer desirable	Social insurance is ultimate aim but urgent need for social assistance system	Basic income guarantee needed with social assistance linked to average wages
Child benefit	May need to be restructured to target needy families, i.e. single parents and those with three or more children	Needs targeting, too many families receive family allowances	Universal family benefits, not means tested as a desired goal	Non-means-tested benefit up to age 16 to be extended to all children in families with three children; further improvements when resources permit
Unemployment	Equipping displaced workers with new skills should be the priority, preferably through private sector, enterprise based training programmes; benefits should be flat rate and eligibility tightened, e.g. excluding new entrants to the labour force; end of hidden subsidy to firms to maintain employment	Disguised unemployed (part-time or forced leave with no pay) need help via establishing proper benefit system	Insurance based favoured, should be work related component and no workfare	Unemployment benefit for 12 months reducing to minimum income
Pensions	Raise the pension age, abolish the early retirement option, reduce the benefits of those who continue to work; eliminate old age benefits to those who do not urgently need them; support the minimum against inflation; consider personal savings accounts	Dependency ration currently unsustainable at nearly 60 pensioners to 100 employed workers; pension age needs review; special allowances, e.g. to war veterans may need curtailing	Pension levels should not be eroded, need to be buttressed to retain value, but age should be increased	Protect minimum to reflect prices; wage related pensions to reflect economic growth; pension age to be raised

Compared with these actors the others are small fry. A possible exception to this can be made for the International Labour Organization. While not equally active everywhere it is, sometimes alongside the UNDP, the consistent opposition to the Bretton Woods institutions in this region. It consistently underplays the Bank's prognosis of crisis. It always suggests that the level of social protection is a policy decision and that higher expenditures backed up by higher revenues (taxes) are possible and even desirable. Only in the need to raise pension age is there always agreement with the Bank. The ILO strategy, which is discussed in more detail below, is to conserve or establish tripartite forms of governance as a means of bringing pressure to bear on IMF influenced governments to maintain social expenditures. While there is some dissent within ILO ranks as to what constitutes best policy advice, something discussed briefly in Chapter 3 and returned to in Chapter 5, this rarely found expression in the country specific advice in the case studies. This advice was always mainstream conservative corporatist, favouring a Bismarckian insurance system backed up by universal social support (e.g. child benefits) and social assistance.

The EU by comparison with these global actors seems to have missed an opportunity to steer income maintenance policy in the region towards the dominant European tradition of conservative corporatism. By delegating its influence to the PHARE and TACIS competitive tendering processes and not asking its consultants to work within a policy framework, it is squandering the potential for consistent and persistent policy influence. The possible corrective to this resulting from the new consensus programme (Chapter 3) came too late to influence events in these case studies. The Council of Europe is always there, is consistent, is seeking to win adherents to its Social Charter, but is very much a quiet background influence.

The OECD seems not to be such an important actor in the region in the sphere of social policy as might have been imagined. Only in Hungary was detailed systematic work undertaken on social policy and here time will tell if it effectively substitutes for the missing ILO and UNDP presence there and cautions the government towards more socially friendly ways of balancing its budget.

Of the governments in the three countries it can be said at this stage that they vary considerably. They have a capacity, if they choose, at the possible cost of economic efficiency, of resisting IMF views. The willingness to play ball with the Bank varies. The Bank cannot achieve what countries do not want to do. Strong trade union presence at national level is a key to resistance to the Bretton Woods institutions. In Bulgaria and the Ukraine the ILO acts as a useful alternative source of external support and advice. Individuals have often played an important part either in encouraging governments to listen to the Bank, or in devising strategies alternative to those emanating from the liberal wing of the Bank.

Our choice of the three countries as representing countries with different degrees of closeness to Europe, countries where the initial trajectory and process of reform were very different, and countries with different degrees of affinity to the Soviet Union seems to have paid off. Clearly Hungary has reformed more of its social policy more rapidly (under Bank and not ILO influence), Ukraine has been resistant to reform (whether of Bank or ILO persuasion) and Bulgaria occupies a middle position. This difference in policy outcome of the first few years of reform is confirmed by the World Bank's (1996: 14–17) comparative assessment of economic and social policy reform in the region. It groups Eastern European and former Soviet Union countries into four categories depending on the degree of economic liberalization, the private sector share of GDP and the extent of asset privatization. Hungary is in the first (fastest) category along with the Czech Republic, Poland, Slovenia, etc. Bulgaria is in the second category along with Estonia, Romania, Lithuania, etc. Ukraine is in the fourth (slowest) category along with Uzbekistan, Belarus, Turkmenistan, etc.

Below the role of some of the organizations in the region is discussed in more detail, drawing upon not only the case studies but also what is known about their activities elsewhere and including the organizations' own self-assessment of their work. An attempt is made here not only to assess impact on country policy but also to analyse how far the policy and actions of the major international organizations have themselves been modified by their encounter with post-communist developed economies.

IMF begins to explicate its hidden safety net advice

Before the advent of post-communist countries in Eastern Europe and the former Soviet Union, the world's developing countries engaged with the IMF in its earlier structural adjustment programmes. What was concluded at that stage about the Fund's impact on and policy towards the poor? Killick and Malik concluded

> (a) that stabilization programmes are liable to have appreciable effects on the distribution of income but that these are apt to be rather complex; (b) that groups of the poor can indeed be among the losers, with the urban working class particularly at risk; (c) that governments adopting Fund programmes are none-the-less free to adopt measures to protect vulnerable groups, although there may be hard negotiations with the Fund over measures which are liable to create large claims on public revenues. (1991: 16)

While nothing would fundamentally change in Eastern Europe in terms of the 'hard negotiations' over measures to protect vulnerable groups, the Fund by 1989–90 had begun to address explicitly how best to protect the poor in the imminent post-communist transition. When the IMF established its East European Department in 1990 it 'had begun to exhibit increased understanding in dealing with the social dislocations which accompany reform. Now the Fund had recognised that in order to convince governments to implement disruptive reforms it must sanction compensatory mechanisms. For instance, the IMF now supports the creation of social safety nets to cushion the impact of enterprise liquidation and inflation in Eastern Europe' (Henderson, 1992: 265). Subsequently a series of IMF staff and working papers which are in the public domain have begun to reveal something of Fund thinking on how best to secure such a safety net. The review of these papers below complements the findings of the research into Fund policy and activity in the three case studies.

An early review of the prospects for and practice of the IMF in Hungary, Poland, Czechoslovakia, Bulgaria and Romania undertaken by a visiting scholar in the IMF's Research Department cautioned that 'a critical problem for all five countries is the transition from a relatively egalitarian and well-endowed social welfare network . . . policy makers will face strong social and political pressures to continue the existing generous social security services' (Bruno, 1992: 767–8). As a consequence the reviewer asked whether 'some fiscal deficit [should] be allowed for the interim period until the tax reform is fully in place'. Kopits, reviewing for the IMF work between 1990 and 1993 in Bulgaria, Czechoslovakia, Hungary, Mongolia, Poland and Romania (as well as Laos and Algeria), concluded that a 'particular challenge consists of providing cost effective social insurance schemes for old age, health care, and unemployment, as well as social assistance for low income families . . . to build and maintain broad-based support for reform it is important to develop measures to shield the poor from the initial adverse effects of adjustment' (1994: 13).

In terms of IMF thinking on how to support the poor in a fiscally suitable way in an inflationary context, Ahmad and Schneider concluded for the countries of the former Soviet Union that 'we would see a continued role for family allowances . . . [and for pensioners] . . . food stamps denominated in quantity terms' (1993: 11). The most systematic internal IMF review of the issue of safety nets was undertaken recently by a group of Expenditure Policy Division staff attached to the Fiscal Affairs Department of the Fund. It is worth repeating the conclusions drawn from their study of Albania, Poland, Romania, Russia, Kazakhstan and Uzbekistan. They conclude that a number of lessons can be derived from the review of country experiences. These were, in abbreviated form:

> First, target groups and benefit amounts should be appropriately determined to achieve the object of social safety nets mitigating the adverse effects of reform policies on the poor . . . Moreover, social safety nets should be designed . . . to maximise the use of existing arrangements . . .
>
> Second, the categorical nature of targeting cash benefits should be maintained, at least in the near term. Effective means testing is not easy, but over time efforts ought to be made to strengthen the institutional capacity for it. Although not ideal, means testing based on formal sector income may reduce the leakage of benefits to unintended beneficiaries, but the possible unfairness of such a scheme – given imperfect assessment of informal sector incomes – suggests caution.
>
> Third, generalized subsidies should be replaced rapidly with targeted cash transfers . . . The remaining subsidies should be targeted to vulnerable members of society as much as possible. Transitory coupon schemes, which can be cost effective, can be resorted to whenever administratively feasible . . .

Fourth, as subsidized credits and transfers to inefficient enterprises are reduced, more effective assistance needs to be provided to unemployed workers. Hidden unemployment should be made open . . .

Fifth, eligibility criteria should be kept tight for cash benefits, and average benefits should be kept at financially sustainable levels. The real value of minimum benefits should be protected from inflation. Modest flat benefits or earnings related benefits with a narrow band would be helpful. Eventually, as available resources increase, a wider band, or a second tier scheme, may be introduced.

Sixth, the base for payroll taxes should be broadened to keep the tax rate as low as possible without undermining the financial viability of benefit programs. A high payroll tax rate increases the cost of labour and tends to reduce wages and the demand for labour.

Seventh, regional differences in demographic and unemployment profiles and developments strongly suggest that the financial resources for pensions, unemployment benefits, and child allowances should be centrally pooled . . .

Eighth, since the primary instruments (targeted subsidies and cash benefits), by design or as a result of weak administration, are likely to leave some vulnerable persons not covered, supplementary social safety nets should be introduced. These could include public works programs, retraining programs for unemployed workers, and assistance (in managerial, legal, and financial areas) for opening small enterprises or self employment . . . Moreover, a limited, locally administered social assistance program would be crucial in minimizing the number of the vulnerable who are not covered. Screening, however, should not depend excessively on income based means testing. (IMF, 1995b, 25–7)

This is important for the lessons learned about the difficulties of operating means tests in fluid economies, and for the consequential need for categorical forms of subsidy and benefit in cash or kind. A fairly substantial social safety net is implied in these conclusions. This is not the IMF of African and Latin American structural adjustment days. Chand and Shome (1995) have explored, for the Fund, the implications of integrating poverty alleviation in this and other ways into the Fund's stabilization strategy for such governments. In other words they have experimented with a financial stabilization model that would not only, as usual, achieve the desired stabilization but also achieve poverty alleviation objectives. They conclude that 'the integrated approach that incorporates the poverty constraint can better achieve the balance of payments target than the traditional approach (which adds on poverty alleviation separately), although at the cost, temporarily, of a higher fiscal deficit and more inflation' (1995: 19).

In the three case studies we have provided evidence of the Fund using some of the measures suggested above in their, still usually hidden, policy recommendations for specific countries.

The World Bank debates what's best

The first substantial internal review by the Bank of its social policy recommendations in the sphere of income maintenance in Eastern Europe and the former Soviet Union was undertaken by Milanovic (1992).

Reviewing the recommendations in the reports on five countries of the former Soviet Union (Russia, Kazakhstan, Kyrghyzstan, Georgia and Lithuania), he concluded that there were several policy areas where a consensus appeared to exist in Bank policy, some areas where differences in recommendations could be explained by the different circumstances of countries, and some key areas where diverse recommendations reflected implicit or explicit disagreements between Bank officials or between the officials and the consultants employed. Consensus appeared to exist in four areas: *social assistance*, where the concern was to redefine the poverty lines; *unemployment compensation*, where there was a need to discontinue benefits for new entrants; *pension commitments* where the statutory retirement age should be increased and equalized for men and women, the lowest pensions should be protected against erosion, and working whilst pensioned should be discouraged (directly by obliging those of pensionable age to choose between wage and pension, or by deducting pension payments in relation to supplementary earned income); and *sickness/incapacity leave* where there was a need to shift some costs to employers.

Disagreements appeared to exist, however, in the following areas. On *universal safety nets*, should there be such a strategy or not? (In the sample of countries examined by Milanovic the case for a universal safety net or minimum poverty line below which nobody should fall was put for Russia and Lithuania, not dealt with for Kazakhstan and Kyrghyzstan, and argued against for Georgia.) On *unemployment benefit*, should benefits be flat rate or wage related? On *pension levels*, should they be equal for all (a state of flat rate minimum) or continue to be wage related (continuing to fulfil the implicit past 'insurance' contract)? On *family allowances*, should they be income tested or universal? (The argument against means testing rests for some Bank personnel on the grounds of the continuing narrow range of income differentials, the absence of administrative infrastructure, and the close association of children with family poverty.) Finally, on *public work* (workfare), the concept of self-targeted public works pro-grammes (as a substitute for means tested social assistance) is defended for some countries.

Table 4.9 indicates the results of a comparable analysis for the three countries of this study, concentrating upon the potential areas of disagree-ment noted above. This can only be a snapshot of policy recommendations at a particular moment in time, but is nonetheless reflective of the issues reviewed above.

In terms of pension policy, while there are still differences of emphasis between those reports that do not argue against wage related pensions and those that do, and between those that explicitly encourage private pensions and those that don't, there is a discernible drift towards a crisis driven, short term flat rate strategy. This was also noted by Vodopivec (1992: 8), who continued the work of Milanovic for the Bank by reviewing more recent reports (Armenia, Estonia, Latvia, Ukraine) and concluded that all reports under current review also advocate flat rate unemployment and

Table 4.9   *World Bank prescriptions for social security and social assistance*

Recommendation	Hungary	Bulgaria	Ukraine
Pensions	Raise pension age; ceiling on benefit; encourage private tier retirement income test	Raise pension age; reduce scope of public pension; encourage private	Raise pension age; retirement income test; reduce average; maintain minimum pension and short term flat rate
Family allowances	Differentiate by number of children; means test	Reduce the universal coverage; need based transfer to low income families	See safety nets?
Unemployment benefit	Shorten duration flat rate for phase II; reduce benefits for some	Flat rate; restrict to dismissed workers	Flat rate; eliminate for new
Safety net	Define nation-wide eligibility criteria and means test	Effective safety net to shield vulnerable groups; provision in kind or food coupons to needy as alternative to cash benefits at local level	Pending income testing and poverty levels differentiated by region benefits to vulnerable groups only; reduce general subsidy

pension benefit. The congruence seems to be a fruit of concerted action on the part of the Bank – powerful arguments against a flat rate benefit reported in Milanovic's study notwithstanding.

In fact, this issue is by no means settled in the Bank, a point mentioned in Chapter 3 and returned to later. In terms of family allowances, there is variable advice which partly presumably reflects actual differences in country policy and differences in the inclinations of report authors and consultants. The general assault on generous, wage related, high replacement rate unemployment benefit continues. In terms of safety net policy, these reports reveal that beyond the common lip service to the concept of a safety net the actual analysis and recommendations vary widely. Where the report for Hungary favoured a national means tested strategy (even though in the event a very locally variable social assistance law has been passed), the report for Bulgaria eschewed this idea in favour of categorical help (even though in the event a national means tested system has been introduced). However, for the 'less European' countries of the former Soviet Union, there does seem to be an understanding now on the part of Bank officials and consultants that continued partial food subsidy and universal entitlements to population categories known to be poor are preferable to unviable means tested strategies. This point is returned to later.

The workfare idea mentioned in the earlier review by Milanovic seems to have fallen out of favour as World Bank policy. This, interestingly, is a strategy that now seems to be favoured by the IMF and is defended strongly by one of its leading advocates inside the Fund on the grounds that means testing in partially monetized and fluid economies is unviable and the dangers of discriminatory practice (such as disallowing access to benefit by prejudiced social workers) can't happen in a work tested system. In defence of the workfare strategy IMF officials also point to the need for the urgent implementation of social protection rescue strategies while longer term, problematic means tested administrative capacity is put in place.

The preceding review of World Bank policy prescription in the field of income maintenance has indicated at least two areas where there is clearly internal dissent and/or confusion among Bank officials and consultants. As was explained in Chapter 3, the expansion of human resources work in Eastern Europe and the former Soviet Union necessitated the recruitment of a large number of new professionals in Washington. These were often Europeans familiar with European Bismarckian systems and sympathetic to the social dimension of European policy. This was to fuel the internal disagreements on these issues. One of the consequences of this dispute was that, on pensions, the Bank was in the unusual position of seeing published, at the same time, by staff and consultants, two differently orientated texts. One of these, a World Bank (1994b) Policy Research Report on pensions produced under a team led by Estelle James, is based in terms of what it says about transition economies partly on a paper by Louise Fox (1994a) entitled 'Old Age Security in Transition Economies'. Louise Fox had been the author of the Bulgarian social security chapter (World Bank, 1991c) within which she had encouraged the development of a private pension scheme and avoided arguing for a national social assistance scheme. Her recommendations relied on severely reducing the public pension provision to either a subsistence contributory flat rate system or a means tested flat rate system, funded by payroll tax or general revenue. In addition, a compulsory funded pillar is proposed, disconnected from the occupational system.

Nicolas Barr (1994), on the other hand, in his chapter on social insurance in a different World Bank volume, set out policy options much more in keeping with existing practice in mainstream European systems. The common ground is the need to raise pension age, and the protection of minimum benefits. The differences are in the scope for state wage related pensions and their private alternatives. Barr argued that social insurance contributions should be shared between worker and employer and the relationship between benefits and contributions strengthened. Private pensions should not be introduced until the necessary regulations structure has been put in place. Beyond this, he argued, 'policy makers have choice about the form of public/private mix in pensions'. A mainstream Western European system would have three tiers and would be very much a partnership between the public and private sectors. The foundation PAYG social insurance pension would have a wider role than mere subsistence and involve only appropriate maxima for contributions and benefits. In addition, there would be mandatory regulated private pensions and voluntary additional schemes (1994: 222).

Within the human resources section of the relevant country divisions, the issue became heated. An internal meeting (November 1993), while perceived by the 'Europeans' to conclude in their favour, was also perceived by the supporters of the flat rate public pillar as laying the framework for further work, demonstrating the relevance of their strategy. The report of the meeting concluded that 'one strategy may be to select a couple of representative countries on which to focus the region's energies and resources for pension reform.' Subsequently, an internal conference was convened to take stock of policy advice in this area (and that of social assistance). The convener was strongly of the opinion that we would be unwise to lock Eastern Europe into the 'costly mistakes' of Western European social security commitments, and saw instead the opportunity for 'institutional leap-frogging' whereby Eastern Europe might fashion schemes more appropriate to post-Fordist flexible production. He had in mind only minimum means and assets tested state pensions. The policy debate, as was demonstrated earlier, unfolded through case examples where the choice of Bank staff and consultants was important.

The struggle between the liberal Californian Girls (as they came to be known) and the European Brighton Boys (where Nic Barr's book was edited) did not end there. Representatives of both camps would have liked to have been responsible for the social policy chapter of the definitive 1996 *World Development Report* (World Bank, 1996) which focused on transition. In the event this coveted task fell to Nic Barr. The influence of the European tradition is evident in the analysis and conclusions of Chapter 4 entitled 'People and Transition'. Some compromise with the liberal camp is also evident and the language used is designed to play down the earlier divisions and build a transatlantic consensus. Of particular note is the reappearance in the report of the sentences on pension policy used earlier by Barr (1994). There are subtle changes, however, as can be seen by comparing the following extracts:

A mainstream *Western European* system would have three tiers and would be very much a partnership between the public and private sectors. The foundation of the system would continue to be a PAYG social insurance pension, with a wider role than *mere subsistence*, although limited by appropriate ceilings for contributions and benefits. The state system would be complemented by a mandatory system of appropriately regulated private pensions . . . The scheme accords a significant role to social solidarity and risks are shared fairly broadly . . . The choice of approach depends on (a) objectives, (b) political arrangements, (c) the economic environment and (d) the social context. (Barr, 1994: 222–3)

A typical pension system in *Europe and North America* has a state pay-as-you-go pension covering more than subsistence, complemented by a variety of regulated privately managed funded pensions . . . The approach accords a significant role to social solidarity and shares risks broadly . . . The precise choice (between this and a Chilean individual funded system) depends on a country's objectives and its constraints. (World Bank, 1996: 83)

On the issue of safety nets and social assistance the report rehearses, as did the IMF, the difficulties of implementing means tested schemes in fluid and egalitarian economies, and concludes that the poor can often be targeted through indications of poverty other than income. It notes approvingly that 'Family allowances are likely to be particularly well targeted in the European transition economies. An income test for all families with children is administratively costly and the larger the informal sector the less accurate it would be. Family allowances – a fixed amount per child per month – are paid without income test throughout Western Europe' (1996: 81). If the 1996 *World Development Report* is taken as an indicator of Bank social policy then it can be concluded that its social policy has been, as a consequence of the encounter with the social guarantees of communism, partly rescued from the private market pension and residualist dreams of the fundamentalist liberals and steered towards a much greater commitment to collectivized, social solidaristic forms of policy and provision. However, as the Hungarian story has demonstrated, Bank personnel on the ground may still be fundamentalist liberals and unsympathetic to Barr's cautious conclusions. Equally, governments under IMF pressure can go ahead and destroy well developed state wage related schemes and means test child benefit against more moderate Bank advice. Equally the social policy conclusions of this report (relevant to about one-third of the world's population) do not sit comfortably alongside the social policy thinking of the Education and Social Policy arm of the Bank responsible for its poverty strategies, described in Chapter 3, which was much more concerned to build an alliance between the interests of the very poor in the South and elsewhere against institutional systems of support for privileged workers.

Nonetheless the 1996 *World Development Report* on the transition from plan to market is important for demonstrating just how much the Bank's thinking on economic and social policy has been influenced by the encounter with communism. Chapter 4 steers a thoughtful course between liberalism with a human face or *social liberalism* and European *conservative corporatism*. To quote:

> Policy makers must recognize the true extent to which large numbers of people are suffering from poverty, insecurity or both. Policy makers have to find a meeting ground between fiscal pressures and the political and social imperatives. People left behind even after growth rebounds and labour markets become more flexible should be able to count on continued government support, including well-targeted social benefits. The elderly in transition economies stand much less chance of recovering their losses and this generation presents a strong case for special treatment. But runaway spending on pensions in transition countries cannot be allowed to continue. Government can address the problem now, by raising the age at which the next generation can retire, and over the long term, by building a pension system that can sustainably support the many generations to come. (1996: 84)

The ILO as bulwark against Bretton Woods

The ILO was quite explicit at the outset of the transition in Eastern Europe as to what its policy objectives were. In a speech by its director in May 1991 (ILO, 1991a) nine areas of concern and policy orientations were enunciated:

1 encouraging social dialogue and tripartism
2 establishing labour legislation and the right to strike
3 facilitating the operation of free trade unions
4 encouraging tripartite formulation of socio-economic policy
5 considering policies appropriate to the issue of East–West migration
6 establishing institutions to facilitate the active labour market
7 helping formulate social security legislation including policy on health, pensions, sick pay, family and unemployment benefits
8 promoting productivity
9 encouraging statistical collection and analysis.

Michael Cichon's (1994b) review of developments in the region could therefore give the ILO some cause for satisfaction. He noted that

> While the pace of reform varies between countries and sometimes even between the different social security subsystems within the country, the aims of the reform processes are remarkably similar. The social protection systems in Central and Eastern Europe, as they are now discussed or emerging from reform processes, seem to follow in broad lines the Central European models which already existed in some of these countries till the late 40's and which combined social insurance with universal and social assistance elements . . . A typical pattern . . . for the reforms can be observed in, for example Bulgaria, Lithuania, Ukraine. (1994b: 52)

Similarly a year later, Cichon noted for the four Visegrad countries that

> the social protection systems of the four Visegrad countries are in the process of transition which can roughly be described as half-way between the old social protection systems inherited from the previous regimes and new pluralistic systems, where the bulk of benefits are provided by contribution financed and, to a considerable extent, self governed social insurance schemes, the state offering subsidiary social assistance and universal benefits such as family benefit . . . the key to success will depend upon whether it is possible to keep short-term fiscal and political aims out of the process of national consensus building. (1995: 10)

This reading of developments suggests that the dominant thinking in the ILO's Geneva based Social Security Department and the Budapest Central and East European Team that a European-style wage related social security system was both desirable and possible in the region was being realized. This, however, oversimplifies both the level of agreement within the ILO as to what should be recommended and the extent of adoption by countries of the ILO viewpoint. In terms of country policy the recent development in Hungary seem to run counter to this optimism. Standing, as we shall see, is far less sanguine about regional development. In terms of country specific recommendations as far as our three case studies are concerned there seems to be not much variation in approach but considerable variation in impact. The presence in the Ukraine and Bulgaria was much stronger. However, there is and has been debate within the ILO, as was suggested in Chapter 3, on a number of issues as discussed further below.

The peculiar history in the region of guaranteed work and hence guaranteed income had prompted Guy Standing, original Director of ILO CEET, to use his position to argue for the applicability in the region of a citizen's income strategy. A unique element of the economic problem facing those who wish to encourage a thriving capitalism in the former Soviet Union and Eastern Europe is the tradition there of guaranteed employment. In effect, guaranteed employment was a form of social security provision. By virtue of work, which everybody had to do, people became entitled to an income. This and the associated food and housing subsidies were the bedrock of the social guarantees of 'communism'. Because everybody worked, the bureaucratic state collectivist system of welfare had, in effect, established an income as a citizenship right. The irony was that the outdated individualist social policy prescription of the IMF was conspiring with the extreme *laissez-faire* economics of the first post-communist ministries of finance to break this citizenship basis of income entitlement just at the moment when progressive social policy thinking within Western Europe was beginning to understand that, because the future labour markets will lead to many not being regularly employed, the West might need to shift from a work based to a citizenship based entitlement to a basic income (van Parijs, 1995). In setting out the alternative versions of a citizenship based income, Jordan (1985) had argued that he was drawn to the conclusion that it was in the countries of Eastern Europe that such policies stood the greatest chance of being implemented.

Standing (1991) and Standing and Sziraczki (1991) have therefore argued that precisely in order to encourage the development of a flexible and mobile labour market in the CIS (and by implication Eastern Europe), the concept of a social guarantee through employment needs to be converted into a social guarantee through citizenship entitlement. Once secure with a basic income, labour will then seek new opportunities to top up this citizenship income. The log-jam of employment in outdated industry and housing in tied flats, which is the mainspring of trade union resistance to economic and production reform, would be broken. There are other arguments to support the case for giving serious consideration to the provision of a non-means-tested basic income as a right or, at the very least, to continue to provide a non-means-tested basic income to unemployed workers for an indefinite period. Julia Szalia and Eva Orosz (1992) have argued that the long gestation of the second economy in Hungary took place in the interstices of the official economy. People simply took time off and resources from the official workplace and built up their second leg of support through petty bourgeois and entrepreneurial activity while still being partly dependent upon their official wage. Because this dual strategy for survival was facilitated for so long, the Hungarian economy now stands the best chance for survival within a capitalist Europe. My point in support of Standing is that because the old culture under bureaucratic state collectivism was summed up in the joke, 'We pretend to work and you pretend to pay us', the new culture should be summed up by the joke, 'We pretend to be unemployed and you pretend to give us benefits.' Concealed unemployment covered with a guaranteed low wage should give way to open unemployment covered with a guaranteed low benefit. Upon the basis of this guarantee, a productive second economy will slowly grow. This way the new and expensive paraphernalia of means tested long term assistance could be avoided together with the impossible policing task of checking who is and is not moonlighting while on benefit. At the same time moonlighting enterprises would have less reason not to legalize themselves. The tax base of the economy would grow. A basic income makes economic and social policy sense.

The campaigning position of Standing on the citizen's income did not however win support within the social security professional team in Geneva. Roger Beattie has insisted in interview that the 'Official ILO view is that an unconditional citizen's income is unrealistic unless *possibly* as a replacement for social assistance, but nothing else.' Cichon has equally determinedly expressed the view that 'In CEE where the direction is more, not less, differentiation the UCI makes zero sense. There is no public support for systems which provide a greater levelling of benefits.' Writing in his personal capacity Standing does now acknowledge the long way that would still have to be travelled if the citizen's income idea were to become policy. He notes in his review of policy changes and continued crisis in the region, which is far less sanguine than that of Cichon, that

There is a third current, too radical and unorthodox to attract more than *sotto voce* discussion thus far. That is to reverse the dominant trends and to opt for building a system of social protection based on minimal universal income protection as a right of citizens . . . In spite of the mafioso tendencies, there is surely enough social solidarity left in the region for this third option to be regarded seriously. Regrettably, other routes look more likely to be taken first. (1996: 252)

The strategy of the dominant position in the ILO to secure European-type social security systems is clearly articulated in the recent ILO CEET publication entitled *Making Social Protection Work* (Cichon and Samuel, 1995). They argue that 'Involving the public in the governance of social protection systems, i.e. bringing the decisions on pensions and other benefits levels out of the back rooms of Ministries of Finance and international agencies to boards of stakeholders in social protection, is one way to empower people' (1995: 4). Through tripartism and public pressure the residualist (albeit safety net residualism) drift of the consequences of IMF involvement can be stemmed. In the same volume, however, an undefeated Standing fires a broadside at traditional wage related benefits and traditional trade union dominated tripartism and argues that 'the realities of high unemployment and unstable work histories . . . must point in the

direction of reducing the link between employment and transfer payments
. . . the governance of social protection systems will have to depend much
more on local community organisations made up representatives of
"flexiworkers"' (1995: 40).

In conclusion, however, regardless of the internal disputes, and notwithstanding that policy developments in the region could still race off in the
direction of liberalism, residualism and privatization, the important role
played by the ILO in the region has been as a bulwark against the disem-
powering impact of the Bretton Woods institutions and their continued
warnings of fiscal crisis. For the ILO there is only a fiscal crisis if governments choose not to raise sufficient revenue to fund adequate social
protection schemes. For its part the ILO reports a degree of satisfaction
with progress in the region. The Fifth European Regional Conference in
Warsaw reported that Bulgaria had ratified 80 conventions, Hungary 63
and Ukraine 50 and that 'a total of 461 ratifications since 1988 were by
new member states' (ILO, 1995c: 116–18).

European based actors have minimal impact despite geography?

Whereas the IMF, the Bank and the ILO have undertaken publicly available reviews and assessments of their work on social policy in Eastern
Europe and the former Soviet Union this does not appear to be the case for
the European Union, the Council of Europe, or the European based
OECD. An assessment of their interventions must therefore be briefer,
based as it is on the relatively small role observed in our case studies of
these actors in the area of income maintenance policy.

The PHARE office did commission recently a review of PHARE funded
work in the field of income maintenance from Igor Tomes but this is not
available to us. The earlier study of the European Community and Eastern
Europe by Pinder (1991) devotes three lines to mentioning the possibility of
PHARE funds being used in the social sector. No systematic programme
analysis or impact appears to be available beyond counts of the percentage
of PHARE funds used in different sectors. In the two case studies eligible
to receive PHARE aid no substantial work on income maintenance policy
had been undertaken by PHARE. However in 1996, after the field work
was complete, it became apparent that under the auspices of the Consensus
Programme a systematic study of the social protection systems of Eastern
Europe was about to be undertaken by the PHARE programme. Country
studies were undertaken and recommendations drawn up in the light of
future EU membership. A review conference was held in late 1996.

In the case of the Ukraine a TACIS project on the social consequence of
enterprise restructuring had got under way in 1994–5 but no outcomes were
yet clear. It leaves it only possible to repeat the earlier comment that,
unlike the IMF, World Bank and ILO, EU PHARE and TACIS work in
this field is unsystematic, dependent upon the individual consultant

employed, and not subject to any European policy constraints. The aid is, of course, in general conditional upon moves towards a pluralist market economy. Association agreements have been used to ensure this broad orientation also. It does seem, however, as the opportunity has been missed for the EU to use PHARE and TACIS to prescribe anything specific by way of social protection policy. The latest Consensus Programme of PHARE may remedy this. The reliance on consultancy firms leads to a curious phenomenon: the effective depoliticization of globalized social policy.

The Council of Europe has worked systematically with ministries of welfare to advise them of the Social Charter and to encourage its signing. This has been done or is imminent in Hungary, Bulgaria and Ukraine. The precise articles of the Charter which these countries will ratify is not yet clear. The minimal requirements of the Charter do at least oblige new countries to have in place a system of either social security or social assistance. Influence as to which parts they should favour has been exerted by existing members informally and formally through various committees. Since ratification procedures take two years and monitoring a further four, it will be some time before reports are completed on the extent to which these new CEE states are considered to be in line with their chosen requirements of the Social Charter.

The concern with the development of social policies which would support the transition to a market economy did not appear to be a fundamental or consistent consideration in the accession of the new CEE members of the Council of Europe. With regard to the countries (Hungary and Bulgaria) in our study which have acceded to the Council, only in the Hungarian case was the country's willingness to sign the Social Charter and 'adapt social security and welfare legislation accordingly' noted favourably in support of the application. In the report on the Bulgarian request for admission there was no mention of social legislation. Political pluralism and the rule of law, as well as respect for the Convention on Human Rights which is compulsory on accession, were clearly of paramount importance. Although there was a broadly shared judgement that none of the countries had at this point made substantial headway in restructuring their pension systems or other social programmes, this did not prevent their accession. The subsequent reluctance of any of the new CEE members to sign up to the Code of Social Security or its protocol (both optional to members), on the ground of cost, are thus not surprising. To support their reluctance, acceding foreign ministers have pointed to the irreverence with which existing members have treated the Social Security Code: only seven members have so far ratified the revised Code, so why should they be any different? This disregard hardly lends credence to the Code as an instrument capable of fulfilling its objectives: 'to enforce minimum standards, but eventually raise social security in all member states to an equally high level'.

The European Social Charter, however, while lacking the coercive power of the European Convention on Human Rights, has become an increasingly useful reference for post-communist states. Reference by socially minded reformers to the obligations of their European Council membership has frequently been used as a means of opposing IMF inspired fiscal policy.

The OECD's Centre for Co-operation with Economies in Transition has undertaken an evaluation of its work overall in the region. This is not available in the public domain. It did conclude that its aims were being achieved. The Czech Republic has joined the OECD and other countries including Hungary in this study will join this century. No specific review of the impact of the Centre's work on social policy in the region is available. Detailed social policy work, other than labour market analysis, has only been undertaken for Hungary and this was discussed earlier. It was a model analysis of high professional competence seeking to reconcile the investment and social solidaristic case for social welfare expenditures and the tight budget constraints. Similar work throughout the region, especially where this has not already been undertaken by the ILO (UNDP), would be highly desirable.

Other UN agencies serve as a social conscience?

In Chapter 3, in comparing the implicit and explicit social policy of the major international organizations, it was concluded that the clutch of UN bodies – UNICEF, UNDP and the research body UNRISD – could be characterized as the global social reformists concerned to increase global redistribution, enhance global social regulation and otherwise help to provide for the needs of or empower citizens to have their welfare needs met in all countries of the world. With the exception of UNDP, which has played an important role in the Ukraine, these bodies have not featured in the case studies. The work of UNICEF has received little comment. A distinction perhaps needs to be drawn therefore between the role of these bodies in the *global* discourse on the future of social policy and global social reform, and their intervention in the *local* politics of social policy in particular transition economies. UNDP, UNICEF and certainly UNRISD appear to be more active at the global level and appear to have less impact on the ground, certainly in the case study countries. When we turn, however, in the next chapter to post-Yugoslav countries where the states and governments have been contested in situations of complex political emergency, the reverse will almost be the case. Here UNICEF will be found to be playing a major role on the ground, in a way that is not always consistent with its global reformist vision, while the Bank sits on the sidelines waiting for a stable government to do business with.

The other UN actor that was considered in detail in Chapter 3 and did not feature in the case studies was the UN Economic Commission for Europe (UNECE). This, along with other UN regional economic commissions, has been targeted for cuts in the early skirmishes about reforming the UN. Nonetheless UNECE has produced regular reports on the economic situation of the wider Europe and, while not addressing social policy explicitly very often, has commented on issues relevant to our concerns (UNECE, 1990a; 1991a; 1992a; 1993a; 1994a; 1995a). In the economic survey of Europe for 1993–4, for example, it was commented that the low rates of unemployment benefit in some countries were an 'ineffective tool of social protection and an insufficient incentive to register' (UNECE, 1994a). Worthy of mention also is the work of the UN affiliated European Centre for Social Welfare Policy and Research. Their report entitled *Welfare in a Civil Society* (European Centre Vienna, 1993), prepared for a conference of European ministers responsible for social affairs, is a model of a comprehensive analysis of the transnational nature of many social policy problems in the 1990s. The thrust of the report was that social values and social rights needed to be addressed in the CEE countries as 'a necessary balance to economic reform'. Welfare, in this report, is 'a minority concern or poor relief, [but] is a comprehensive and universal policy'.

At a general level, rather than at the level of individual country case studies, it is possible to discern these organizations' views on aspects of income maintenance policy as expressed in their publications. In terms of the UNDP a distinction needs to be drawn between the UNDP Human Development Report Office, which annually produces the global social reformist orientated *Human Development Report* discussed in Chapter 3 and the Operations Division of the UNDP, also in New York – and in turn between that and operations on the ground in the region. In our two case studies where the UNDP was active the work did reflect the orientation of the Human Development Report Office. Local *Human Development Reports* supporting an ILO-type defence of social protection were important interventions in local debate and policy making. It is significant here that one of the Report Office staff accompanied the UNDP mission to the Ukraine. The UNDP Operations Division in New York, however, when interviewed, did not appear to put much stress on defending state social protection measures in its budget plans. The UNDP's Annual report on *Human Development at Work* (UNDP, 1992a), for example, stressed 'encouraging the dynamism of the private sector' specifically in social provision. The Operations Division Office report on the region (UNDP, 1993b) commented that 'Support is needed for changing people's mentality and convictions; people's drive for shouldering increasing individual and social responsibility for jobs, food, shelter and social security, [needs nurturing].' The UNDP Operations social policy expert stressed that her job was not to steer development work towards any preconceived UNDP policy solution. Others in the UN offices of the Economic and Social Council feared that, in operations terms, the UNDP had 'taken on the Washington [Bretton Woods] agenda'. Little work apart from the creation of local *Human Development Reports* appears to have been undertaken, however, by UNDP operations in our three countries.

UNICEF is the agency of this clutch that must be singled out for special attention. Through the dynamism of key individuals, not only is it acting as an important player in the global social policy discourse as reviewed in Chapter 3 but it has acted as the social conscience of the world in relation to the social costs of transition in Eastern Europe and the former Soviet Union since 1989. The three Regional Monitoring Reports produced out of the Florence Child Development Centre's Offices (UNICEF, 1993a; 1994; 1995b) under the direction of Cornia have had a major impact in heightening concern about the increased impoverishment of the populations, the declining living standards, the rise in mortality and morbidity rates and the increase in disorder and crime. These reports have not only put indicators of social development (or rather social deterioration) as high on the agenda as the IMF would want to put the public sector borrowing requirement or the World Bank the rate of economic 'growth' but have also challenged the orientation of some of the advice initially offered to countries in the region. The latest report comments 'Untimely, naive, partial, poorly sequenced and – at times – completely erroneous policies, some of them introduced on the advice of Western experts, have been an important and frequent source of welfare deteriorations' (1995b: vi). In place of this advice, the UNICEF Florence Office acting under an initial mandate 'to provide technical support to rethink policies for child survival, development and protection' now argues that a policy for 'transition with a human face' which is 'needed to ferry the economies of Eastern Europe towards a modern, democratic, efficient, and equitable society' must be guided by seven principles. These are stated as (1995b: vi):

1 Achieve and maintain stable macroeconomic balance while avoiding deflationary shocks and fiscal adjustments focusing only on public expenditure cuts.
2 'Build the market' by means of privatization that promotes widespread shareholding, eliminates 'barriers to entry' and relies on a clear regulatory framework (but which does not privatize health and education).
3 Develop a poverty alleviation strategy focusing more on the promotion of employment and self-employment, active labour market policies (for retraining, wage subsidies and public work schemes), income policies (raising minimum and social sector wages in relation to the average wage) and an improved transfer payment system. The latter should correct the present intergenerational bias against children and the working poor, by raising, for instance, public expenditure on family allowances by 1–2 per cent of GDP.
4 Sustain past achievements in health, education and child care with a 'package of key priority programmes' aimed at preserving maternal and child health services, controlling the sharp rise in 'paternal mortality', maintaining past standards and coverage in primary education, and restoring pre-transition kindergarten enrolment levels. Resources for these activities can be obtained through the reallocation of funds towards these priority programmes and the implementation of tax reform. User fees should be applied only in specific cases.

5 Develop a modern legal system for the protection and deinstitutionalization of at-risk children and adolescents, and create a network of youth institutions.
6 Develop a child and family policy promoting family stability and helping the growing number of incomplete families through income transfers and support services.
7 Monitor – continuously and in detail – the evolution of the situation of children and families.

It is the hope of the Florence Office that UNICEF's National Programme of Action now being discussed with the governments of Hungary, Bulgaria and Ukraine as well as other countries in the region will contribute to this shifting policy.

As we saw in Chapter 3 UNICEF does not believe, however, in only shouting from the sidelines. In the past, in its campaign to encourage the World Bank to rethink its structural adjustment policy and adopt a poverty focus, and now, in its work in Central and Eastern Europe, it believes in working with the Bank in order to influence it. In 1993 the CEE/NIS team of UNICEF decided to approach the Bank with a view to more formal collaboration and joint missions in the region. It was seen by UNICEF, according to the *aide-mémoire* of that meeting that such a collaboration would 'increase UNICEF's impact in CEE countries' would mean that 'UNICEF would be in a stronger position to influence Bank policy in the social sector' would 'increase UNICEF's access to Bank information'. Possible disadvantages were seen to include 'compromising UNICEF's independence to criticise the activities of the Bank', and 'UNICEF being seen by host governments in the negative light by which the Bank is viewed at times'. On 13 September 1993 it was agreed between the World Bank Central/Southern European Department and the CEE/NIS Section of UNICEF that 'UNICEF would participate in Bank missions, beginning on a trial basis in some selected countries. It is desirable that at least two UNICEF persons participate in each mission.' This is an important initiative that might prefigure the future relationships between other UN agencies and the Bretton Woods institutions which will be discussed further in Chapter 6. The initiative came too late to have discernible impact on the ground in any of the countries in our sample.

Some conclusions

This chapter has reported a detailed analysis of work on income maintenance social policy in three East European post-communist countries by the World Bank, EU, ILO, IMF, OECD, Council of Europe, UNICEF, UNDP and other international organizations. On the basis of this research we reach three kinds of conclusions: first, on the nature of the advice of agencies in terms of how far they reflect the diverse political strategies for welfare discussed in Chapter 2; secondly, and more specifically, regarding the impact of transnational influences on social policy; and finally, concerning the implications of these findings for certain approaches to analysis within relevant social sciences.

First, it is concluded that each agency is not systematically identified with agency specific social policy prescriptions and that these agency prescriptions are not identifiable only with a particular welfare regime approach to policy as reviewed in Chapter 2. Rather what has been demonstrated is that the international discourse about desirable governmental social policy, already discussed in Chapter 3, is being held in the region but is shifting and cross-cuts agencies. *In other words, for most agencies examined we have identified some internal disagreements about policy prescription, variability in policy prescription and shifting policy thinking over time.* The global ideological struggle over appropriate social policy in Eastern Europe and the former Soviet Union is continuing apace, but different positions are not always tidily equatable with different agencies and do not always get articulated the same way or with the same impact in different countries.

The advice flowing from the EU to the East is not systematically European conservative corporatist advice. The struggle between Euro-liberals and Eurocorporatists is reflected in the failure of DGV Social Affairs to control advice flowing from DGI which handles the PHARE programme. The competitive tendering in PHARE, combined with the power of recipient governments to influence tender outcomes, leads to PHARE activity in the social policy sphere, which is surprisingly little in the countries studied, being undertaken by consultants of unknown policy persuasion. The social policy thinking of the OECD appears, as we suggested in Chapter 3, to be undergoing a paradigm shift from American liberalism to some form of commitment to socially regulated capitalism, but this has only been articulated in any detail for Hungary. Within the Council of Europe, the Social Affairs Directorate appears to wish to rethink the charter or legal rights approach in the social policy field, to engage in a discourse which involves breaking the distinction between income from work and income from benefits, but the major work of the organization in the region has been to encourage signing up to the existing Social Charter. Within the World Bank it is perhaps most evident that a heated and hard fought struggle of ideas and policy prescriptions is under way. Here we identified a 'camp' associated with European wage related state funded social security systems and a 'camp' associated with a flat rate – possibly means and assets tested – residual pensions policy. The presence of the Bank is everywhere and its tenacity is noteworthy. On balance, however, we suggest that Bank policy in the region has been as much influenced by the existing social guarantees of communism as the Bank has succeeded in undermining them. Within the ILO it appears there is a conflict of opinion between those in the Central and East European Team who favour a traditional European conservative approach combining state social security with universal social support and safety net means tested social assistance buttressed by tripartite forms of governance, and those who have advocated something more like a citizen's income approach to replace the guaranteed income from work under the old regimes, although this view has not found expression in country specific recommendations. The ILO clearly works best and has most influence where tripartism is well established. Sometimes, however, the ILO appears to be in danger of talking to the old guard instead of the new and can be accused of preventing economic reform. The IMF is a permanent and usually hidden backdrop in the region, forcing a shift to a safety net variant of policy. Its ability to impact, as is the case for the Bank, depends on the willingness of government to collaborate and the political and social relations in the country. Henderson (1992) suggested that Fund impact in the region depended on state structures, political processes and state–society relations. This work reinforces that analysis. UNICEF, while not especially active in each country, has provided an indictment of the worst aspects of monetarist driven structural adjustment. The UNDP has, in places, lent support to the ILO resistance to IMF and Bank policy.

Within this cross-cutting global discourse acted out in the region we have demonstrated that the classic worlds of western welfare capitalism – liberalism, conservatism, social democracy – are present but we have also begun to show that the existing paradigms of welfare policy and strategy are breaking down in the face of the deconstruction of work and security and the encounter with the social guarantees of communism. Within the World Bank there is clearly an attempt by some, that may not be successful, to leap-frog beyond what is conceived of as the doomed and now unsustainable social security structures of Europe to a residual means tested safety net for parts of Eastern Europe and the former Soviet Union. This strategy, which we are inclined to call social liberalism (liberalism with a human face), is not yet clearly articulated. The exact meaning of a universal safety net is not defined. the problems of means testing coupled with privately managed and fully funded pension schemes are not clearly thought through. The IMF inclination towards a work test and food for work kind of safety net is not entirely shared by this wing of the Bank. Perhaps the IMF thinking can be regarded as a workfare variant of social liberalism. Equally the encounter with post-communism has strengthened the arm of those urging the Bank to embrace a 'European' commitment to welfare. This contrasts with the different form of leap-frogging that was identified in the thinking of some individuals in the ILO. Here it has been suggested that the social security policy appropriate to a post-industrial situation in the former Soviet Union should embody a citizen's income, available to all without test of means, which would facilitate the flexible economic participation required. This thinking is not shared by the main body of the ILO which is still strongly conservative corporatist.

In other words we are convinced that social policy making in Eastern Europe and the former Soviet Union *is* a testing ground for different western social policy strategies but that this competition between ideas and

Table 4.10　*Global discourse on the future of social policy as articulated in Eastern Europe and the former Soviet Union*

Welfare ideology	Type of social policy prescription	Agency sometimes promulgating
Welfare as burden	Liberalism (USA historically)	IMF (historically), OECD (historically)
Welfare as social cohesion	Conservative corporatism (German historically)	EU, World Bank, ILO, OECD, UNICEF
Welfare as redistributive commitment	Social democratic (Sweden historically)	UNICEF?
Welfare as investment	Investment infrastructure (South East Asia)	OECD, World Bank
Welfare as safety net	Version (a) universal means tested safety nets	EU, World Bank
Welfare as workfare	Version (b) universal workfare safety nets	IMF
Welfare as entitlement	Citizenship income	Individuals associated with ILO, Council of Europe

strategies now embraces a radical citizenship income and a social liberal version of social policy which sometimes finds reflection in agency thinking. Very tentatively we suggest in Table 4.10 a typology of social policy advice flowing eastwards and an association of particular agencies with the different types of advice. This discussion of the emerging global discourse and its implications for the global governance reform agenda will be returned to in the final chapter.

Secondly, more specific conclusions about agency impact can be drawn from the research reported in this chapter. These are noted below, and some of these points will also be picked up and woven into the discussion in the concluding chapter after we have reviewed the rather different case studies of post-Yugoslavia in the next chapter.

1　Major international organizations are involved in shaping post-communist social policy with varying degrees of impact.

2　The advice of different agencies often pulls in opposite directions (e.g. World Bank and ILO).

3　Conflicts between agencies (e.g. IMF versus ILO and/or UNICEF) are reflected in internal conflicts within countries (ministry of finance versus ministry of labour).

4　The encounter with the social guarantees of communism has heightened debate and discord within and between several of the international organizations.

5　An element of the competition of ideas within and between organizations reflects a competition between fractions of global capitalism (e.g. USA versus EU). Advice from the West cannot be read off as monolithic western economic imperialism.

6 The epistemic community within and around the Bank and IMF (Kahler, 1992) has changed as a result of the encounter with the post-communist transition. New policy ideas not categorizable as either traditional US liberalism or European conservatism are emerging within this community.

7 Governments, and social and trade union movements, can and do make a difference and can welcome or block advice coming from different organizations.

8 'Entrepreneurial' individuals working within a commitment to a set of values have had a significant impact on the global social policy discourse and, less often, the advice to individual countries.

9 The capacity of an international organization (e.g. UNICEF) to engage effectively in the global social policy discourse may not be matched by its capacity to effectively intervene in particular countries.

10 There is a random and uncontrolled element in agency advice but this is more the case in some organizations (e.g. EU) than others (e.g. IMF). This random and uncontrolled use of consultants, where it occurs, leads to the depoliticization of supranational social policy making.

11 Different international organizations have different capacities to influence social policy and are having different impacts in different countries. The financial clout of Bretton Woods does not guarantee an impact. The strength and determination of national trade union and allied actors can facilitate ILO intervention.

12 The trajectory of social policy reform in the region, as a consequence of western intervention, remains evenly balanced between an IMF/World Bank encouraged social liberalism (e.g. Hungary) (liberalism with a safety net) and an ILO/UNICEF encouraged European welfare conservatism (e.g. Bulgaria). A post-communist conservatism which is resistant to both reform agendas may be maintained only at the cost of increased economic efficiency (e.g. Ukraine).

Finally, this study leads to certain insights and conclusions regarding the social science disciplines that contribute to the study of globalization and social policy. In terms of economics this study adds support to those who argue that the subject should be concerned not with mathematical models but with real economics, which comprises the political decisions (motivated by economic and other considerations) about regulation and redistribution of national and supranational actors. In terms also of economics the study reveals the very explicit and contested political nature of decisions that lie behind the World Bank's and IMF's 'economic' advice to government. In terms of political science, the obverse is true. It reveals that the locus of politics and policy making is shifting from the overt national political forums to exchanges of e-mail between human resource and other professionals inside the global economic organizations. Formal politics has yet to catch up and invent the accountable transnational constitutional framework within which it could operate. In terms of the study of international organizations and international relations the study adds weight to the argument of those who insist on the relative autonomy of international organizations in the shaping of the intergovernmental business of transnational policy making. That is not to say that the study shows that states have lost their sovereignty; rather that it shows in the interaction of governments and supranational authorities, decisions are made that those states are happy (more or less) to subscribe to and endow with some authority. This echoes the conclusion of Hirst and Thompson (1996: 90) that 'sovereignty is alienable and divisible, but states acquire new roles even as they cede power; in particular they come to have the function of legitimating and supporting the authorities they have created by such grants of sovereignty'. Finally it is clearly confirmed that social development studies has to emerge from the ghetto and enter a dialogue with comparative studies of the social policies of the developed and post-socialist world. Strategies for welfare in the South and strategies for welfare in the East clearly need to be evaluated alongside each other. The final chapter picks this up in terms of the discussion of the dialogue that is currently taking place between the global poverty lobby, global NGOs, global labour standards experts and global human resource specialists.

5

Non Governmental Organizations and Global Social Policy in Conditions of Conflict

This chapter seeks to address a range of issues and themes which have been noted earlier, but have had insufficient attention paid to them thus far in the book. In particular, the emphasis is on the social policy and social development role of non-governmental organizations (or NGOs), of various kinds, which are increasingly important actors in the sphere of global social policy. In particular, the role of such organizations in conditions of conflict, which can be seen as increasingly 'normal' in the global context, is addressed. We do this primarily through a case study of post-Yugoslav countries which have severely tested the claims of supranational and regional organizations, and of national and supranational NGOs, to engage positively in the spheres of security, preventive diplomacy, peace building, justice and human rights, as well as in the general social welfare agenda of health, income maintenance, social protection and poverty relief.

The case study raises issues concerning two other themes which have been relatively underdeveloped thus far. The first is the issue of migration in the context of global social policy. The mass forced migration caused by the wars of the Yugoslav succession sorely tested the world refugee regime developed under the auspices of the United Nations High Commission for Refugees (UNHCR). In particular, of course, the pressure on Western European countries to accept large numbers of refugees from the wars occurred at the time of the development of a new migration regime of 'Fortress Europe' which sought to eliminate border controls within EU member states but to prevent mass migration to those countries from, in particular, Eastern Europe and the former Soviet Union. The relationship between migration and global integration is, of course, a highly complex one which deserves, and has had, numerous texts devoted exclusively to it (Castles and Miller, 1993; Harris, 1996; Richmond, 1996). We cannot repeat these arguments here, other than to assert that migration is itself a transborder question in which movements of people, like movements of capital and commodities, impact on social welfare structures.

A second issue concerns the development of 'ethnicized nationalisms'. The development of ethnic identities in post-communist countries in Central and Eastern Europe and the former Soviet Union affects crucially notions of citizenship and its implications for political, civil and social rights. The resignification of ethnicity as a powerful, if imagined, leitmotif in the building of national sovereignty is a major challenge to notions of global regulation and governance built on principles of human rights. The construction, deconstruction and reconstruction of ethnicity, and of ethnic relations, pose fundamental questions for the analysis of global social policy. The relationship between ethnicity and social welfare regimes, expressed earlier in terms of a continuum of 'ethnic nationalism', 'assimilationism', 'multiculturalism' and 'antiracism' (Chapter 2), is addressed here through a particular case study which shows that, in fact, global and supranational agencies and different kinds of NGOs employ contradictory strategies, and hold competing visions, regarding these alternatives.

Non-governmental organizations and social welfare

The term 'non-governmental organizations' or NGOs is now widely used, as NGOs have assumed a huge importance in the sphere of social welfare, but it is rarely defined and, indeed, is often used interchangeably with the sociological concept of 'civil society' (Stubbs, 1996b). In fact, in the US literature, the term is much less used than the concept of 'not-for-profit organizations'. In the UK, a much used term is 'the voluntary sector' although, increasingly, this includes organizations where staff are employed as well as those based exclusively on more traditional ideas of volunteering. Often, the term is also collapsed into the notion of 'associations of citizens' which form around shared interests and concerns which might, of course, have a social welfare role. Increasingly, debates about the 'welfare mix' refer to the balance of provision between the public sector, the for-profit private sector, and the not-for-profit or 'third sector'. Again, this is often described in terms of state, market and civil society (Kolarič et al., undated).

Willets (1996: 8) has helpfully categorized international organizations and the shades of meaning attached to non-governmental organization involvement in them. First are intergovernmental organizations such as NATO where NGO involvement is minimal, and intergovernmental organizations such as the UN where NGO involvement, via consultative committees, is routine. Second are hybrid international organizations which involve NGO in their structure but where sometimes governments dominate (e.g. ILO) and sometimes NGOs and governments share power (e.g. International Committee of the Red Cross). Third are international non-governmental organizations within which category are NGOs which have different kinds of relationships to government. These are those (e.g. International Union of Police Federations) made of government employees, those (e.g. International Planned Parenthood Association) where government funding is routinely welcome, and finally those (e.g. Amnesty International) where government funding is not routinely welcome.

Notwithstanding the multiple problems of inconsistent terminology and definition, there is one fundamental problem when discussing the relationship between NGOs and global social policy. By defining NGOs as 'not government', there is an implicit pull to the sphere of the nation state as the most important actor in government. However, large NGOs, often with annual budgets rivalling or exceeding the GDPs of nations in the South and the East, are, as we shall argue, major contributors to global debates on social policy and social welfare and, more importantly for our purposes here, are major providers of social welfare throughout the world. They are in the business of governance at national and global level. In the context of the less developed world, and particularly of Africa and Latin America, NGOs have been a major theme in the development studies literature and major actors in implementing policy. Cleary (1996) had documented the extensive and increasing use of NGOs by the World Bank in Africa. This practice is set to develop further. The World Bank, in its strategy to co-opt the poor (and challenge corporate and trade union interest) into its social development strategy for lower income countries, discussed in Chapter 3, will make increasing use of NGOs to reach the parts governments can't or won't reach. This has not been a feature of Bank work in the countries in our earlier case studies and this is reflective of the low involvement of NGOs in Bank implementation strategy in the region (Cleary, 1996). The work of NGOs in post-communist Central and Eastern Europe has tended to be studied more from a perspective of pluralist political science examining NGOs as one provider among many in the welfare mix (Coble, 1995; Siegel and Yancey, 1992). There has, therefore, been little systematic analysis of different NGOs, in relation to social policy, which compares them in the so-called First, (former) Second and Third Worlds.

A rare exception to this is the work of Mark Duffield, a UK development studies scholar who has mainly studied sub-Saharan Africa but who also compared the 'complex emergencies' of Angola and Bosnia (Duffield, 1994) and has, most recently, written of NGOs in terms of the 'globalization of public policy' (Duffield, 1996b). His work challenges many orthodoxies in the field of humanitarian assistance and social development. His argument is that the increasing channelling of resources through nongovernmental organizations by western and supranational aid agencies, which began in the 1970s following disillusionment with 'infrastructural' aid programmes channelled through government, has led to the residualization of state welfare in the region. This danger of NGOs substituting for effective public policy has been noted by other commentators. Green observes that 'in extreme cases (large NGO presence combined with weak government and civil society) they engender fragmentation, incapacitation, and client creation to a degree that generates major resentment, not least among the by-passed domestic social sector actors' (1995: 75). It has also been argued that this process benefits as much the global middle class of aid professionals as it does the poor (African Rights, 1994; Stubbs, 1996a).

In the post-communist context, this strategy could join with the distrust of the social state to add strength to the new 'residualist' social welfare strategy (which we have termed social liberalism), resulting in a new 'convergence' between the East and the South, partly dressed up as 'social development', 'participation', 'empowerment' and 'civil society'. Bosnia-Hercegovina and other post-Yugoslav countries, and other complex political emergencies in the former Soviet Union, could be the locations where the World Bank's poverty strategy for the Third World and its poverty strategies for Central and Eastern Europe confront each other. The liberal wing of Bank thinking might win support against the European conservative corporatist wing in this context.

This view that NGO are active participants in the residualization of social policy is only one side of the argument, however, since it ignores the role of some international NGOs in pressurizing supranational bodies to place issues of social justice, social integration and equality on the global agenda. Without the interventions of agencies such as Oxfam, for example, we doubt whether the critique of structural adjustment policies and of the environmental and cultural impacts of economic development would have been addressed to quite the extent which they have. In addition, of course, many international NGOs have been able to open a space for local and regional NGOs from the South to have a voice in global arenas (Mayo and Craig, 1995). Willets (1996), after all, has argued that such NGOs are the conscience of the world. The post-Yugoslav countries represent a significant case study to address these debates and complexities.

There is clearly a need to discuss NGOs and civil society in relational terms (Stubbs, 1996a), in terms of historically specific global, regional, national and local social relations. Crude functionalist typologies of the roles of NGOs in democracies and in emerging democracies are unhelpful, as is measuring 'civil society' by the numbers of associations registered in a particular country. The relationship, however, between different NGOs, national and local governmental structures, and global agencies is a fruitful area of study. A key distinction to be made is between supranational, international, national and local nongovernmental organizations.

Supranational NGOs are the 'major players' in the aid and development world, operating in a wide range of countries, often across borders, and working on an ever widening, and apparently unconnected, set of issues: water and power supply construction, emergency food aid, building kindergartens, emergency health projects, community development programmes, and so on. Duffield (1996a) terms these agencies 'multi-mandated'. Most are in a competitive marketplace bidding for large contracts from supranational and regional agencies, most importantly UNHCR and other UN agencies, and the EU, as well as from the aid administrations of the United States (USAID) and Western European countries (such as the ODA in the UK).

In real terms, NGOs doubled their income in the decade 1975–85 (Clark, 1991), and there is every indication that this trend has accelerated in recent years, with the proportion of aid going to the larger NGOs also increasing so that some, such as Catholic Relief Services and Oxfam, have annual budgets on a par with the aid budgets of some Western European governments. Oxfam, for example, whose mandate includes 'the relief of suffering arising as a result of war or any other cause in any part of the world' (Whittaker, 1983), now works in some 65 countries in Africa, Asia, the Middle East, Latin America and the Caribbean, and Eastern Europe and the former Soviet Union (Oxfam Supporter Services, 1995).

International NGOs work in a more limited range of countries, often building up specialist expertise around a particular theme or issue. Most importantly, however, they are based in one country, most often the USA or a Western European country, and their work in other countries can be in partnership with national NGOs or with the aim of promoting the development of such NGOs in their countries of operation. A number of small western NGOs flooded into Central and Eastern Europe immediately after 1989 (Save the Children, 1994). Some of these are now quite large and have begun to challenge the major players for dominance of the market (the best example is Scottish European Aid which has won major UNHCR contracts in Bosnia-Hercegovina). In addition they have been joined by more established NGOs and by an emerging breed of 'foundations' of which the most important is the Open Society Fund associated with billionaire businessman George Soros, and which have faced little scrutiny by sociologists or social policy scholars.

National NGOs were formally discouraged prior to 1989 in all of the countries of Central and Eastern Europe, although some linked to, for example, Caritas or the Red Cross did function, and others began to operate in more liberal atmospheres in the 1980s in some countries. These organizations have grown immensely since 1989 although, as will be clear from the case study below, their development has been uneven and varied. Most of these organizations are, at best, tolerated by government and rarely seen as partners; Slovakia and Croatia, for example, are both trying to pass laws which will severely limit the development of the NGO sector. Many work as pressure groups in the field of human rights, and operate as alternative media as well as working in social welfare and social policy. Most obtain funding, albeit erratically, from diverse western sources.

Local NGOs are those which are more grassroots or community based, focusing on issues of concern to a community, region, ethnic group or section of the community rather than operating throughout the country. Many of these derive from independent women's initiatives, helplines, shelters and so on, which developed in some countries in the 1980s; others focus on the needs of Roma groups, on refugees and so on. Many survive through the work of volunteers and from small donations, including, in some countries, money from local and central governments. There is often an inability on the part of these small NGOs to attract funding from the World Bank and other donors precisely because they are too small!

The study of non-governmental organizations is of fundamental importance in any study of globalism and social policy. Increasingly, supranational and international programmes, including UNHCR, EU PHARE and so on promote the work of partner NGOs as providers of social welfare services. This trend has a complex relationship to questions of national sovereignty and some have suggested that the need for governments to regulate the NGO sector has been under-emphasized (Adiin-Yaanshah, 1995; Adiin-Yaanshah and Harrell-Bond, 1995). In the wake of the report on UN intervention in Rwanda (Milwood, 1996), which argued that many NGOs were ineffective, claimed competence which they patently did not have, and may have contributed to deaths, a major review of the role of the 'sub-contracting' of humanitarian relief and social development to NGOs is likely to occur. There are clearly parallels here to the critical points made in Chapter 4 regarding the unregulated use of consulting firms as agencies offering social policy advice to the region under PHARE and TACIS programmes.

Globalization and complex political emergencies

Supranational and international NGOs operate in a global environment which is, of course, changing; however, it should be remembered that NGOs are key constructors of the terms of debates about how the world is changing. This is at its clearest in the notion of 'complex political emergencies' which, it is argued, these NGOs are uniquely placed to deal with. Mark Duffield (1994) has defined this concept in a way which relates it directly to the core themes of globalism and social policy, suggesting that they contain three key elements:

1   They take place in areas of the global economy which are increasingly marginal, in strategic and economic terms.
2   The crises are prolonged by the emergence of predatory political formations which require the crises for their own survival.
3   Interventions from North America and Western Europe in such crises are problematic and increasingly centred on the delivery of humanitarian assistance.

Whilst these are crucial points, we would suggest, rather, that conflicting mandates and visions of various agencies, including UN agencies, regional organizations and NGOs themselves, contribute to these crises. In addition, the definition of what are 'marginal' areas, strategically and economically, is itself a contentious issue between the agencies.

Wars and conflict

Whilst in Chapter 1 we argued that there is a need to go beyond traditional international relations frameworks, which concentrate almost exclusively on military and security questions and address also the globalization of social and environmental questions, there remains a need to examine the renewed development of localized conflicts in 42 countries in 1993, sharing a large number of common characteristics including: multiple tensions; civilian involvement; brutal violence; use of widely including available light weapons; increased importance of media coverage; long duration (half of the conflicts in 1993 had been under way for more than a decade); mass population movements; and lack of a clear resolution. Duffield states that the UN recognized some 26 of these situations as 'complex political emergencies' (1994: 7), requiring humanitarian interventions under the UN umbrella, covering some 59 million beneficiaries with an estimated relief requirement of over US$4.5 billion. An increasing role for global agencies and NGOs working in these situations has led to a serious questioning of the ways in which humanitarian assistance might operate, unintentionally, as a support for war as a viable social and economic system (UNRISD, 1995b: 123).

There are convincing arguments to suggest that these conflicts point to a 'new zone of insecurity' (Duffield, 1994) and to a new split between a 'zone of peace' and an enlarged 'zone of turmoil' (Singer and Wildavsky, 1993), although, in our view, the effects of globalization make this distinction increasingly problematic. As John Keane (1996: 4–9) has argued recently, interlinkages between these two zones, including global arms production and mass migration, as well as media coverage, mean that the effects of wars in particular spaces have wider social consequences. In addition, they pose new challenges relating to the role of supranational regulatory institutions, including supranational politico-judicial arrangements which seek to criminalize certain kinds of state (and substate) violence. The clearest example of this is the, thus far ineffective, War Crimes Tribunal in The Hague which, some have suggested, should be the precursor of a wide ranging international court (Grant, 1994). The feature of 'ethnic cleansing' which is a common element in these war situations should be recognized as a form of 'implicit social policy' entailing a particular, if obscene, vision of how society should be organized (ODA, 1995b), which, of course, tests the development of supranational regulatory agencies and mechanisms to the limit.

Forced migration in context

A second key element of complex emergencies is the extended crisis of forced migration. The number of refugees in the world has risen inexorably since UNHCR was founded. In 1970, there were an estimated 2.5 million refugees throughout the world; by 1983 the figure was closer to 11 million, and by 1992 there were some 18.2 million refugees, of which almost a quarter were in Europe or the former Soviet Union, the region which, largely because of the Yugoslav crisis, showed far and away the biggest rate of increase in the last decade. The role of UNHCR as the organization primarily responsible for the world's refugees has, therefore, become increasingly important. As well as seeking to influence policy and practice concerning refugees, the UNHCR intervenes directly, principally in the field of protection of refugees. Increasingly, the other key elements of refugee crises – the need for shelter, humanitarian assistance and community social services – are developed through partner NGOs.

The definition of what is to constitute a refugee developed in the very different context of the immediate post Second World War period. The 1951 Convention, extended by a 1967 protocol, still governs practice today, defining a refugee as: 'a person who is outside his or her former home country owing to a well-founded fear of persecution for reasons of race, religion, nationality, membership of a particular social group or political opinion, and who is unable or unwilling to avail himself or herself of the protection of that country, or to return there for reasons of fear of persecution' (UNHCR, 1993: 11). The Convention is fraught with problems of interpretation and, significantly, does not include victims of generalized violence (Joly, 1992), so that many who fled the wars of the Yugoslav succession were granted only temporary status and must return when it is deemed safe (this is already occurring with Croatian and Bosnian refugees in Germany).

A second problem is that, whilst UNHCR's mandate can be extended to 'internally displaced' persons and 'at-risk groups' within the general population, it is increasingly the case that the needs of refugees are met by agencies different from those working with other non-refugee sections of the community. This can, itself be a source of tension and of problems in terms of social policy where the needs of equally poor people are handled differently, as will be discussed below. Following the end of the cold war, between 1990 and 1995, the number of persons displaced within the borders of their own countries has risen to over 25 million, exceeding the number of refugees (US Committee for Refugees, 1996: 20).

The rise of ethnicized nationalisms

The most complex conjunction of recent times is that between social relations which have become increasingly globalized and those which have become narrow, parochialized and ethnicized, through the assertion of particular kinds of 'identity politics' and, in particular, through the rise of ethnicized nationalisms. Nowhere is this more apparent than in the post-communist countries of Central and Eastern Europe and the former Soviet Union where, along with the processes of liberalization and (partial) democratization, have come reworkings of national and ethnic antagonisms and the increasing tendency of large, multi-ethnic, states to split into smaller, single ethnic (or single ethnically dominated) states. This is often expressed as a consequence of the collapse of communism as if authoritarian regimes simply 'suppressed' national and minority questions whereas, as a number of scholars have reminded us, national questions were always of central importance in these regimes.

The most useful definition of ethnicized nationalism, indicating that it is a process reworking 'imaginary' constructs, has been provided by Kaldor and Kumar, who see ethnicity as involving the forming and reforming of collective identities through custom, religion, language and so on, and hence, ethnicized nationalism involves movements which assert ethnic identities as the primary basis for building nation states (Kaldor and Kumar, 1993: 12–13). The sheer complexity of questions of ethnicity and of minorities in Central and Eastern Europe is immediately apparent. In some senses 1989 represented not only the collapse of communism in the region, but the beginning of the end of imperial domination which can be traced through the period of Austro-Hungarian and Ottoman empires and of the Soviet empire. The range of minority situations is also complex, encompassing at least five types (of which the first four are discussed in Foucher, 1994: 17):

1 communities not linked to a defined nation state or spatial entity, the most obvious example being the Roma or gypsy communities ranged throughout the region
2 communities maintaining cultural and linguistic links with a defined nation state of origin but geographically very distant from it, such as the German minority in the former Soviet Union
3 communities living close to a co-national state but not on the boundary with it, such the Hungarians in Romania
4 communities living close to their state of origin or identification, such as Albanians in Kosovo or Hungarians in Slovakia
5 communities that, since the formation of new states, no longer are part of a majority in a larger state but are a new minority in a smaller one, such as ethnic Russians in the Baltic states, and Serbs in Croatia.

The issues of minority rights and of countering ethnicized nationalisms have posed major challenges to supranational agencies, in particular the European Union, the Council of Europe, and the Organization for Security and Co-operation in Europe (OSCE). These questions have coincided, and interlinked, with two other major issues: the war in former Yugoslavia, and the rise of racism, fascism and xenophobia in the countries of Western Europe and, in particular, in the newly reunited Germany, targeting minorities from the South and East, Roma, and asylum seekers. The complexities and contradictory approaches, inter- and intra-agency, in the fields of minority rights, parallel those already discussed in terms of social welfare. In particular, the tension within what might be termed a 'stick and carrot' approach, rewarding positive practice and criticizing (and ultimately expelling or refusing admission to) those states where bad practice prevails, is fraught with difficulties. The argument that there are legal, or technical, solutions to questions of racism is, of course, one which has been challenged by scholars of race and ethnic relations in Western Europe. In addition, there seems to be a bias so that some countries, such as the Czech Republic, are rewarded for their 'western' economic orientation and something of a 'blind eye' is turned towards their exclusionary citizenship laws (Beck, 1995). Equally it has been argued that intervention by western agencies in the ethnic affairs of nations has exacerbated the situation by encouraging the articulation of resource claims in minority rights terms while paradoxically refusing the transfer of resources to such states because they are not governed by the moral values of the West (Chandler, 1996). This echoes the challenges discussed in Chapter 1 to the ethical claims of the West and suggests that the new morality of equal minority rights is a new cloak for covering western regulatory intervention.

In sum, the phenomenon of complex political emergencies which is compounded by war, by forced migration, and by the rise of ethnicized nationalism presents a very different context for international agency involvement than the relatively stable, uncontested situations in Hungary, Bulgaria and Ukraine. As we shall see below it leads to a much greater role being played by multi-mandated NGOs, brings organizations like the OSCE and Council of Europe more sharply into focus, and makes problematic the more 'normal' interventions of the World Bank and ILO. It also makes more problematic the 'normal' social policy issues. Territorial and sovereignty disputes exacerbate historically derived social security claims, movements of people affect housing and social assistance entitlements, and redefinitions of citizenship affect entitlements in these spheres also.

From former Yugoslavia to post-Yugoslav countries

Research in post-Yugoslav countries

The case study which forms the core of this chapter derives from research work undertaken since 1993 in post-Yugoslav countries, primarily Croatia and Slovenia but, also, more recently, Bosnia-Hercegovina. It has also been informed by consultancy work undertaken for the UN in Macedonia (Deacon et al., 1996). It has some commonalities with the research detailed in Chapter 4, notably a concern with the role of global and supranational agencies, but also many points of difference. Crucially, the main focus is with social development and social reconstruction in the context of a conjunction of war, complex political emergency, mass forced migration, and ethnicized nationalisms. This encompasses the relationship between traditional social policy concerns and questions of provision for refugees and displaced persons, peace-building projects, and broader participatory social development initiatives. The conjunction of social policy and social development, noted earlier, is hence joined by refugee studies, peace studies, and race and ethnic relations.

The research has, as its main focus, the role of different types of nongovernmental organizations and the forms of relationships with national and local government and with global and supranational intergovernmental agencies in social reconstruction and social development. The work has involved participatory research in a refugee camp in Croatia, and collaboration with a range of non-governmental organizations and with social policy scholars at the University of Zagreb, as well as the submission of advice and guidance to ODA as part of a research project on Croatia and Slovenia (Stubbs, 1996b).

Uneven development and the Yugoslav crisis

The research is not primarily an attempt to add to the millions of words which have been written about the 'destruction' (Magas, 1993), the 'breakdown' (Yugofax, 1992), the 'tragic death' (Denitch, 1994), the 'disintegration' (Cohen, 1993), 'the fall' (Glenny, 1992), the 'ending' (M. Thompson, 1992) or the 'unmaking' (Wheeler, 1993) of Yugoslavia. The question of the 'Yugoslav exception' in terms of the history of communism and post-communism in Central and Eastern Europe is, however, relevant. It is certainly true that few non-specialists living in Western Europe knew very much about the complex make-up of Yugoslavia from its first incarnation in 1918 to the post Second World War state which, after settlement of external border disputes with Italy in the 1950s, included six republics: Bosnia-Hercegovina, Croatia, Macedonia, Montenegro, Serbia and Slovenia. Later, Serbia was divided into Serbia proper and two autonomous provinces, Kosovo in the south and Vojvodina in the north which, until the ending of their autonomous status in 1990, had many of the characteristics of republics.

The other key feature of Yugoslavia was that it was a multi-national or multi-ethnic entity in which every national group was a minority. The definition of different groups changed over time, and, as many commentators noted, traditions of mixed marriages and of increasing numbers of people describing themselves as 'Yugoslav' until the 1980s were also important factors. Nevertheless, by the time of the new federal structure in 1974, there was a fairly clear pattern of diverse groups living in different republics and autonomous provinces. Table 5.1 shows the ethnic composition of Yugoslavia and the constituent republics in 1981.

Whilst it is crucial to challenge the racist myth of 'the Balkan mentality' as underpinning the dissolution of Yugoslavia, there is a need to recognize that the country, as constituted in 1918, had the 'fault line' of the Austro-Hungarian and Ottoman Empires running through it, and contained people of Catholic, Orthodox and Muslim religions. In addition, Yugoslavia was split asunder during the Second World War with Tito's Partisans winning a war of liberation and civil wars against Croatian and Serbian nationalists (the Ustashe and Chetnik movements). The victory was, however, at a huge internal cost, with an estimated 1.7 million people killed and some 300,000 being expelled or migrating (Madzar, 1992; Mesič, 1992).

The nature of Yugoslav society after the Second World War and, in particular, the nature of the development of 'self-management' following

Table 5.1 *Ethnic structure of Yugoslavia and constituent republics, 1981*

	Population (Million)	Montenegran	Croat	Macedonian	Muslim	Ethnic groups (5) Slovene	Serb	Albanian	Yugoslav	Other
Yugoslavia	22.4	2.58	19.75	5.97	8.92	7.82	36.30	7.72	5.44	5.51
Bosnia-H.	4.1	0.34	18.38	0.05	39.52	0.07	32.02	0.11	7.91	1.60
Montenegro	0.6	68.54	1.18	0.15	13.36	90.52	3.32	6.46	5.35	1.54
Croatia	4.6	0.21	75.08	0.12	0.52	0.55	11.55	0.13	8.24	3.61
Macedonia	1.9	0.21	0.17	67.01	2.07	0.03	2.33	19.76	0.75	7.67
Slovenia	1.9	0.17	2.94	0.17	0.71	90.52	2.23	0.10	1.39	1.77
Serbia (total)	9.3	1.58	1.60	0.53	2.31	0.13	66.38	13.99	4.75	8.74
Serbia (Proper)	5.7	1.35	0.55	0.51	2.66	0.14	85.44	1.27	4.78	3.29
Kosovo	1.6	1.71	0.55	0.07	3.70	0.02	13.22	77.42	0.17	3.14
Vojvodina	2.0	2.13	5.37	0.93	0.24	0.17	54.42	0.19	8.22	28.33[1]

[1] Predominantly Hungarian

Source: Vojnič, 1995: 88–91

the break with Stalin in 1948, is hotly contested (Allcock et al., 1992; Ramet, 1985; Simmie and Dekleva, 1991). Allcock et al.'s assertion that 'self-management' was both a real attempt to decentralize and, to an extent, democratize social and economic relations, and a legitimatory symbol designed to maintain the monopoly of the ruling party over fundamental aspects of the system, seems most valid. The historical development of 'self-management' has also to be related to the complex national question in Yugoslavia. At the same time the existence of market socialism as an element of the 'self-management' led to the earlier introduction in Yugoslavia of unemployment compensation schemes more attuned to European models.

Importantly, Yugoslavia's unique strategic position 'between East and West' meant that, throughout the 1970s, it was able to maintain what the World Bank (1975) described as a 'very highly developed' social security system, offering higher social welfare provision than Central and Eastern Europe and the former Soviet Union. This boom period of the 1970s, buttressed by economic loans and credits, and continued urbanization, created high expectations, which in the crisis of the 1980s could no longer be met.

There are few studies of the relationship between 'self-management' and social policy, which is surprising given the nature of the system – neither straightforwardly capitalist nor state bureaucratic, but rather combining 'development with decentralization' (World Bank, 1975). The unique features of the 'Yugoslav experiment', in which public services were run by a supposedly voluntary combination of self-managed productive enterprises and local communities, seemed to mean, at least in the 1970s, that Yugoslavia would have been best placed to respond to the end of the Cold War and move smoothly to a European social market economy with associated social security systems. The decentralizing impulse seems particularly important, whereby federal laws established certain minimum standards, but local associations were responsible for establishing benefits and collecting funds. The central question, however, of the balance between 'equity' and 'efficiency' remained problematic within each republic and, more importantly, within the federation as a whole.

In addition, Yugoslavia opened its doors to the West in a way unlike any of the countries in the Soviet sphere of influence. This was a two-way process with large numbers of tourists, visiting mainly the Croatian and Slovenian coasts, and relatively unrestricted travel to, and opportunities to work in, the countries of Western Europe. By 1971 over a million Yugoslavs were working in Western Europe (Mesič, 1992: 180), and remittances home were a crucial part of the development of an informal social welfare system.

However, the 'national question' remained unresolved with very different attempts, at different periods, to produce either an overarching integrative 'Yugoslavism' or a more devolved federal structure with considerable levels of regional and ethnic autonomy. The conjunction of nations, republics and

Table 5.2   *Indices of gross domestic product in Yugoslavia
and constituent republics, 1959–89 (Yugoslavia = 100)*

	1959	1969	1979	1989
Yugoslavia	100	100	100	100
Bosnia-H.	75	69	65	68
Croatia	116	123	127	126
Macedonia	64	69	68	65
Slovenia	170	187	204	197
Serbia proper	101	97	99	104
Kosovo	39	34	28	26
Vojvodina	113	111	115	119
Montenegro	62	75	65	73

Source: Vojnic, 1995: 80–1

Table 5.3   *Other regional variations in Yugoslavia, 1971–9*

	Industrial productivity 1976 (Yugoslavia = 100)	Illiteracy rate 1971 (%)	Secondary education 1976 (%)	Prop. in agriculture 1977 (%)	Unemployment 1979 (%)
Yugoslavia	100.0	15.1	15	39.4	14
Bosnia-H.	87.3	23.2	11	42.5	17
Croatia	105.4	9.0	19	33.3	6
Macedonia	80.4	18.1	11	42.1	28
Slovenia	115.6	1.2	23	19.5	1
Serbia proper	100.3	17.6	15	45.8	20
Kosovo	78.0	31.5	7	50.1	38
Vojvodina	99.7	9.0	17	39.7	13
Montenegro	80.2	16.7	14	37.9	19

Sources: Singleton, 1979: 13; Woodward, 1995: 53

religions was and is highly complex, and the administrative machinery that Tito set in place, to manage the succession of a rotating president drawn in turn from each of the republics before disappearing into oblivion, needed little to upset it. In the 1980s economic crisis, a democratizing 'civil society' movement in Slovenia, and repression against the Albanian majority in Kosovo ushering in an assertive, authoritarian populist Serbian nationalism under new Serbian President Slobodan Milosevič, was certainly enough. In addition, the army and security apparatus, highly centralized and to an extent dominated by a particular segment of Serbian society, constituted almost an autonomous republic in their own right.

The extent of 'uneven development' within Yugoslavia with unusually large differentials in per capita income and other social welfare indicators, took on an added dimension since the differences tended to coincide with ethnic boundaries (Madzar, 1992: 71). As Tables 5.2 and 5.3 show, differentials between the poorest and the richest regions showed no signs of diminishing, with regional policies being thwarted by republican elites and, of course, by the tendency of western investment to further polarize the divisions.

The context of social welfare in Yugoslavia was, therefore, complex. Milanovic's work for his PhD, and later whilst working at the World Bank (1975), suggested that Yugoslavia had an exceptionally high level of equality, although some of the highest levels of inequality occurred in the poorer parts of the country. None of this was particularly a source of tension in a country experiencing high rates of economic growth, buttressed by revenues sent home and by loans and credits. In the 1980s, however, as growth rates declined, there was a serious problem. The extent of the slump in the 1980s is illustrated by the rate of growth in unemployment from under four per cent in 1980 to 17 per cent in 1988 (Woodward, 1995: 52), the change in the rate of inflation from very low figures in the early 1980s to 1,300 per cent in 1989 (1995: 54), and the drop in the GDP which by 1990–1 was falling at 15 per cent per year (1995: 55).

These figures would have eroded the social welfare base of a stable democracy. Combined with the death of Tito, the existence of an elaborate federal structure (which meant that, as Branka Magas wrote following a visit in May 1988, 'Yugoslavia as such exists only at the level of the federal bureaucracy and the army. In reality, the country has been divided into separate units, each living its own life, each burdened with its own specific problems' (1993: 136)), and the collapse of the Soviet Union (so that Yugoslavia's unique position between East and West had been lost), the effects were dramatic. Real personal incomes decreased throughout the 1980s, being worth less in 1986 than in 1970, with almost half of all families surveyed in 1988 reporting that they were occasionally short of money for food or other essentials (Simmie and Verlič-Dekleva, 1991: 107–8).

The pressure on the federal structure was exacerbated by the resurgence of Serbian nationalism associated with the rise to power of Slobodan Milosevič. The tension between competing nationalisms and, in particular, between 'unitarian nationalism' linked to ideologies of a 'Greater Serbia' and 'autonomous nationalisms' linked primarily to demands from Slovenia and Croatia for greater autonomy and control over revenues, came to a head with the rise to power of Milosevič, who annexed the autonomous republics of Kosovo and Vojvodina and strengthened the power of Serbia within the federation through the development of a Serbian nationalism. The ideology of 'Greater Serbia' can be seen as an inter-republic and intra-republic hegemonic strategy through which old elites, galvanized by Milosevič, sought to retain power. As such, it could be jettisoned when no longer useful, in favour of, variously, a re-assertion of supposedly socialist centralism, or even of free market liberalism. The conflicts unleashed, however, developed their own dynamics. Yugoslavia was to be transformed from an East European country best placed to make a smooth transition to a capitalist welfare system to a fragile mosaic of states some of which were to find themselves on the receiving end of global humanitarian assistance rather than technical social policy advice.

Post-Yugoslav countries: a chronology

We cannot address the conflicts with any degree of sophistication here. The chronology in Table 5.4 provides some basic pointers to the war in Slovenia in June 1991, in Croatia from July 1991 onwards, and in Bosnia-Hercegovina from April 1992. The 'rump Yugoslavia' of Serbia (including Kosovo and Vojvodina) and Montenegro claims for itself the title Federal Republic of Yugoslavia (FRY). Other recognized sovereign states are Slovenia, Croatia, Bosnia-Hercegovina and Macedonia. Hence there are five really existing states in the region so that the epithet 'post-Yugoslav countries' is used here in preference to the commoner term 'former Yugoslavia' which has little analytical sense and can be seen to distort the picture by harking back to a pre-existing Yugoslavia.

Of course, only Slovenia's sovereignty is secured. Croatia is slated to regain control over Eastern Slavonia, a UN protected area, peacefully, within one to two years, having resorted to force in May and August 1995 to retake other parts of its territory, producing a mass exodus of Serbian people who are estimated to constitute only three per cent of the population now compared with some 12 per cent in 1991. Bosnia-Hercegovina has, under the Dayton and Paris peace accords of December 1995, been divided into two entities with a planned fragile and clumsy centralized authority which few believe will work. The entities – an increasingly shaky looking Croat-Muslim Federation and the Serbian Republic – exist across a series of cease-fire lines with few long term prospects for peaceful coexistence. Macedonia has achieved recognition but under the title Former Yugoslav Republic of Macedonia (FYROM), largely because of objections to the use of the name Macedonia from its EU partner and neighbour Greece, which argued that it implied territorial aspirations to Northern Greece. The Federal Republic of Yugoslavia (Serbia and Montenegro) continues to be isolated in the international community, although Milosevič's presentation, by self and others, as 'peace maker' has succeeded in having sanctions lifted and may lead soon to recognition.

The story of the 'post-Yugoslav countries', then, is one which joins post-communism, war and economic crisis. The 'uneven development' which grew throughout the 1980s can be seen to have been perpetuated and extended through the wars. In addition, there is a shortage of information about the social welfare context of each country. In most of the key guides to social policy and development, there is almost no mention of post-Yugoslav countries with the exception of Slovenia (ISSA, 1994a) for example. Yugoslavia appeared in the UNDP *Human Development Reports* of 1991 and 1992, only to disappear subsequently and not be replaced by any of the post-Yugoslav countries (UNDP, 1991; 1992; 1993a; 1994; 1995a; 1996). Even the valued monitoring reports of UNICEF (1993a;

Table 5.4 *A chronology of post-Yugoslav events*

1986	
September	Serbian nationalist petition signed by a number of oppositional intellectuals published in Belgrade
1987	
September	Slobodan Milosevič becomes president of Serbia
1990	
April	Elections in Croatia produce victory for the newly formed HDZ (Croatian Democratic Community) with Franjo Tudjman as its leader
September	Serbia abolishes autonomous status of Kosovo and Vojvodina
September	Slovenian assembly amends constitution to allow possibility of secession from the federation
1991	
March 16	Serbian autonomous region of Krajina within Croatia proclaimed
June 25	Croatia and Slovenia declare independence
June 26	Beginning of unsuccessful intervention by JNA (Yugoslav People's Army) in Slovenia
October 8	Croatia and Slovenia formally secede from Yugoslavia
1992	
January	UN negotiated cease-fire in Croatia sets up UN protected areas (UNPAs) and the stationing of UN troops as UNPROFOR
January 15	European community and a number of other countries recognize independence of Croatia and Slovenia
April 6	Bosnia's independence recognized by EC
	Karadzic declares Serbian Republic of Bosnia and Hercegovina
May	Seige of Sarajevo intensifies
May and June	Thousands of refugees arrive from 'cleansed' areas of Bosnia into Croatia
July	First stories about Serbian concentration camps in Bosnia appear in the Western press
September	Serbs effectively control two-thirds of Bosnian territory; only the eastern enclaves of Srebrenica, Zepa and Gorazde, together with parts of Sarajevo, remain unachieved military objectives
October 25	First fights between Bosnian army and Bosnian Croat army, HVO begin around Prozor
1993	
April 16	Srebrenica declared a 'safe area' – a term late extended to five other areas
April	Full scale conflict between Muslims and Croats in Bosnia begins
June	Bosnian Croat army, HVO, drives Serbs out of Mostar stories of camps run by Bosnian Croats emerge
July	Bosnian Serb forces complete capture of Srebrenica with 40,000 Muslims fleeing
October 23	Massacre by Bosnian Croats of Muslim villagers in Stupni Do
1994	
February 5	Mortar bomb attack in Sarajevo's central market place kills 69 people, adding to the nearly 10,000 people killed in Sarajevo alone since the fighting began
February 10	Nato ultimatum to Bosnian Serbs to withdraw heavy weapons from around Sarajevo
March 2	Formal inauguration of Bosnian-Croat Federation in Bosnia signed in Washington

(continued overlead)

Table 5.4   *(continued)*

1995	
May	Croatian action retakes Serb held western Slavonia, prompting a new refugee exodus
July 11	Srebrenica falls to Bosnian Serbs: some 10,000 men are unaccounted for, most presumed to have been massacred
July 28	Croatian forces overrun Bosnian Serb towns of Grahovo and Glamoc
August 4	Croatian Army assault on Krajina begins: whole area is under Croatian control within a week, and almost 200,000 Serbs leave
September	Richard Holbrooke's shuttle diplomacy creates agreement on peace plan dividing Bosnia between Croat-Muslim federation (51%) and a Serbian 'entity' (49%)
December	Agreement signed by Izetbegovic, Milosevič and Tudjman in Dayton and then in Paris
1996	
May	Refusal of Croatians in Mostar to accept outcome of Mostar elections in which Muslim parties win a majority: puts planned September national elections and whole Dayton agreement in Jeopardy
September	Elections secure victory for nationalist Serb, Croat and Muslim parties, suggesting a bleak future for an ethnically mixed Bosnia

1994; 1995b) only report Slovenian data. Many statistics have not been gathered, partly through the real disruption of war but also because of a failure to appreciate the importance of tracking 'normal' indices of welfare and development in the context of war and contested sovereignty. Summary indicators are, however, provided in the World Bank (1996) report for three of the ex-Yugoslav countries; these are reproduced in Table 5.5, along with comparable data for the neighbouring states. For Macedonia, Croatia and Slovenia clearly the already existing inequalities of the former Yugoslavia have multiplied massively. Data for Bosnia would confirm this. Serbia has no doubt declined dramatically on several indicators.

The context and extent of agency interventions

International organizations, both of the intergovernmental kind like the World Bank and EU, and especially of the NGO kind, have been and are therefore intervening in a patchwork of very different post-Yugoslav countries governed under very different policies and in very different contexts. The issue of 'uneven development', crucial in the post-war history of Yugoslavia, takes on an added importance in the context of war, forced migration and territorial reconfiguration. As Table 5.5 showed, the economic and social development contexts are uneven. Table 5.6 captures the differences between all post-Yugoslav countries in terms of the extent of ongoing political emergency, the economic situation, the degree of territorial integrity, the extent of forced migration and the characteristics of the form of governance. It is suggested here that while Slovenia and

Table 5.5   *Contemporary economic and social indicators in the region*

	GDP growth rate 1995 (%)	GNP/capita 1994 ($)	Infant mortality 1994 (per 1,000 live births)	Life expectancy at birth 1994 (years)	Secondary school enrolment 1993 (%)
Macedonia	−4.0	820	23.8	72.7	54
Croatia	2.0	2,560	10.9	73.5	83
Slovenia	5.0	7,040	6.5	73.6	89
Albania	6.0	380	31.0	72.8	78 (1990)
Bulgaria	3.0	1,250	15.3	71.2	68
Greece	–	7,700	8.0	78.0	85
Turkey	–	2,500	62.0	67.0	61

Source: World Bank, 1996

Table 5.6   *Post-Yugoslav countries compared*

	Political emergency	Economic situation	Territorial integrity	Forced migration	Political/economic framework
Croatia	Partial	Fair	Partial	High	Ethnicized authoritarian capitalism
Slovenia	No	Good	Yes	Low	Conservative corporatist capitalism or liberal capitalism
Bosnia	Yes	Very poor	No	Endemic	War, contested
Macedonia	Potential	Poor	Yes	Low	Emerging conservative corporatist or liberal capitalism
Serbia	Partial	Poor	Yes	High	Ethnicized authoritarian post-communist conservative

Macedonia might be hovering between economic and social policies of a liberal and conservative corporatist kind, Serbia is trapped in a post-communist conservatism overlayed with an ethnicized nationalism, and Croatia is ruled under an increasingly authoritarian and ethnicized nationalist form of government. Bosnia-Hercegovina remains in a war condition in which separate ethnicized entities appear most likely to co-exist in a loose and unstable, formal state.

Table 5.7 captures the differential intervention of international organizations in these contexts, together with an indicator of the extent of NGO national activity. The case studies below analyse and provide evidence for the situation in more detail, but in sum the key points of similarity and difference are already evident. Slovenia, with no contested sovereignty,

Table 5.7 *NGOs and global agencies in post-Yugoslav countries*

	National NGOs	international NGOs	Main focus	Supranational agencies	Main focus
Slovenia	High	Low	Social development	EU PHARE	Economic and social development
Croatia	Medium	Medium	Psycho-social help	World bank	Economic and social development
Bosnia-H.	Low	High	Humanitarian aid	UNTRANS	Peace building
				EU	Aid, psycho-social help
				IFOR	Peace enforcing
				UNHCR	Refugees
				OSCE	Human rights
				EU, World Bank	Elections, reconstruction
Serbia	Low	Low	Refugees	UNHCR	Refugees
Macedonia	Low	Low	Conflict prevention	UNPREDEP	Conflict prevention
				World Bank	Economic and social development
				OSCE	Human rights

might be expected to have the 'normal' relations of East European states with the major international organizations but in fact external intervention has been relatively limited. The debates between social liberal and conservative corporatist approaches to economic and social policy are taking place largely between a strong civil society and the government. The country is on the fast track to joining the EU and has benefited from PHARE money. Macedonia is in a similarly near 'normal' situation but with much more significant World Bank loans in the social assistance field and enterprise closure field. However, a major thrust of external intervention here has been to prevent the development of ethnic tensions. UNPREDEP, the United Nations Preventive Deployment Force, had determined that a focus of its intervention should be not military or political but social, adding a further example to support our thesis of the socialization of global politics. This work and its outcome (Deacon et al., 1996) is described in the case study below. Serbia remains a pariah with little international organization involvement except by UNHCR to help refugees. Croatia is a mixed bag, with some 'normal' relations with the World Bank emerging now that there is more territorial integrity. EU support has been through its aid arm (ECHO) rather than PHARE and has concentrated on psycho-social work in the wake of war trauma. Considerable NGO involvement is evident in peace building, in humanitarian relief and help with refugees, but this has distorted normal social provision. Bosnia-Hercegovina remains the key site of complex political emergency, where the World Bank and EU are still standing on the edge waiting seriously to activate their pledge to fund reconstruction. Both organizations note the need to move from emergency intervention to long term social policy making but have so far been unable to do so. In the meantime the field has been open to a wide array of international NGOs providing a variable residual kind of welfare support in lieu of effective public policy by a fragile government. The OSCE monitors human rights. Worthy of note is the low profile of the ILO in the region, reflecting the disruption and instability to its normal intervention caused by war and instability.

The focus of many of these interventions and of our research, as the case studies reveal, is broader than the narrow focus of income maintenance policy in our other case studies in Chapter 4. The concern is with the broader definition of social policy as embodying a vision of social development (ODA, 1995b). At the same time because of contested circumstances even the interventions in the narrower income maintenance fields are, to varying degrees, made more complicated. Some of these have been mentioned earlier. A full check-list of the complications might be:

1 The pension and other rights accrued under the former Yugoslav scheme were not automatically honoured by Serbia for the 'breakaway' states. Negotiations between funds continue.
2 Bank accounts in the former Yugoslav Bank were frozen for citizens of 'breakaway' states, immediately impoverishing certain people.

3 Croatia has made offers of citizenship entitlement (e.g. pensions) to Croats in Bosnia while refusing, in practice, citizenship entitlements (e.g. pensions) to some Serbs and Muslims in Croatia. Similar uses of citizenship as a system of exclusion exist elsewhere in the region.

4 Population movements have cut across normal housing tenure and ownership entitlements, including reallocation of properties previously owned by the Yugoslav army.

5 Workplace closure in the context of war has disrupted rapidly the entitlements to workplace welfare and undermines normal trade union pressure for social security.

6 Competing claims on local social assistance offices arise from the locally poor population and the influx of refugees.

7 Distribution systems used by NGOs bypass and delegitimate normal local agency responsibilities.

8 The increased pressures on resources of those injured or made homeless together with demobilized soldiers create impossible demands on normal government systems.

9 The sudden cessation of remittances from abroad with the closure of EU borders to workers has altered informal welfare systems which historically had plugged holes in the safety net.

10 The religious or ethically earmarked character of some aid potentially exacerbates difficult local social relations.

11 Resettlement allowances for returning refugees (offered, for example, by Slovenia to Muslims returning to Bosnia and by Germans to Roma returning to Macedonia) distort normal income maintenance systems and local income distribution patterns.

In the following sections the interventions of international organizations in the variable circumstances of ex-Yugoslav countries are described in more detail.

Slovenia: civil society, social movements and social development

The case of Slovenia, as is clear from the above, is quite exceptional in the post-Yugoslav context, since we are discussing the most developed of the former Yugoslav republics, in which 1980s discussions were dominated by the claims of social movements and civil society, and where the state, and local government, have funded national nongovernmental organizations since the late 1980s. Furthermore, Slovenia, partly because of its status as a single ethnic state (Silber and Little, 1995), was allowed to secede from Yugoslavia following a brief war in June 1991 which did not affect, to any great extent, physical and social infrastructure. It was the first, and for a long time until Macedonia joined in 1996 the only, post-Yugoslav state to be a member of the Council of Europe and appears on the 'fast track' towards Nato and European Union membership, not least as its economic performance continues to outshine even that of Hungary and the Czech Republic.

Slovenia responded to the refugee emergencies in first Croatia and then Bosnia-Hercegovina at best half-heartedly, although it is true to say that many Bosnian refugees integrated into Slovenian society given the presence of Bosnians, in the past, as migrant labour from other former Yugoslav republics. Indeed, the argument that the presence of refugees was high enough to stimulate progressive social welfare practice but low enough not to induce a crisis within the system is persuasive, since the total reached, at its peak, some 75,000 people or little over four per cent of the population (Ramon, 1995), provided one recognizes the progressive practice to be framed within self-consciously exclusionary criteria for citizenship introduced by the government.

The 'battle for civil society' in Slovenia between 'progressive currents' reflected, in the 1980s, by such forces as the women's movement, independent trade unions, alternative mental health and children's rights movements, and peace and ecology, and what has been termed 'conservative currents' including, crucially, the Church and nationally oriented movements (Kužmanič, 1995), is now played out in terms of social policy and non-governmental organizations. The tension between an anti-oppressive imperative, based on complex theorizations of marginality, and a new conservative corporatist framework modelled on developments in Austria, is a key struggle. What is not disputed is the leading role of national non-governmental organizations in this – a fact seemingly acknowledged by global agencies and international NGOs working in Slovenia.

The insights of Zinka Kolarič, Ivan Svetlik and colleagues in the University of Ljubljana, in arguing for a 'welfare mix' based on 'integrated independence' of the NGO sector in relation to the state, whereby there is a low degree of control, a medium degree of state financing, and a high degree of communication and contact, are important. They argue further;

> The non-profit sector as a service provider could occupy second place in the structure of the Slovenian welfare system (Kolarič and Svetlik, 1987) following the public sector and preceding the private for-profit sector. Thus a new type of welfare system could be formed, which would not be completely identical with the social democratic, liberal, or conservative corporate models (Esping-Andersen, 1990) but would include elements of all three. (Kolarič et al., undated)

In the context of sustained economic growth which represents the beginnings of Slovenia's integration into the economic markets of the developed world, a broad based political stability and generally positive human rights record, and a strong national non-governmental sector, it seems appropriate to designate the Slovenian model as one which provides for 'social development' without the presence, in any significant form, of supranational or global agencies as regulators, distributors or providers. Although there is an argument which suggests that Slovenia, through its uniqueness and complex position, actually fares worse than similar countries in terms of aid and development resources, the more positive elements of a thriving indigenous non-governmental sector compensate for this.

In particular, the range of work undertaken within the non-governmental sector is wider than that found in other post-Yugoslav countries and focuses, particularly, on what Darja Zavirsek (1995) has termed 'social innovations in the spheres of mental health, working with women, and child care'. Most initiatives are relatively small and their growth has been more 'developmental' than 'crisis-orientated' and, moreover, such organizations are beginning to have an influence in the statutory sector. There are tendencies towards a 'technocratic' approach to provision, and social welfare organizations are disproportionately operating in the capital, Ljubljana, but the standing of the sector as a whole bodes well for the future.

Those international organizations who have been involved, including Save the Children (UK), have recognized the strengths of the non-governmental sector and sought to develop capacity rather than to compete, as service providers, or support only the interests of one client NGO. There are possibilities, moreover, for Slovenia to play a role in the development of initiatives throughout Central and Eastern Europe. The sophistication of the sector means that there would be real problems for supranational and international agencies to impose their own agenda. As such, Slovenia represents a particular case study in the development of global social policy which suggests that, perhaps, the development of a real, progressive, nascent civil society is a prior condition for sustainable social development. Hence, the neglect of the role of global agencies in social policy in Svetlik's (1992b) collection seems to be less an intellectual and practical oversight than a recognition of the nature of the Slovenian exception.

Croatia: NGOs and forced migration

The Croatian situation is far more complex, contested and contradictory. The fact that it was primarily in Croatia that the wars and destruction in post-Yugoslav countries first began, should not be forgotten. Few now remember that, in the early days of the conflict, the UN set up its headquarters in Sarajevo rather than risk basing its operations in the Croatian capital Zagreb (Rieff, 1995). The ways in which Croatia, after Slovenia the most developed Yugoslav republic, was defined by international and global agencies and, in its turn, how sections of Croatian society responded to their presence, form an important case study.

The war in Croatia, which began in the summer of 1991, was effectively ended with a cease-fire and a UN brokered peace agreement in early 1992 which recognized Croatian sovereignty over the whole of its territory but allowed for effective local Serbian control of four UN protected areas:

Table 5.8   *Displaced persons and refugees in Croatia, October 1994*

	Displaced	Refugees	Total
Totals	196,870 (52%)	183,038 (48%)	379,908
Age:			
0–14	37,471 (19%)	47,104 (26%)	84,575 (22%)
14–25	28,723 (15%)	32,291 (18%)	62,014 (16%)
25–59	85,403 (43%)	67,048 (37%)	152,451 (41%)
>59	44,273 (23%)	36,595 (20%)	80,868 (21%)
Gender:			
male	93,087 (47%)	72,450 (40%)	165,537 (44%)
female	103,783 (53%)	110,588 (60%)	214,371 (56%)
Accommodation:			
organized	53,102 (27%)	30,466 (17%)	83,568 (22%)
private	143,768 (73%)	152,572 (83%)	293,340 (78%)

Source: UNHCR, 1994

Sector East, beyond Osijek and including Vukovar, an oil and agricultural area more integrated into Serbia proper; Sectors North and South, the so called 'Krajina' or military frontier areas bordering Bosnia and including Knin; and Sector West in western Slavonia, centred on the divided town of Pakrac. Following a renegotiation of UN peace-keeping forces' mandate in March 1995, renaming them UNCRO rather than UNPROFOR, the Croatian army launched successful attacks in May 1995 to regain western Slavonia and, in August 1995, to regain the Krajina areas. Sector West remains under UN authority with UNTRANS meant to oversee the transition to Croatian control within one to two years.

The war had many devastating effects on the Croatian economy: Croatia no longer controlled a third of its territory; vital road and rail networks were disrupted; and income from tourism dropped to virtually nil (Ramet, 1996). In addition, the crisis of displaced people from the areas which remained under Serbian control combined, from April 1992, with a huge influx of refugees from the fighting in Bosnia-Hercegovina, was a major concern. At the height of the crisis of forced migration at the end of 1992, Croatia accommodated over 700,000 forced migrants as registered refugees and displaced persons: the numbers of unregistered refugees probably took the real figure much higher (Isakovič, 1993; Mesič, 1993; Meznarič and Winter, 1993; Puljiz, 1992). At the last count, before the May 1995 actions, Croatia accommodated 380,000 people, almost 10 per cent of the total population. Their distribution in terms of status and type of accommodation is indicated in Table 5.8.

There is a far greater range of foreign and supranational agencies including non-governmental ones operating in Croatia than one finds in other post-communist countries in Central and Eastern Europe. A large number of organizations co-ordinate or are involved in humanitarian relief and psycho-social programmes dealing with the effects of post-war trauma.

Croatia offers a case study in the problems of aid, familiar in the development studies literature, in a European setting. Similar economic and political effects of aid, including imbalance in the terms of trade, challenges to national independence, and influencing political objectives, can be observed. In addition, humanitarian aid may reinforce processes of ethnicization. For example, supranational bodies such as UNHCR define their work primarily in terms of the needs of refugees, leaving the needs of internally displaced persons to government who then must seek foreign agencies to help. In any case, aid agencies may insist upon an explicit religious or ethnic basis to the entitlement to aid. Whilst the main Muslim and Catholic agencies operating in Croatia and Bosnia-Hercegovina have stated policies on non-discrimination, they recognize that, in practice, these are difficult to implement 'on the ground'.

One of the clearest critiques of refugee policy and practice in Croatia has come from Barbara Harrell-Bond and her colleagues from the University of Oxford Refugee Studies Centre (Elliott, 1993; Harrell-Bond, 1993). Some of this work seems to see the problems as a product of the unthinking application of a particular model of relief work in which refugees are marginalized and seen as helpless; in which foreign agencies and supranational bodies assume host governments could not manage, or manage fairly, a refugee assistance programme; and where humanitarian aid is disguised nonetheless as non-political (see also Harrell-Bond, 1986). Of most relevance to our concerns is the argument that relief models have exacerbated tensions between refugees, internally displaced people and local communities. As each of these groups receives different help, from different agencies, based upon different assumptions and philosophies, it is not surprising that divisions are exacerbated. It is not hard to imagine how accusations about one group being favoured, or privileged, at the expense of others can link in with an ethnicized nationalist agenda. The social policy implications of localized competition between impoverished local communities, Croatian displaced people, and refugees have not yet been systematically researched. There is a readily apparent confusion, however, in terms of which agency is responsible for whom, with resources in cash and in kind being distributed by different governmental and local governmental agencies (the Office for Displaced Persons and Refugees and Centres for Social Work), supranational agencies (particularly UNHCR), the Red Cross, and national and international NGOs.

The question is further complicated, however, by Croatian involvement in Bosnia-Hercegovina where almost 20 per cent of the population are ethnic Croat and where the concentration of these in the south-west of the country, in Hercegovina, has a strong resonance in Croatian politics. The involvement of Croatia politically and militarily in Bosnia-Hercegovina is addressed further in the Bosnia case study below. Here, there are two key issues. First, the way in which ethnic Croats in Bosnia were able to apply for and obtain Croatian citizenship further led to a situation where ethnicity rather than residence became a basis for entitlement to various social welfare benefits and housing. Secondly, the war between Muslims and Croats in Bosnia occurred when Croatia itself was host to large numbers of Muslim refugees even after it effectively ended an open border policy in 1993. Currently some 25 per cent of registered refugees in Croatia are ethnic Muslims, the overwhelming majority being ethnic Croats (US Committee for Refugees, 1996).

As is increasingly the trend in the South, global, regional and national aid agencies tended to bypass central and local government and to work through non-governmental organizations. A number of questions are beginning to be asked about the possible negative effects of foreign NGOs, many of whom had no previous European experience. The main concern is whether the pattern of foreign NGO activity is related to need. It may be that many foreign NGOs operate in areas which produce considerable duplication of services, and tend to concentrate on specific, short term, prestigious projects rather than on helping to build up a needs based infrastructure of care. The assumptions upon which projects are based, including their relationship to social welfare provision more generally, are not always clearly spelt out. In addition, the form of delivering services may be inappropriate, based on culturally specific models of intervention which cannot be transferred uncritically to Croatia (Deacon et al., 1994).

In contrast to Slovenia, Croatia had a less developed voluntary sector in the 1980s with the exception of Caritas, the relief wing of the Catholic Church, and a number of independent women's initiatives. A number of Croatian NGOs were created, from scratch, as a direct result of the crisis of war and forced migration. These organizations have experienced a skewed development in terms of priorities and funding, primarily through the emphasis on the 'emergency' context, and the prioritization of work with refugees rather than with a range of groups in need within the general population. UNHCR funded a small number of Croatian NGOs at quite high levels from 1993 onwards, producing a reliance on this funding and real problems when, as occurred in subsequent years, it declined (Stubbs and Sertic, 1996). Of particular importance is the way that the pattern of crisis orientated funding prompted the development of administrative and bureaucratic structures whose main interest becomes their own survival. As a consequence NGO social welfare activity is, actually, less cost effective than is often imagined.

The emphasis of extended NGOs on work with refugees has tended to produce a parallel welfare system which is distorting in terms of the prioritization of need, salary structures within agencies (foreign nationals and local Croats earn more working for UNHCR than for Croatian social services), and so on, as well as promoting a competition for scarce resources between forced migrants and the local poor. In addition, a competitive marketplace has been created in which local NGOs, to survive, are forced to reproduce the categories, assumptions and practices of their foreign funders. It is not simply that NGOs do what funders want; rather, processes of negotiation and of alliance develop in which certain common emphases are created and certain other possibilities are ruled impossible. The creation of a 'globalized new professional middle class' who, regardless of their country of origin, tend to speak a common language and share common assumptions, seems to be a key product of the 'aid industry' as exemplified in Croatia (Stubbs, 1996a).

Further, partly because of the marginalization of governmental structures, and partly because of the importance of what Bogdan Denitch (1995) has termed 'grassroots nationalism', a number of NGOs have developed which have close financial, personal or ideological ties to the ruling party in Croatia. This challenges an assumption that NGOs are, in all cases, contributors towards a non-nationalistic civil society. The relationship of different agencies to ethnicization is also complex. Some organizations are self-consciously, implicitly or explicitly, ethnically exclusionary – reserving their services for members of one ethnic group. Many are assimilationist, arguing that their services are 'open to all' whilst failing to develop personnel, service monitoring, and review practices which would ensure, through sensitivity to cultural difference, that this was actually the case. On the other hand inappropriate emphasis on culture and ethnicity – either in terms of a celebration of difference (multi culturalism) or in terms of power relations (anti-racism) – can also be observed in the values and practices of some supranational and international agencies operating in Croatia. A recent example concerns the exodus of the majority of the Serbian population from western Slavonia in the weeks following the Croatian army action in May 1995 to take back territory from rebel Serb control. The assumption of UNHCR was that the Serbian population was at great risk and so they helped to organize convoys to take those who wished to leave, conveying them to parts of Bosnia and eastern Slavonia where, in fact, men were immediately mobilized. Similarly international agency meetings at one point focused on the plight of the Serbian community in and around Pakrac. The problem was that no local social welfare agencies, particularly the Red Cross and Centre for Social Care, were invited. In fact, what many of the international agencies saw as discrimination against Serbs was little more than the routine slowness of the Croatian welfare bureaucracy. That is not to whitewash the Croatian authorities. Indeed it is the case that the aftermath of the Croatian army actions in the Krajina areas in August 1995, where far fewer international NGOs operated, involved widespread and systematic abuses of human rights.

Another policy issue in the context of the crisis of forced migration in Croatia is the way in which social and community development approaches were under-emphasized compared with what has been termed a 'psychosocial approach' based, in particular, on an assumption that large numbers of refugees and displaced persons were suffering from 'war trauma' or post-traumatic stress disorder (PTSD). The emphasis on psycho-social approaches seems to derive from, at least, three different directions. First, there had been a criticism in other refugee situations that the only needs attended to were the immediate needs of survival – shelter and food – and that other needs, particularly psychological, tended to be denied. The setting of a 'war in Europe' hence allowed for a remedying of this imbalance. Secondly, the suffering of refugee and displaced communities was, certainly in the early days, defined primarily through stories of systematic rape of women and children. The ways in which feminist organizations, and feminist ideas, influenced the response is important. Thirdly, Croatian and Bosnian professionals, particularly psychologists, also reacted in accordance with their own frameworks and approaches, and it is certainly the case in Croatia that psychological approaches have more influence and prestige than social work and community development approaches. Hence, from a relatively progressive set of imperatives, a new orthodoxy was created which shaped the terrain in which non-governmental organizations would compete for scarce resources. It was only in 1996, five years after the beginning of the crisis, that the United Nations Development Programme opened an office covering the whole of Croatia, so that, at last, economic and social development issues could be given a higher priority.

There has also recently been more concerted support for human rights organizations within Croatia, as well as for alternative media. These organizations, together with a network of women's organizations, and peace groups, can be said to form some kind of alternative 'civil society' seeking to promote democratic values. Croatia is on the verge of admission to the Council of Europe, despite an unprecedented delay at the final stage because of concerns including the aftermath of events in Krajina, a constitutional crisis over the wish of the opposition who won in the recent elections to appoint a mayor of Zagreb, lack of media freedom, and Croatia's continued refusal to disown Croats in Bosnia who have failed to recognize the outcome of elections in Mostar. Admission would allow for Croatia to be involved in PHARE and other European programmes. The World Bank has been working quietly in the background in Croatia for a number of years and policy changes reflecting its involvement are now being debated. There is evidence that contradictory advice is being given, with the debate between European and liberal perspectives, noted in the previous chapter, also being played out here. Despite the involvement in Croatia of Sipos, of the 'European' wing within the Human Resources Operations Section, the possibility of introducing a pension scheme based on the Chilean model is under discussion (World Bank, 1995f). A huge number of early retirees within the past few years has prompted this perceived crisis in the pension system in Croatia. As the war fades there is therefore a return to more 'normal' relations with international organizations in Croatia, but the uneven development within the country, heightened by the war, is likely to lead to the coexistence for the time being of these more normal relations and the distorting influences arising from the continuing involvement of international NGOs.

Bosnia-Hercegovina: genocide and the politics of humanitarianism

Bosnia-Hercegovina has been the place where many of the hopes of the 'new world order' have completely collapsed. The extent of destruction and of population displacement is on a scale seemingly unimaginable in post Second World War Europe. Estimates of the number of people who have died in the war in Bosnia-Hercegovina vary, although conservative estimates suggest that the figure is between 200,000 and 300,000 (Ramet, 1996: 317). Add to this the fact that some 1.3 million Bosnian people are refugees in other countries, significant numbers are displaced within Bosnia itself and there is only a minority of the population still living where they lived before the war. The appalling cost of attempts to divide ethnically the most multi-ethnic of all Yugoslavia's republics is apparent from figures such as these.

The Dayton and Paris peace accords, which maintain a loose central government structure in Bosnia-Hercegovina, with governmental positions rotating according to complex formulae strangely reminiscent of Tito's era, have effectively divided Bosnia-Hercegovina into two entities: the Croat-Muslim (or Croat-Bosniak) Federation, which will control 51 per cent of the territory, and the Serbian Republic of Bosnia, which will control the remainder. The peace agreement is enforced by IFOR, a Nato based force, including a significant number of US troops, which is scheduled to stay in Bosnia-Hercegovina for one year. A civilian component is set up with the appointment of Carl Bildt, previously the EU's chief negotiator, as the High Commissioner for Bosnia-Hercegovina in Sarajevo.

The agreements also contain clauses on human rights, the return of refugees, national, cantonal and local municipal elections and co-operation with the international investigation and prosecution of war crimes. All of these agreements have been seen, by various commentators, as unrealistic and as being backed by little real power to enforce co-operation. National and cantonal elections have been held but local ones were postponed until September 1997. A great deal of faith is put in the World Bank and European Union led reconstruction plan which is meant to allow for all parties to see the economic value of peace and reconstruction in a country where, in 1993, industrial production was estimated to be only five per cent of 1992 levels (Ramet, 1996) and where demobilization adds to the already chronic problem of unemployment. The plan, therefore, introduces a new supranational division of labour into Bosnia-Hercegovina with Nato leading on peace enforcing; the USA leading the political settlement; UNHCR leading refugee and resettlement issues; World Bank and EU leading on reconstruction and development; and OSCE leading on human rights and the elections. In addition, non-governmental organizations are now being encouraged to shift from an emergency focus to questions of reconstruction and development.

In this section, we cannot address adequately the social policy implications of the new peace agreement. Things move so rapidly that it would be foolish to make more than a number of general comments. However, it is possible to look back at the role of international agencies in Bosnia-Hercegovina and address the lessons that might be learnt from the evident failure to stop genocide, ethnic cleansing, territorial division, and massive forced migration.

There is an evident parallel between Bosnia-Hercegovina and Rwanda, where a recent report sponsored by the Danish government suggested that:

> the essential failures of the response of the international community to the genocide in Rwanda were (and continue to be) political. Had appropriate political decisions been taken early on, it is apparent that much of the humanitarian operation subsequently required would have been unnecessary. In effect, humanitarian action substituted for political action. (Milwood, 1996: 11)

Similar conclusions have been made by diverse writers including the journalist David Rieff in *Slaughterhouse: Bosnia and the Failure of the West* (1995), and in the academic work carried out by a team led by Larry Minnear and published as *Humanitarian Action in the Former Yugoslavia: The UN's Role 1991–1993* (1994). Despite their very different styles, they point to the absence of a clear operational goal for UN agencies, the confusion between different parts of the UN and, through a definition of its role as 'neutral', the development of the UN as another party to the conflict, having to spread disinformation and to maintain certain kinds of untenable positions.

Nowhere are the dilemmas more clearly illustrated than in the reaction of UNHCR, charged with the protection of refugees, in the face of 'ethnic cleansing' which, as an ODA report argued recently, is itself a form of 'implicit social policy'. The High Commissioner for Refugees, Sadako Ogata, expressed the dilemma succinctly in November 1992:

> In the context of a conflict which has as its very objective displacement of people we find ourselves confronted with a major dilemma. To what extent do we persuade people to remain where they are, when that could well jeopardise their lives and liberties? On the other hand, if we help them to move, do we not become an accomplice to 'ethnic cleansing'? (in Minnear, 1994: 64)

Minnear suggests that there were policy shifts and policy confusion within UNHCR over this central issue which again, of course, illustrates the impossibility of a humanitarian role in the context of a failure to intervene politically or militarily to stop such actions. Minnear suggests that UNHCR found its role as lead agency difficult and was unable to mobilize sufficient resources to build networks of community social services. In addition, thousands of expatriate staff came and went, often within a very short timescale.

Mark Duffield (1994), in his analysis of UNICEF's work in Bosnia and Angola, makes the important point that Bosnia-Hercegovina was and is a case of a 'strong state' becoming an emergency. Linkages between the population and well-developed civil, professional and social infrastructures were undermined by war, genocide and 'ethnic cleansing'. His suggestion that many of the foreign NGOs who intervened in Bosnia-Hercegovina, at best, failed to work to restore those linkages and, at worst, actively contributed to their further deterioration, is a salutary one. The rise of the 'multi- mandated' NGO in Bosnia-Hercegovina and, to an extent, in Croatia is illustrated by the example of the US NGO International Rescue Committee (IRC), the vast majority of whose funding is from USAID, which administers an 'umbrella grant' for non-governmental organizations working on trauma and reunification, delivers humanitarian aid, administers a seed programme, and operates its own social welfare and mental health services. In 1993, IRC's budget for its Bosnian operation, of some US$50 million, was more than UNICEF's budget for the entire region. IRC, like many foreign NGOs, administered what Duffield has described as 'own brand projects' which, 'whilst of benefit to the immediate beneficiaries, have little connection with the existing professional and civil structures' (1994: 65). The consequential failure to develop effective longer term social policies has been noted by the resident World Bank social sector experts, who concluded in May 1997 that 'a serious attempt is missing to help the government develop a strategy for a streamlined and affordable program of social benefits beyond the emergency phase' (World Bank, 1997: 1). In terms of medical care policy similar sentiments are expressed by the medical coordinator of the European Commission's Humanitarian Office (ECHO) in Sarajevo, who notes 'two entities, three currencies and three health systems are in place fifteen months after the Dayton agreement . . . for the time being no clear policy from the EU in the health sector is evident' (Sole, 1997).

The failure of foreign NGOs to work with civil and professional struc- tures stands in some degree of contrast to the work of international organizations such as UNICEF and the World Health Organization (WHO). The World Health Organization's mandate, 'to protect the mental health of populations in former Yugoslavia during the conflict and prepare national mental health services for post-war development' (Buus Jensen, 1994: 72), whilst resting on an unhelpful split between emergency based provision during conflict and post-war reconstruction, does address the question of mental health infrastructure and does necessitate an under- standing of, and ability to work with, existing infrastructure. UNICEF has operated according to a similar model, in terms of its mandate to protect vulnerable women and children, particularly in the field of education.

In general, however, emergency based humanitarian aid in Bosnia- Hercegovina became a substitute not only for political action but for social sectorial interventions too. The failure to work with existing social welfare infrastructures, combined with a disregard for any element of planning within an 'aid as temporary substitute social policy' approach, is bound to make post-war reconstruction in the social sector more difficult. The slippage from 'social service' interventions to a new orthodoxy of 'psycho- social' interventions also encourages a 'trend' approach to 'own brand' provision where 'target groups' are identified less on the basis of need and more according to particular trends and fashions in terms of both which groups to work with and what regions to work in (Summerfield, 1996).

The division of Bosnia-Hercegovina into two 'entities' – a Croat-Muslim Federation, linked through a confederal arrangement with Croatia, and a Serbian entity, effectively linked, ultimately if not immediately, with Serbia proper – also poses key problems for supranational agencies. In addition, of course, it raises the spectre of 'Greater Croatia' and 'Greater Serbia' increasingly challenging any notion, however tenuous, of an independent sovereign Bosnia-Hercegovina. Parts of the Croat-Muslim Federation in Bosnia-Hercegovina continue to operate as 'the Croatian Republic of Herceg-Bosnia' which, in turn, has strong links to Croatia in terms of infrastructure (telephones, car registration), politics (the ruling party is HDZ), finance (with the Croatian currency, the kuna, widely used), and economics (professionals are paid the equivalent of Croatian salaries). These links are having an impact on social policy in a number of ways. The social insurance funds of Bosnia-Hercegovina are effectively split between a Bosnian fund operating in the Bosnian majority areas and a Croat fund operating in the Croatian Republic of Herceg-Bosnia. Specialist hospital treatment is available in Serbia or Montenegro for those in the Republic Srpska and in Croatia for those in the illegal Croatian Republic of Herceg-Bosnia, while no such facility exists for those in the Muslim majority areas of Bosnia-Hercegovina (Sole, 1997). The ability to obtain Croatian citizenship and settle in Croatia remains a key element of the balance of power in the region. The issue is illustrated dramatically in key divided centres such as Mostar, under EU administration but where attempts at reunification have been resisted, sometimes violently, by leading Croatian politicians, and in Gornji Vakuf, where an invisible front line divides the town. 'Strengthening the federation' has been seen as a major objective by USAID, in support of the US led peace plan in which a strong federation plays a key role. However, the attempt to reward authorities where power is shared with lucrative aid and reconstruction programmes has run into difficulties. The western project to restore a multi-ethnic society in the wake of the Dayton peace settlement may yet, as the September 1996 elections suggest, flounder on the rocks of continued ethnicized nationalism. The broader question of how to treat the Serbian entity of Bosnia-Hercegovina, in which indicted war criminals continue to hold high office in breach of the Dayton agreement, is even more complex. Few international organizations work in that territory and there is a reluctance on behalf of donors to invest, partly because of this and partly because of the degree of instability which they see. There appears little or no prospect of refugees and displaced people returning to territory held by a different 'ethnic group', so that the future prospects for Bosnia-Hercegovina remain bleak. The development of grassroots organizations, building civil society and alternative political conceptions, tends to be lost in the aid politics of the multi-mandated NGOs and the sheer size of reconstruction effort needed.

Increasingly, supranational agencies are identifying 'building civil society' as a central objective. However, this tends to support the already existing multi-mandated NGOs and, indeed, supposedly local NGOs created in their image. It is far more difficult for small, grassroots agencies to present themselves as credible to, say, UNHCR, who are used to dealing with NGOs with large budget lines. In addition, the development of a national network of NGOs is hampered by huge problems of communications and of mistrust between different areas, the erosion of the middle class base inside Bosnia-Hercegovina, and the absence, at least in the social welfare field, of civil society activities in the 1980s. The prospects of even beginning to discuss social policy in Bosnia-Hercegovina in any normal sense of the word remains, therefore, remote at this time, although the World Bank has made some progress in discussing pension reform in both entities of the country.

Indeed, as Susan Woodward (1996) has argued recently, post-Dayton there has been a lack of co-ordination between the military and civilian components, combined with the absence of any coherent strategy for sustainable peace. In effect, the process allows ethnicized blocs to pursue their wartime objectives through other means: the ways in which regis-tration for the 14 September elections tended to cement ethnic cleansing is an illustration of this. Delays in the availability of reconstruction funds for economic and social development, precisely because the conditions for lending imposed by the main agencies require a 'normality' which nowhere exists in Bosnia-Hercegovina, mean that reconstruction has become the Achilles' Heel of the peace process, fuelling economic rivalry between the entities and within the Croat-Muslim Federation.

Serbia and Montenegro: post-communist crisis, continuity and change

The lack of attention to questions of social welfare and development in the rump Federal Republic of Yugoslavia of Serbia and Montenegro reflects the relative absence of supranational agencies and, in particular, of international NGOs. The isolation of the Serbian regime which culminated in sanctions which, demonstrably, resulted in severe hardship for the most vulnerable part of the population, including refugees, also led to a relative failure to support the development of an alternative 'civil society' in Serbia. More agencies are involved in Kosovo which has been seen, for some time, as the most likely site of an extension of the conflict and where, of course, a state of emergency, direct rule from Serbia, and systematic human rights abuses of the Albanian majority have been in place for almost a decade.

The refugee crisis in Serbia and Montenegro is, itself, also relatively under-discussed. Figures from 1994 suggest that there were some 450,000 refugees in Serbia and Montenegro, or some five per cent of the total population. The exodus from Croatia in 1995 suggests that the true figure is probably now closer to 700,000. The Serbian regime has reacted in contradictory ways to such refugees, at times welcoming them as 'fellow Serbs' suffering from the 'genocide' of neighbouring regimes, at times using them as an (unwilling) part of its demographic policy of settling more Serbs in Kosovo, at times by mobilizing men the moment they arrive in Serbia and, most recently, by trying to prevent entry and forcing relocation in Bosnia. As of late 1994, only a very small proportion, some six per cent, of refugees lived in organized accommodation, most of which is in any case quite small, with no more than 200 people on average, compared with the large refugee settlements in Croatia.

UNHCR has very few partner NGOs in Serbia, and hence tends to work more closely with government and to provide services directly. This has encouraged, ironically, the possibility of more integrative services and a closer correspondence between provision for refugees and provision for local poor, although, in the context of sanctions, this has also been problematic. There are more organizations from countries more sympathetic to Serbia's position internationally and, in particular, from Orthodox charity organizations, although again this is less pronounced than the presence of Catholic and Muslim aid agencies in Croatia and Bosnia-Hercegovina. The development of self-help programmes for refugees has tended to be at the expense of government taking any responsibility. Most care is through family, friends and other 'private' arrangements, which has simply led to an extended reproduction of poverty.

As a post-communist conservative government, clinging to power, the regime distrusts NGOs and has made a particular example of the Open Society Foundation, attempting to close it as illegal. Other civil groups work in the fields of human rights, law, peace education and so on, and also face continued problems with the authorities which, at best, ignore them and, at worst, react in a hostile way to their activities. Some organizations close to the government, such as organizations of the disabled which existed previously, are treated differently. In addition, the state, together with 'experts', has sought to regulate the activities of all NGOs through requiring detailed scrutiny of their programmes (Parun-Kolin, 1996).

Serbia and Montenegro faced huge economic crises in the early 1990s linked to, but predating, the imposition of sanctions by the international community. Gross domestic product in Serbia halved between 1990 and 1993 (Parun-Kolin, 1996) with inflation at the end of 1993 reaching a high point of 178,882 per cent, prior to stabilization measures which mean that the annual rate is now closer to 100 per cent. Importantly, as Parun-Kolin argues, 'the state appears as the centre of the criminalization of the economy' with a 'grey economy' and war profiteering creating a 'new elite' of less than 10 per cent of the population, increasingly differentiated from an 'extended poor' including the professional middle class. Given the departure of some 300,000–400,000 young people, including the most highly educated, the prospects for future social development in Serbia also remain problematic.

The absence of a viable 'third sector', combined with a for-profit sector benefiting a new, quasi-criminal, elite and introducing the worst kind of privatized provision in, for example, health, also poses a huge threat to the development of social policy. The need to continue popular welfare programmes whilst facing huge economic problems has led to a situation where promises are made which cannot be fulfilled and where poverty is constantly redistributed 'by shifting priority from one fund to another' (Parun-Kolin, 1996).

Serbia is now the most multi-ethnic of all post-Yugoslav countries, with ethnic Serbs constituting no more than 65 per cent of the total population, with Albanians very much the majority in Kosovo, and with Hungarians a significant minority in Vojvodina. The huge discrepancies in terms of economic, social and demographic development between Serbia proper and Kosovo and, to a lesser extent, Vojvodina also pose huge question marks about the ability of the regime in Belgrade to continue to manage the tension between continuity and transformation. The reluctance to allow supranational organizations and international NGOs to monitor the human rights situation in Kosovo is one example of the likely tension which will arise as Serbia reintegrates into the new global order. Parun-Kolic's point that Serbia and Montenegro now lag behind other countries in the region in terms of the openness of the economy, amount of investments, established international relations, technological co-operation, decentralization of economic and degree of privatization, and been thrown back 'thirty or forty years', seems even more pertinent when questions of political development, human rights and social policy are added. How far the key global policy agents, including the World Bank and IMF, will be able to counter this remains an open and hugely complex question.

Macedonia: stability or wider war?

The description of Macedonia as 'unstable in a stable way' (Mickey, 1995) seems most pertinent, since this small republic has avoided large scale conflict yet faces continued tensions in the social, economic and political spheres. Four factors all operated together to contribute to a degree of instability. First, the transition from Yugoslav republic to an independent nation involved the loss of Yugoslav markets, frozen Yugoslav bank accounts, and, most importantly, the forced closure of many of the largest unproductive enterprises which had been located in Macedonia in an attempt to counter its underdeveloped status within Yugoslavia. Secondly, economic sanctions against Serbia also disproportionately affected Macedonia. Thirdly, the economic blockade imposed by Greece in protest against the use of the name 'Macedonia' effectively deprived the republic of any southern trade. Fourthly, the existence of an Albanian minority concentrated in the west of the country, with strong grievances from the old system, continuing into the present, and concerned with events in Kosovo, also contributed to instability. Experiencing a 50 per cent reduction in GNP since 1989, and with unemployment officially at 30 per cent the country clearly faces major problems, although Ramet's (1996) suggestion that it now resembles more of a Third World economy seems overstated.

Despite the relative impoverishment, Macedonia has the most 'normal' relations with the major international financial organizations of all ex-Yugoslav countries. The International Monetary Fund, the World Bank, the European Bank for Reconstruction and Development, the European Union through PHARE and the European Community Humanitarian Organization (ECHO), the Council of Europe, the Organization for Security and Co-operation in Europe, UNICEF, and perhaps less prominently the ILO, are all playing a part. The UNDP does not have a presence, although it is funding a development plan/project, in collaboration with the Macedonian Academy of Sciences and Arts and the Ministry of Development, to formulate macroeconomic strategies for the country. In addition, there is considerable bilateral financial assistance.

The World Bank has agreed to provide an IDA loan worth US$14 million in the field of social reform and technical assistance. Its four components are designed to:

1   facilitate the restructuring of socially owned enterprises through action to reduce the individual and community impacts of worker dislocation
2   improve the provision of social benefits and the collection of payroll contribution for social benefits
3   improve public awareness of the rationale for reform policies
4   support the continuing implementation of the enterprise restructuring economy.

In the context of the work on benefits, the World Bank has enabled the government to propose a modification to its social assistance system which reduces the amount payable in terms of a revised poverty line, differentiates this by region and tightens aspects of eligibility. This is yet to be implemented and work is under way to enable actuarial pension calculations. But no major thrust towards privatizing pensions is currently evident. Certainly, the Bank's resident representative in Macedonia is of the opinion that there is little point in gratuitously destroying established state social security systems so long as they can be made financially viable.

The Organization for Security and Cooperation in Europe (OSCE) established a monitoring mission to Macedonia in September 1992. Originally concerned with border spillover problems from the north, it has recently also developed a broader concern with the internal threats to stability. The OSCE High Commissioner on National Minorities has focused his efforts on issues concerning the education and the broader participation of ethnic Albanians in Macedonian society. He has also ensured that 'appeals for a progressive staffing of the military and police at all levels, by adequately reflecting recognised nationalities, be the subject of annual progress reports by the Council for Inter-Ethnic Co-operation' (Kroč, 1996: 318).

In 1993, the United Nations deployed the UN preventive deployment force, along the border between Macedonia and Serbia, to be involved in classic UN peace keeping and deter aggression from Serbia. Significantly, this force included United States ground troops and cemented a degree of US support for Macedonia. The force was renamed UNPREDEP and given a degree of autonomy from other UN missions in the region with the appointment of Henryk Sokalski as the Special Representative of the Secretary General. UNPREDEP's mission was extended for another six months to November 1996 and, as well as undertaking traditional military and political peace-keeping duties, Sokalski has sought to develop a social dimension to UNPREDEP's work, part of which involved a social development mission making recommendations regarding social policy, social development and international co-operation (Deacon et al., 1996).

The mission followed the analysis of Kroč which suggests that several factors have increased the salience of the ethnic Albanian-Macedonian cleavage within the socio-political life of the newly independent republic during its transition:

> Despite the participation of the ethnic Albanian political parties in coalition governments, their unilateral and confrontational actions including boycotting the referendum on independence and vote on the Constitution have led Macedonians to question ethnic Albanian loyalties and intensified the Macedonians' sense of insecurity. On the other hand, the Macedonian radical nationalists' drive for control of the State and the political agenda have especially intensified the Albanians' sense of 'second class citizenship' and justice. (1996: 298)

This mission asked: what role can social policy play in the constructive management of such inter-ethnic conflicts? How can preventive diplomacy be implemented via reforms in the way social policy and services are operated? In common with the experience learned from conflict resolution in other situations of ethnic tension (Stubbs, 1996a), it pointed approvingly to the work of international agencies in funding and encouraging programmes operating at the grassroots level in Macedonia, which are also exemplary in terms of promoting cross-ties.

> The basic concept behind such programmes is to support the establishment of local NGOs such as women's groups, parent–teacher and other associations. Such programmes increase society's capacity to withstand inter-ethnic tensions, particularly by giving local people skills to solve problems that become 'ethnicised' in ways that reframe and depoliticise the issue at stake. The point here is that many schools provide for education in Albanian and Macedonian and such groups are, therefore, an ideal mechanism for encouraging collaboration across ethnic divisions on a practical social development task. This empowerment of a multicultural, but inter-ethnically collaborative civil society must be the key to rescuing the issues from posturing politics. (Deacon et al., 1996: 48)

If Macedonia is to emerge from its difficult circumstances, as a state that embodies a multicultural respect for difference that does not become inter-ethnic indifference and distrust, then, the mission argued, the search for jobs and equivalent activities beneficial to the society and further measures to reduce poverty and deprivation are most vital. The attempts to foster societal integration should be interconnected and underpinned by practices and principles that foster the goals of multiculturalism. 'Pluralism and multicultural hegemony can be contributed to by dialogue and discussion across ethnic divisions, by public policy that secures a greater degree of equal opportunity between groups and by administration involving ethnic groups collaborating together in the management of their own affairs' (Deacon et al., 1996: 49). The role of international, national and local NGOs in Macedonia seems less contentious than in many other post-Yugoslav countries, with the exception of this focus that many have in relation to ethnic tensions which may not always be perceived as positive by government. If those in Macedonian politics who favour multi-ethnic coexistence prevail then the prospects for the future stability and prosperity of this small corner of post-Yugoslavia are good.

Some conclusions

This chapter has addressed the question of globalism and social policy in the context of conflict, forced migration and ethnicized nationalism, through case studies of post-Yugoslav countries. In the process, we have examined a wider range of debates and of agencies than in Chapter 4, including, centrally, the role of non-governmental organizations, be they supranational, international, national or local. A number of conclusions can be drawn from the case studies, which make more complex the analysis reached so far in this book.

1 The studies point to the need to widen the definition of social policy to address the complexities of humanitarian agency interventions, and international security agendas, together with questions concerning migration and refugee regimes. The role of supranational agencies in terms of regulation, distribution and provision in conditions of conflict necessitates a closer link between social policy, development studies and refugee studies.

2 The studies point to the importance in the region of the conjuncture of war, political emergency, mass (forced) migration, and post-communist transition. The importance of addressing the social policy context of such complex emergencies should not be understated. The range of agencies the nature of interventions, and the development of contradictions differ in a number of ways, from those addressed in the previous chapter where the focus was on more stable countries. The competition between agencies and the competing social visions, described in Chapter 4, is made more complex in these conditions. In particular it introduces the distinctive contribution of international NGOs which engage in their own agendas often in parallel to and without a dialogue with either

government or other international agencies. Their anti-poverty agendas appropriate to the South appear alongside the social policy prescriptions relevant to reforming European countries. There is a silence rather than a discourse between these positions. At the same time the independent philosophy and practice of NGO, funded as they are from abroad rather than by national governments, can lead to the undermining and marginalization of normal governmental social policy mechanisms.

3   International agencies play a complex and contradictory role in relation to questions of national sovereignty and territorial reconfigurations between and within post-Yugoslav countries. The replacement of a 'former Yugoslav' agenda with one which emphasizes the Croat-Muslim Federation in Bosnia-Hercegovina is reflected in the uneven development of agency involvement. Clearly the major international organizations (World Bank, ILO), in order to intervene in the conventional policy advisory way, require, paradoxically, a settled national sovereignty with which to do business. Conversely situations of complex emergency open the door to the different interventions of global NGOs who substitute for effective government public policy. Organizations like UNICEF and UNDP which, we have argued in Chapters 3 and 5, are the global social reformists at the level of the global discourse get caught up in these complex emergency situations in actually funding, via subcontracting, international NGOs who are effectively operating residualist welfare systems in the absence of effective public policy. At the same time the studies have added weight to the concern that such substitution by NGOs for public policy is undertaken in unregulated ways. International NGO intervention, rather like the intervention of consultancy advice elsewhere in the region within TACIS and PHARE (Chapter 4), falls outside the frame of any democratically responsible policy framework.

4   The case studies begin to address the different welfare regime affinities of different religious interests. This is reflected in support for different states and entities, constituted parties within the conflicts, and different territorial and political solutions. Orthodox, Catholic and Muslim non-governmental and governmental intervention plays a part in sustaining ethnic difference and preventing multi-ethnic policy solutions in some of the case studies. Comparative and global social policy analysis has hardly begun to understand the impact of such affinities on trans-national and national policy making in the Balkan region or elsewhere.

5   The key global social policy definers discussed in the previous chapters, particularly the World Bank and the International Monetary Fund, only play a similar roles in post-Yugoslav countries where there is a trend, as in Slovenia, Macedonia and latterly Croatia, towards the normalization of global social policy making. Their commitment to working in this way only in legitimated regimes can perpetuate uneven economic and social development. The World Bank and European Union reconstruction programme for Bosnia-Hercegovina poses new challenges for both organizations.

6 The case studies begin to point to an under-researched issue in social policy, namely the significance of ⟨diaspora effects⟩ including: remittances home from *émigrés* and guest workers; mobilization of funds and support for particular parties by those active in diaspora politics, many of whom return to play key roles in nationalist administrations; and the setting up of diaspora based NGOs which, under the notion of 'humanitarianism', intervene to support particular regime based ideological projects.

7 The case studies highlight the uneven development of foreign and national in different post-Yugoslav countries. The balance between the two relates to the context of supranational agency definitions, the extent of political emergency and humanitarian crisis, the extent of regime legitimacy, the nature of professional identities and interests, and the extent and nature of nascent civil societies and social movements.

8 As an extension of this, the nature and effectiveness of national and local NGOs also vary between different post-Yugoslav countries. The relative absence of national NGOs in Macedonia and Serbia contrasts sharply with the flowering of NGO activity in Slovenia. Croatia, and even more so Bosnia-Hercegovina, represent case studies of the problems of national and local NGO development including: strong reliance on foreign funding and assumptions; mutual distrust with governmental structures; trends in service provision unrelated to need and the growth of a new globalized professional middle class.

9 The uneven development of agencies' commitment to promote forms of provision which are 'integrative' between refugees, displaced persons and impoverished local communities is also demonstrated. This relates to the complex ways in which agencies produce and reproduce particular notions of 'ethnicity' and points to the need to extend, or even rework, the distinction made previously (Chapter 2) between 'ethnic nationalism', 'assimilationism', 'multiculturalism' and 'anti-racism'. One of the key problems is whether, by focusing on ethnic divisions, international agencies encourage claims for resources based on ethnicity rather than on another factor. At the same time international agencies are reluctant to stop the search for ethnic pluralist solutions for fear of reinforcing an ethnicized solution to the problem.

10 The studies, particularly the Macedonian example, reinforce one of the arguments of the book that the global politics agenda, or the global international relations agenda, is increasingly concerned with social rather than military matters. To prevent instability in Macedonia UNPREDEP focused on how social policy might better regulate relations between ethnic groups.

The need, suggested by the findings of this chapter, to combine the core concerns of social policy with those of development studies and, indeed, of refugee studies and peace studies is best expressed in terms of the notion of 'livelihoods'. By defining social policy as 'any policy developed at supra-national, state, local or community level which is underpinned by a social vision of society' and which, when operationalized, affects the rights and abilities of people to meet their livelihood needs (ODA, 1995b: 26), we can better address a range of global issues and concerns. Clearly, war, genocide and mass forced migration, expressed by the epithet of 'complex emerg-encies', threaten livelihoods in extreme ways. Questions of entitlement, capacity and sustainability, and their converses of need, vulnerability and distortion, are of immense importance in an ongoing debate about 'social integration'. The case studies of post-Yugoslav countries demonstrate the shortcomings of supranational agencies in the face of a conflict in Europe. The terms of these shortcomings and even failure are not unknown to commentators on the African situation. However, they do pose particularly acute questions about how to address causes rather than symptoms, build capacity rather than parallel provision, promote real civil society rather than opportunistic international NGOs and, above all, sustainable peace rather than a balance of ethnic terror. It is to questions such as these in the context of a global governance reform agenda that we turn in the next chapter.

6

The Prospects for Global Social Policy

The argument of the book recapitulated

This book has been about the impact of globalization on the making of social policy. It has argued and demonstrated that globalization (a) sets welfare states in competition with each other, (b) raises social policy issues to a supranational level, and (c) generates a global discourse on the best way to regulate capitalism in the interests of social welfare East and West, North and South.

Global social policy as a practice of supranational actors embodies global social redistribution, global social regulation, and global social provision and/or empowerment, and includes the ways in which supranational organizations shape national social policy.

The classical concerns of social policy analysts with social needs and social citizenship rights becomes in a globalized context the quest for supranational citizenship. The classical concern with equality, rights and justice between individuals becomes the quest for justice between states. The dilemma about efficiency, effectiveness and choice become a discussion about how far to socially regulate free trade. The social policy preoccupations with altruism, reciprocity and the extent of social obligations are put to the test in the global context. To what extent are social obligations to the other transnational?

The entry of the former 'socialist' economies into the global capitalist arena has coincided with a period of intensified global economic competition which has contributed to the flexibilization of labour which, in turn, has challenged the viability of the traditional work based European social security and income maintenance systems.

This book and the research upon which it is based have demonstrated three arguments in this context. First, the making of post-communist social policy has been very much the business of supranational and global actors. Secondly, in post-communist conditions of national stability and uncontested borders the key international players are the formal intergovernmental and international organizations like the World Bank, IMF, ILO, EU, etc. Thirdly, by contrast, in post-communist conditions of complex political instability and contested borders the field is left much more open to international non-governmental organizatons.

Within this context and in the absence of any adequate formal global forum for the articulation and contestation of alternative social policy programmes, a hidden global discourse has emerged within and between the human resources divisions of these global organizations. The future for welfare not only in the East but by implication elsewhere is being resolved in the interplay between these global actors and the constrained decisions of national governments. In summary an argument can be constructed, on the basis of the analysis in the preceding chapters, that develops as follows:

1 Western welfare states have differed in how they provide for the welfare needs of their citizens. The social democratic regimes of Scandinavia and the social security (conservative corporatist) regimes of much of Europe have met human needs more effectively than the *laissez-faire* or liberal regime of the USA.

2 However, global economic competition between West and East, North and South, including competition with regimes that carry few social obligations, tends to erode the social security provisions of Europe.

3 Equally, the level of economic development and associated social security provided historically in the privileged northern and western countries may not (it is suggested by some) be demographically or ecologically sustainable if replicated on a world scale.

4 Additionally, the patterns of work upon which the social security structures of privileged northern and western countries have been predicated are being eroded by models of flexible employment and the associated tendency to create casualized and marginalized labour.

5 All of this leads to a set of conflicting interests articulated in alternative social policies and reflected in the prescriptions of different agencies described in this book. These conflicting interests may be represented schematically as: capital versus labour; securely employed versus casualized; Europe versus the USA versus elsewhere; North versus South; and present versus future generations.

6 Within this complexity and in the move to freer global trade the progressive social security structures of Scandinavia and Europe come to be seen by the South as privileged and unsustainable protectionism of core workers in the North.

7 In other words the North accuses the South of social dumping: competing unfairly by denying their workers basic rights and decent social conditions. The South accuses the North of social protectionism: refusing access to markets to conserve the social welfare privileges of the few. The ILO can't sanction the use of social clauses in world trade because it also represents the South. The World Trade Organization won't complicate international free trade agreements with social clauses.

8 In effect, the global playing field of economic and social policy within which free trade can take place is being set by the competition between agencies and ideas that have been analysed in this book.

9   In other words, the conclusion might be that the influential social liberalism of the IMF and Bank identified in this book as a prescription for post-communist and other developing countries, while contributing to the erosion of social democracy and conservative corporatism in the North, might be laying the foundation of a global social safety net policy. The alternative radical project of a citizen's income, which would also erode traditional social security structures, has yet to find significant support within the intra- and inter-agency discourse identified in this book.

10 To summarize, the opportunity created by the 'collapse of communism' for the global actors to shape the future of social policy has been grasped enthusiastically by the dominant (social liberal) tendency in the World Bank. In alliance with social development NGOs who are being given a part to play especially in zones of instability, a social safety net future is being constructed. This NGO support combined with the political support of many southern and some East European governments is challenging powerfully those defenders of universalist and social security based welfare states to be found in the EU, the ILO and (not withstanding their influence on the 1996 *World Development Report*) in smaller numbers in the Bank. Ineffective so far are the lone voices calling for a global citizenship income.

This last chapter develops some aspects of these conclusions. In the next section the concept of a global social policy discourse is examined in more detail. The shifting nature of the epistemic communities in and around the global organizations and their impact on policy information is discussed. In the following section the current global governance reform agenda which could impact on policy outcomes is reviewed. The contending ideas for the reform of the UN, the accountability of the Bretton Woods institutions, the strengthening of the G7 and the World Trade Organization, and the search for the empowerment of citizens through a global rights agenda are examined.

The chapter then turns to the prospects for and the desirability of what I call a global social reformist project. Such a project would involve significant global *redistribution*, a mechanism for global *regulation* that would provide for more than a safety net playing field for world trade, and important elements of global social *provision* and *empowerment*. The forces leading towards this project and the obstacles and objections to it are reviewed. Finally the implications of this book for the subject matter of social policy are considered. A global social policy research agenda is suggested.

The global social policy discourse: the significance of epistemic communities

How decision makers define state interests and formulate policies to deal with complex and technical issues can be a function of the manner in which the issues are represented by specialists to whom they turn for advice in the face of

uncertainty . . . epistemic communities [networks of knowledge based experts]
play a part in . . . helping states identify their interests, forming the issues for
collective debate, proposing specific policies, and identifying salient points for
negotiation. (Haas, 1992)

It has long been accepted that one powerful epistemic community in the
context of economic structural adjustment programmes is that made up of
macroeconomists in the World Bank and IMF and their counterparts close
to and in the governments of developing countries. The period of relatively
willing adoption by developing countries of the recommendations of this
epistemistic community in the 1970s and 1980s has been explained by the
'close alignment between a cadre of national economic technocrats and the
international financial institutions' (Kahler, 1992: 127).

Suggestively Kahler concluded that conditionality would widen in the
1990s but that 'these efforts to shape national policies will be undertaken in
societies, such as Eastern Europe, whose political features and adjustment
paths differ significantly from those on which past lessons have been built'
(1992: 132). One aspect of the studies reported in this book has been to
shed light on how the nature of the epistemic communities seeking to
influence economic and social policy has changed as a consequence of their
encounter with the social expectations and inherited social obligations of
post-communism. One aspect of the change was the recruitment, described
in Chapter 4, of new human resources specialists to the operations division
of the Bank dealing with the post-communist transition. Rooted more in
the traditions of Europe with its Keynesian and Bismarckian history, these
new technicians engaged (and are still engaged) in a heated controversy as
to how to define the limits and possibilities for state social welfare spending
in the region. The new members also found listening ears in some of the
economists and social policy technicians in the post-communist transition
economies. The outcome has been both the importation into the Bank of
elements of conservative corporatist thinking and the softening of the
liberal fundamentalists towards a social liberal (safety net) position. A
second aspect of the change was the greater openness of the governments of
the region to the influence of the epistemic community of labour and social
standards defenders in and around the ILO and Council of Europe. The
ministries of labour and social affairs of post-communist countries shared
the same values and concerns with the defence of labour rights and
inherited pension and other entitlements. This has led to open clashes
between this and the social liberal community of the Bank in the region.
The emerging social costs of the transition began to be publicized by yet
another epistemic community that I earlier called the global reformists.
Spokespersons for UNICEF, UNDP, etc., who have constituted a kind of
global poverty lobby, a global social conscience, have had a voice in this
story. The post-Yugoslav story has highlighted in addition the presence of
international non-governmental organizations, an emerging global middle
class of professional interventionists, who have contributed their distinct
analysis of the problem of what is to be done about poverty in complex

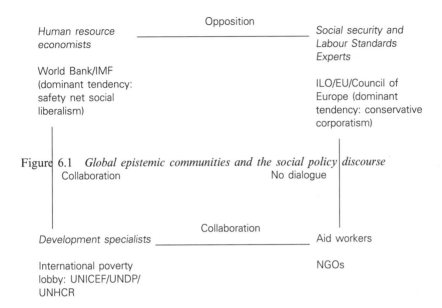

Figure 6.1   *Global epistemic communities and the social policy discourse*

political emergencies. The post-Yugoslav story has revealed the paradox that epistemic communities like the articulate spokespeople for UNICEF and UNDP may represent at the level of global discourse a social reformist set of ideas, while in practice their operational counterparts in the field (especially in the context of complex emergencies) may be implementing through subcontracting a residualist substitute for effective government social policy.

The study has thrown light on the paradigm shifts taking place, partly as a result of the encounter with post-communism, inside some of these epistemic communities. It has highlighted the emergent and unresolved discourse between and within the overlapping epistemic communities. It has suggested how alliances between fractions of these communities have contributed to significant shifts in the content of global social policy making.

Figure 6.1 in schematic form suggests that the long established neo-liberal macroeconomic epistemistic community in and around the Bank and IMF has had to share intellectual and political space with not only new European recruits to its own organization (not on the figure) but also the ILO influenced labour standards epistemic community and, in a few countries, also the global poverty lobby expertise associated with UNICEF and UNDP. In the wings, but powerful in post-Yugoslavia and other complex political emergencies, has been the cadre of the international non-governmental organizations. The emergent and perhaps dominant social liberalism or safety net strategy has emerged in part as a result of alliances between some in the Bank, some in the NGOs, and perhaps some in the

Table 6.1   *Global social policy discourse*

Ideology of welfare	Regime type	Income maintenance	International agency sometimes associated
Existing worlds of welfare			
Burden	Liberalism (USA)	Residual public assistance	IMF
Social cohesion	Conservative corporatism (Germany)	Social insurance	EU ILO World Bank (one tendency)
Investment	SE Asian (Confucian?)	Individualized funds	OECD World Bank
Redistributive commitment	Social democracy (Sweden)	Insurance and citizenship entitlement	–
Future worlds of welfare			
Safety net	Social liberalism	Means and assets tested social assistance and social support	World Bank (dominant tendency) Compliance of NGO poverty lobby?
Citizenship entitlement	Futuristic	Citizen's income	ILO (Individuals) COE (Individuals)
Welfare failure	Social neglect	Self reliance	NGOs in practice

operations arm of the international poverty lobby less concerned with the interests of labour. This powerful alliance of one Bank tendency of international NGOs, and of some in the global poverty lobby is leading to the marginalization within the global social policy discourse of traditional defenders of labour and social security standards. This outcome is exactly as prescribed by Graham (1994b), discussed in Chapter 3. Other backcloth epistemic communities contributing to the social policy and social regulation dialogue include the global environmental lobby (Rio, 1992) and the global women's lobby (Beijing, 1995).

Table 6.1 suggests in summary form the prescriptions for the future for social policy as exemplified by income maintenance policy that have emerged from fractions of these transnational policy communities. It is not, as was hypothesized in Chapter 3, that particular supranational organizations were associated with particular policy positions and that these reflected the dominant national interests underpinning these organizations, but rather that debate and disagreement have become truly transnational and global. The e-mail exchanges between the global civil servants prefigure a global politics that has yet to find a democratic and accountable form.

The old world of unreconstructed fundamentalist liberalism associated with the IMF is on the wane within the global discourse (even though it has clearly not died as a strategy for domestic US politics, as the emasculation of the federal system of aid to families with dependent children testifies). Equally challenged is the social democracy of Scandinavia (which finds no global defender) and the conservative corporatism of Europe. As prescriptions for a post-communist and post-Fordist future of labour insecurity, there are the new contenders of social liberalism (safety net liberalism) and of a citizenship income. The one world that straddles the old and the emergent is the South East Asian concern with personal investment and savings for individualized social security accounts. The global financial institutions can no longer be written off as unconcerned with the poor and with social policy. The question now is the adequacy and appropriateness of their explicit social policy and their explicit strategies for combating poverty. In terms of the Bank one question is whether those seeking to win it to a more European conservative corporatist kind of income maintenance policy (and their allies in the EU and ILO) are able to defend this strategy against continued accusations of the outdatedness and economic and demographic inviability of it. The other question is whether the safety net with personal savings social liberal strategy makes the most sense for post-communist and developing economies or whether it will still be challenged within those countries for limiting unnecessarily the scope for pooled risks and shared social solidarity. For the dominant tendencies in ILO and its allies the challenge continues to be the viability of defending labour standards in a world of flexible and disappearing labour. For the citizenship income lobby the issue remains of winning more political support. For some citizens in some countries the real prospects for their social policy may be neither of these global prescriptions but an entire collapse of the welfare state where unregulated NGOs substitute for effective public policy. For the conceptualization of this outcome as a system of social neglect I am indebted to Branko Milanovic of the World Bank Policy Research Department.

Regardless of detail a broader political and moral question is whether it is helpful to see some of those in these epistemic communities who are concerned to fashion either a global social safety net or a global citizen's income as being on the side of the angels, as the humanizers of capitalism globally. Are they, alternatively, like national social reformists of old, to be accused of creating a fig-leaf to cover naked global imperialism?

It has been an implicit assumption of this book that the struggle for better global and national social policies is partly a struggle of values and ideas. It has become an empirical conclusion of this book that this struggle of values and ideas is now being waged inside the World Bank (and the other international organizations) rather than merely inside the state. Can we indeed conclude that we are witnessing, whether in the guise of social liberalism or a citizenship income future, the emergence of a new humanizing and civilizing world hegemony countering fundamentalist liberalism that 'is expressed in universal norms, institutions, and mechanisms which lay down general rules of behaviour for states and those forces of civil society that act across national boundaries' (Cox, 1993: 62)? Is, on the other hand, such a judgement an infantile delusion? Adler and Haas (1992) concluded that:

Among the necessary conditions for minimal progressive change in international relations are the redefinition of values and the reconciliation of national interests with human interests in general, such as security, welfare, and human rights. To the extent that epistemic communities make some of the world's problems more amenable to human reason and intervention they can curb some of the international system's anarchic tendencies, temper some of the excesses of a purely state-centric order, and perhaps even help bring about a better international order.

Cox, however, concluded that

there is very little likelihood of a war of movement at the international through which radicals would seize control of the superstructure of international institutions . . . one tactic for bringing change in the structure of world order can be ruled out as total illusion (1992: 64)

Whether Adler and Haas or Cox are right depends on what constitutes 'radical', what constitutes a desirable 'change in the world order', and whether the choice between liberal cut-throat global capitalism or socially regulated global capitalism matters. To be sure, a post-capitalist socialist world order, and the struggle for that within international institutions, can be ruled out as total illusion for now. If, however, the movement towards the social regulation of global capitalism is regarded as radical and a change in the world order then the evidence of this book suggests that a war of movement at the international level is in progress. These broader issues of what constitutes a global social reformist project, whether it would constitute a global counter-hegemonic project, how an alliance for it might be built or obstructed, and even whether such a project is desirable, will be returned to in the section after next. We turn now not to this grander project (illusion) but to the practical steps that are being canvassed for in terms of those aspects of the reform of global governance that have a relevance to the making of global social policy.

The global governance reform agenda

In the next section I want to address at a schematic level what I will call a global social reformist project. The elements of this will include a call for more global social redistribution, more global social regulation, and more global social provision and/or empowerment. The possibilities of and obstacles in the path of such a project will be assessed. Whether such a project should be categorized as being on the side of the 'global angels' or merely another trick of the imperialist 'global gangsters' (Wheeler, 1996) will be addressed then. This section is concerned not with the schematic dream but with the faltering actual steps that are being taken, or at least being seriously debated, to improve the way the world is governed in terms of the goal of better meeting human needs.

There are a number of partially contending, partially parallel and overlapping strategies, often implicit, being articulated by members of the interconnected epistemic communities identified in the previous section and by others. Global human resource specialists, the global poverty lobby, the global labour standards and social security experts, and the global non-governmental organizations are contributing to a discourse not only about specific social policy recommendations for particular countries, as this book has demonstrated, but also about global governance. A casual review of the relevant political science, international relations, and political economy periodicals will reveal a number of parallel themes within this global governance discourse. All are directed at containing the threat of a post cold war global disorder and seeking to establish a more humane and socially just new world order. Some of the themes in these communities are picked up spasmodically by significant national and regional political leaders. Five themes or strategies or proposals are picked out for brief comment below. These are:

1   regulating global competition
2   making the Bretton Woods institutions more accountable
3   reforming the United Nations
4   strengthening global political, legal and social rights
5   empowering international civil society.

I make no pretence that there is anything original in these themes. They reflect, among other sources, the conclusions of the Commission on Global Governance (1995), the thinking of the United Nations *Human Development Reports* (UNDP, 1990: 1991: 1992: 1993a: 1994: 1995a), the contribution of the United Nations Research Institute for Social Development (UNRISD, 1995b), the reflections upon these themes by Held (1995), the valuable contributions in edited volumes by Griesgraber and Gunter (1995; 1996: 1997) and many other sources. These sources are not read by students of the social policy of developed welfare states and, as I argued in Chapter 1, they need to be.

Regulating global competition

At root is the problem that 'global integration can destroy hard won social gains in many countries – driving them down to the lowest common denominator in a competitive market – or, on the contrary, integration can begin to raise social standards towards levels attained in the most successful cases' (UNRISD, 1995a: 40). The future welfare states will depend partly on how they compete in this global marketplace and partly on the rules of the game that regulate this competition, on the political decisions made about this.

A recent articulation of the conflicting global interests bound up with the issue of free trade and social standards was provided by the French President in the context of the G7 Summit in Lille on 2 April 1996. He argued that public opinion in the West could accept that lower wages, less extensive social security and different labour laws enabled developing countries to compete successfully for export markets. But other aspects of labour markets in developing countries would not be tolerated. 'Can it be accepted that fundamental rules of social democracy be so grievously stretched in this great world wide market? Can more or less disguised forms of adult or child slavery be tolerated? The citizens of our countries are becoming better and better informed about such forms of abuse and rightly judge them to be intolerable' (*Guardian*, 2 April 1996). Apparently the festering row among the West's leading industrial nations over linking free trade to human rights burst into the open at this G7 summit (*Guardian*, 2 April 1996). The European Commission call for minimum global labour standards threatened to split the G7 down the middle. Padraig Flynn for the EC argued that 'free collective bargaining, free association, and the abolition of child labour are fundamental rights'. Britain and Japan claimed, to the contrary, that the move was an attempt to defend the high cost economies of the West from international competition and represented protectionism by the back door. The issue surfaced again at the subsequent G7 summit in Lyons in June 1996. This summit, interesting for its involvement of not only the G7 nations (France, Germany, the USA, the UK, Japan, Canada, Italy), which represent only 12 per cent of the world's population, but also for the first time the heads of the World Bank, the IMF, the World Trade Organization and the UN concluded in both its economic and political communiqués that there was a need, in the context of freer trade, to combat social exclusion (*Observer*, 30 June 1996). Chirac concluded that 'Globalisation holds out advantages in terms of growth but also carries dangers of exclusion for nations and individuals. Certain safety barriers have to be introduced.' The conference 'recognised that there is a will to address the relationship between trade and internationally recognised core labour standards' (Group of Seven, 1996: 7). These were subsequently discussed in Singapore in December 1996 at the meeting of ministers at the World Trade Organization. As we noted in Chapter 3, the declaration of that meeting only served to confirm the continuing divisions of opinions and interest regarding this topic.

A stepwise progress towards such global regulation of labour standards is likely to be the reality. First, northern governments could use their own national regulations or labour and social standards to enforce them on the operation of their own firms operating abroad. Secondly, regional associations of governments playing host to TNC investment could establish common ground rules for that region (e.g. the Association of South East Asia States). Thirdly, intergovernmental agreements could ensure common standards (Gleckman and Krut, 1995). Eventually, of course, only a common purpose between consumer interests in the North (not wishing to purchase goods made by child labour) and emergent worker interests in the South (seeking to limit child labour) expressed through a network of social and labour organizations would ensure that transnational corporations saw the necessity of the social regulation of their activities. This argument has earlier been put forward in the context of the common interests of women as consumers in the North and workers in the South, by Mies (1986) and in the context of a discussion of fair trade by Barratt-Brown (1993). Within the context of this twin pressure of a globalized labour and consumer movement the constitutional proposals (see below) to give greater power to UN bodies to oversee the regulation of global trade could become practical, feasible politics.

Running counter to the concern to regulate global trade in the interests of labour and social standards are those who argue that the globalization of trade can and should be reduced. A sea change is argued for whereby future strategy in the interests of global ecological concerns and the sustainability of local economies should focus on relocalization and renationalization of economic development and management. Herman Daly on leaving the World Bank argued that 'Ten years from now the buzz words will be "renationalization of capital" and the "community rooting of capital for the development of national and local economies", not the current shibboleths of export-led growth stimulated by whatever adjustments are necessary to increase global competitiveness' (Cavanagh, 1994: 116). This is echoed by Lang and Hines (1995) in their concern to protect the environment against the damaging consequences of increased global trade. Elsewhere they argue that 'The purpose of political economy should be to build up diversified local economies in place of the warehouse or global assembly-line units of today' (1996: 113). The importance of this argument notwithstanding, the likely future is the slowly increased social regulation of increased world trade.

Making the Bretton Woods institutions more accountable

This book has demonstrated the importance of the IMF and Bank in shaping the character of the social policy of countries in transition. The proposal has been often repeated in critical discussion of the Bretton Woods institutions that they should be made more accountable for policies they effect and promulgate. At present they are accountable to the governments that fund them proportional to the capital provided. Modestly the Commission on Global Governance (1996: 34) suggests that voting strength should reflect gross domestic product based on purchasing power parity. More radically it argues that 'the time is now ripe for a global forum that can provide leadership in economic, social and environmental fields. It would be more broadly based than the G7 or the Bretton Woods institutions and more effective than the present UN system' (1996: 155). A proposal is made for an Economic Security Council which would be more broadly representative of all large economies (measured in purchasing power parity terms), regional associations and smaller states. It would provide a policy framework within which the Bank, IMF and WTO would work. Others more enamoured of the effectiveness of the existing UN Economic and Social Council and wanting a greater voice for the

South have proposed the accountability of Bretton Woods to ECOSOC (UNRISD, 1995a).

Arguing that it is not a matter of either making the Bretton Woods institutions more accountable to the countries that fund them according to a measure of the size of their population, or subjecting them to a reformed UN Economic Security Council, Singer (1995) proposes that reforms in voting systems for both the Bretton Woods institutions and the UN are needed and that, once this is undertaken, the two could work more closely alongside each other, with the Bank and IMF focusing on harder finance issues and the UN focusing on 'softer' social policy issues. 'The system of decision making in the Bank and Fund could be democratized and moved in the direction of the present UN system, while the UN system could be made more realistic and moved in the direction of the Bretton Woods system' (1995: 18). Majorities of both donor countries (Bank and Fund) and all countries (UN) might be needed for policy agreement. The share in power over economic and social policy by a reformed UN Economic Security Council would simply be an institutional reflection of the trend analysed in Chapter 1 that the substance of global politics is shifting from military matters to economic and, latterly, social matters. Preventive diplomacy by the UN now involves the analysis of social policy (Deacon, 1996). Power sharing by reformed Bank, Fund and UN would merely reflect this.

At stake is not only the question of accountability of Bretton Woods but also the role. While there is general agreement among the rich capitalist countries that the IMF credit of last resort role is important there is more debate about the role of the Bank. Regardless of the populist politics of the USA which might want to curtail the Bank, most opinion is concerned with the scope of the Bank's brief. Put simply, should the Bank as a development agency not simply deal, as Singer suggested, with hard financial matters but continue to expand its brief not only to the environment and to poverty alleviation as described in this book but also to taking over (for example, from the UNHCR or the UN's Bureau for Humanitarian Assistance) a responsibility for refugees and humanitarian disasters? The question is whether the UN social agencies should be given greater resources and responsibility for shaping national and transnational social (and other) policies or whether the Bank replaces them. In the context of the G7 summit in June 1995, and the fiftieth anniversary of the UN in March 1996, calls were made not only for the United Nations Conference on Trade and Development (UNCTAD) to be abolished but even for the ILO's role to be reconsidered. Subsequently at the G7 meeting in June 1996 the ILO issue appeared to have been dropped and indeed the communiqué thanked the ILO for the quality of its work. The IMF, World Bank, WTO and UN Secretary General, however, were invited to the meeting to discuss among other things concrete proposals to abolish UNCTAD and UNIDO. The Bank and the World Trade Organization between them could end up not as partners with the UN as Singer wants but, as Susan Strange and Fabrizio Sabelli (1995) have suggested, as the global ministries for education, health, environment, welfare, trade and labour, leaving the IMF as global ministry of finance.

The significance of the moves to different kinds of accountability for the subject matter of this book is not however immediately obvious. A heated controversy within the epistemic community has been documented with regard to the social policy prescriptions of the human resource specialists of the Bank. Had they been open to the public scrutiny of a reformed Economic Security Council, or to the UN Economic and Social Council, it is not clear what differences in the balance of influence of the sides in this debate would have resulted. Greater global accountability may not throw more light on the social policy options for the future.

Reforming the United Nations

It is impossible to do justice to the volumes written on the need for the reform of the UN. The importance of the topic for the future of the ILO, WHO, UNESCO, UNICEF, UNDP, UNHCR and the other global social reformists identified in Chapter 3 as having a distinctive voice in world social affairs can't, however, be under-estimated. As a bulwark against Bretton Woods (Chapter 4) the ILO stands out in our analysis. There could be little confidence that the WTO could perform the same job, even if as has been argued above, the WTO should have to uphold labour and social standards in its regulatory work. UNICEF and UNDP stand out as critics of existing global policy and practice and their disappearance would be a severe blow to progressive opinion, notwithstanding the acknowledgement made in the light of the ex-Yugoslavia story that, in practice, subcontracted NGOs working for UNICEF and UNDP can end up playing a part in a residualist social policy.

The horns of the dilemma appear to be that, as presently constituted and managed, some of the G7 nations will continue to give little credence to the UN work in the social field, but if reformed in the way some of the northern industrial nations are suggesting, the UN will become an institution less open to the influence of the smaller nations of the South. The price that might have to be paid for a UN that is taken more seriously by the developed and large economies is that it becomes more subject to the interests of these developed nations. To put it differently, to ensure that it is a UN Economic Security Council that contributes to the regulation of global trade with a view to protecting labour and social standards, it might have to be a UN reconstructed to better reflect the interests of developed nations.

The G7 summit of June 1996 seemed to take a concrete step in the direction of reforming the UN in order to preserve it and to take further the idea of IMF, World Bank and UN agency collaboration rather than competition. It was proposed that ECOSOC be strengthened by the appointment of an Under Secretary General who would rationalize the several development agencies of the UN (e.g. UNDP/UNICEF). The expectation would be that for each country where the global agencies intervened, 'UNDP, other agencies, the World Bank, IMF, the WTO and regional development banks could work together . . . in the preparation of country strategy reports . . . Regular meetings of donors in each country should be organised . . . The resident UN co-ordinator or the World Bank . . . could organise these meetings' (Group of Seven, 1996: 14). The problem, of course, is that calls for increased co-ordination of agencies (in particular co-ordination of UN bodies and the World Bank) avoid the fact that the issue is not only one of co-ordination but one of divergency in thinking about social and economic development, as evidenced in our analysis of the global social policy discourse. Giving the Bank the economy and the UN the soft social questions will not end this controversy over strategy and policy.

The crisis of the UN is also one of financing brought about by the continued reluctance of the USA to contribute its required share of resources. It is also one of overlapping and poorly co-ordinated divisions among specialized agencies. It may also be a crisis of internal management styles. The Commission on Global Governance (1995: 344) has called for a reformed Security Council to share power more appropriately to the new distribution of economic power, for an annual Civil Society forum to involve international civil society (global NGOs), for the Economic and Social Council to be replaced by the Economic Security Council described above, and for a United Nations Adviser or Directorate for the advancement of women. The draft communiqué, which was eventually watered down, of the G7 summit in June 1995 called for (a) consolidation and streamlining of organizations in the economic and social fields, (b) examination of the role of bodies such as UNCTAD in the light of the establishment of the WTO, (c) arranging for high level sessions of the Economic and Social Committee to take more responsibility for issues of public concern, and (d) the reduction of costs.

A crisis appeared to be unavoidable in early 1996, despite the supportive words spoken by Clinton at the fiftieth anniversary celebrations of the UN. Unpaid dues from member states at 31 December 1995 were $2.3 billion compared with $1.8 billion in 1994. The USA owed $1.2 billion, or half the total. By comparison Russia owed $455 million, Germany owed $23 million. US resistance to maintaining its proportional commitment which reflects GNP prompted the Secretary General to recommend in February that the US contribution should be limited. He proposed a ceiling of 15 per cent or 20 per cent of the UN budget from any member state. The USA's proportional contribution should have been 25 per cent. EU diplomats who together contribute 35 per cent of UN expenses objected. Against this backcloth plans were being made to cut staff by 10 per cent and to reduce activities in a number of areas. In the event the USA did pay a large proportion of its arrears but the crisis served only to highlight the equivocal nature of support among some developed nations for the UN as currently constituted.

Over recent decades the periodic financial crisis of the UN has generated proposals for forms of global taxation that are not dependent upon the political whim of national governments. The Brandt Report of 1980 first raised the issue, and more recently the UNDP has pressed for forms of global taxation. At the UN World Summit on Social Development in 1995 the Tobin tax first proposed in 1972 became a serious candidate for discussion. This would be a small tax levied on currency transactions (0.5 per cent). The target would be international financial speculators which has a ring of justice about it given that it has been the free movement of finance capital that has contributed to the competitive challenge to welfare states. The UN Secretary General has proposed a tax on international air travel. A recent review of options concluded that 'the airport tax surcharge seems the simplest and least controversial idea, if political pressure for global revenue were to develop. The Tobin tax remains the scheme on which most work has been done . . . but there is little political pressure to translate it into action' (*ODI Briefing Papers*, February 1996: 4).

The discussion of alternative ideas for levying a global taxation for global redistributive purposes has been coupled to the problems that the IMF and Bank have in reconciling the development needs of nations to which they lend money and the interests of the shareholding countries who provide the resources. The need not only of the UN but possibly of a reformed UN and reformed Bank collaborating alongside each other for independent sources of finance has been reviewed recently by Girvan (1995: 27).

With the UN under strong financial and political pressure from the developed nations to reform if it is to be granted a greater role in world governance, is there a southern view on the prospects? The South Centre exists to promote South solidarity, to foster convergent views and approaches among countries of the South with respect to global economic, political and strategic issues: to act as, in effect, a policy think-tank for the G77 group of nations. It is chaired by Julius Nyere. Its views on the UN reform debate were clearly set out recently (South Centre, 1995). It argued that 'the UN must be empowered to deal with matters pertaining to the world economy . . . Improved co-ordination between an enlarged G7 and the IMF are insufficient and unacceptable. This function must be reassigned to the UN' (1995: 33). It continues: 'the opposition to a strong and dynamic UN is political and profoundly ideological, and is largely concentrated in a few states whose establishments prefer not to strengthen a forum in which their domestic and global policies can be challenged or trimmed' (1995: 35). While important, this runs counter to the idea that it is precisely some of the northern states who are seeking global social regulation and some of the southern states who have seen the possible advantage to them of unregulated free trade. The debate is not only a North–South one but cross-cuts both hemispheres, with adherents of liberalism and social regulation, of UN power and Bretton Woods power, to be found North and South.

Strengthening global political, legal and social rights

The concern of this book that the social citizenship rights of people in economies in transition are being shaped by the ideas circulating in the global financial institutions leads us directly to ask what the prospects are for the laying down for all countries of minimal global citizenship rights. The Commission on Global Governance has argued for a global civic ethic: 'We believe humanity as a whole will be best served by recognition of a set of common rights and responsibilities. It should encompass the rights of all people to a secure life, equitable treatment' (1995b: 336). Dharam Ghai has argued too that 'in a fragmented and somewhat inconsistent way, the world seems therefore to be moving towards a debate on global citizenship similar to that which marked the affirmation of certain inalienable rights within advanced industrial societies' (UNRISD, 1995a: 170). Baubock (1994) has elaborated the case for and obstacles to the establishment of transnational citizenship rights. Held (1995) has called for the creation of a new International Human Rights Court reflecting on a global level the work already done on the European continent by the Strasbourg Court of Human Rights of the Council of Europe.

These increasingly frequent calls for global citizenship rights of the political, legal and socio-economic kind are, of course, a subject of heated dispute. Are these ethical concerns of the emerging global civil society whose spokespeople are usually international NGOs on the side of the 'guardian angels' in their concern to humanize global capital, or are they merely providing a new legitimation for western imperialist forces to claim global hegemony under post-war conditions; are they actually working for the 'global gangsters' (Wheeler, 1996)? This debate will be returned to in the next section where the political status of the global social reformist project is addressed.

In practical terms at present there are three instruments which have formally been adopted by the UN. The 1948 Universal Declaration of Human Rights was adopted without dissent. In 1966 the International Covenant on Civil and Political Rights and the International Covenant on Economic, Social and Cultural Rights were tabled and came into force in 1976 after they had been ratified by 35 countries. Humana has documented the extent to which these rights are adhered to and has reported 'an improvement over a five year period which is unparalleled in history' (1992: i). In compiling the guide he is dismissive of those who would argue the relativist case that some Muslim or other countries governed by religious laws do not, in practice, wish to be bound by these conventions. 'If the indicators have to bear the label of being Western liberal . . . then the guide will have to live with such criticism' (1992: 8).

In terms of socio-economic rights and, say, the right to social assistance these global conventions are silent, although the right to work is acknowledged. On the European level, of course, the Council of Europe's Social Charter is more explicit about this. The real issue is whether any practical meaning backed up by judicial force could be given to the idea of the right to social assistance. In terms of the global discourse on income maintenance that this study has documented, two futures are emerging. The safety net future with the right to a means tested social minimum, set at levels appropriate to the country, could be said to be the dominant global tendency. The alternative citizenship entitlement to an unconditional minimum income, again set at a level appropriate to the country, has many defenders (van Parijs, 1995; Purdy, 1996) and is included in the discussions of the experts advising international organizations.

It is not fanciful to suggest that some decades hence either the right to social assistance or the right to a mininium income could be enshrined as one of the global citizenship entitlements that the reformed UN system would expect its member states to uphold. In terms of steps on this road Katarina Tomasevski (1995) has argued for a human rights impact assessment to accompany Bank lending. This would parallel the environmental impact assessments agreed after the 1992 Rio conference. The Bank's concern to see established social assistance schemes as documented in the case studies in this book is seen by her as a move in this direction. In the longer run social citizenship rights of global citizens everywhere could be enhanced by a global social security pact (Green, 1995: 43–6) whereby resource transfers from richer countries (raised by the taxation systems discussed earlier) could take place to poorer countries on condition that these were used by governments to increase the access to livelihood of all citizens.

Empowering international civil society

Within the context of making the Bretton Woods institutions and/or the UN agencies more accountable a greater role is being argued for and given to international NGOs. 'Global governance . . . now involves not only governments and intergovernmental organisations but also non-governmental organisations, citizens' movements, transnational corporations, academia, and the mass media' (Commission on Global Governance, 1995: 35). The results of the post-Yugoslav case study in Chapter 5 and the critical appraisal of the role of NGOs in Rwanda (Milwood, 1996) suggests that this is not an unproblematic development. The elision between international civil society and NGOs begs questions about which elements of civil society are being 'represented' and which others effectively disempowered. The extent to which NGOs are increasingly dependent for their existence upon the funds of official intergovernmental organizations begs questions about their independence and autonomy. This challenges the simplistic view (Willets, 1996) that NGOs are the conscience of the world. The trend, however, to more NGO involvement is clear. In financial year 1994 50 per cent of World Bank projects had provision for NGO involvement. A principal element in the Bank's poverty strategy is to conduct poverty assessments and these increasingly involve participatory research projects with local NGOs. In the context of targeting resources on the most poor the Bank is stepping around the potentially corrupting obstacles of state agencies and delivering resources to localities.

The World Summit on Social Development and the previous and subsequent summits have been characterized by active NGO involvement in agenda setting. In the wake of the summit UNRISD (1995a: 25) analysed four approaches to summit follow-up within the international NGO community. These are developing alternative thinking, defining specific targets for implementation, establishing a non-governmental monitoring system, and lobbying for United Nations reform. The report cautions however against exaggerated claims that NGOs represent the poor at the grassroots: 'It is widely agreed that NGOs are often less accountable to the intended beneficiaries of their support than to their financial donors' (1995a: 34). Among some of the most determined defenders of the Economic and Social Council of the UN are NGOs who have won recognition rights from the Council. This NGO involvement has of course complicated the process of negotiation, agenda setting, and decision making in ECOSOC. In 1994 there were 980 NGOs accredited to ECOSOC. This could be one of the reasons why those impatient with the existing work of the UN in the economic field are calling for a streamlined Economic Security Council, and propose hiving off NGO involvement to an annual NGO assembly.

In this context Hirst and Thompson (1996: 191) have argued that the emerging form of global governance should be understood as one whereby states, even though they have ceded some powers to international organizations, continue to be important actors both in influencing international organization policy and in agreeing to implement such agreed supranational policy. Because of this the empowerment of global civil society in relation to global governance takes place partly through the traditional forms of national democratic accountability. International NGOs are here ascribed the role of informing such traditional electorates:

> Such representation is very indirect, but it is the closest to democracy and accountability that international governance is likely to get. The key publics in advanced democracies have some influence on their states and these states can affect international politics. Such influence is the more likely if populations of several major states are informed and aroused on an issue by the world 'Civil Society' of transnational non-governmental organisations. (1996: 191)

This approach differs sharply from the more visionary picture painted by Held (1995: 279) of a future cosmopolitan democracy whereby a global Parliament, with revenue raising capacity, shares global governance with an International Court which empowers global citizens to take their 'local' national governments to court if they deny them their basic citizenship rights which would include a 'guaranteed basic income for all adults' (1995: 280).

This section has not been able to do other than review briefly the global governance reform agenda. The details of the debates will change over the next decade but the themes are likely to remain the same. The calls for

greater social regulation of economic competition, for greater accountability of the international financial organizations, for reform in the UN,
for the strengthening of global political, legal and social rights, and for the
further empowerment of international civil society will increase and be
increasingly heard.

The politics of and prospects for global social reform

In the last paragraph of the study of the consequences for social policy of
the collapse of the Soviet and East European communist regimes, it was
asserted that

> Our conclusion is . . . not that in the struggle between capitalism and socialism
> capitalism has won . . . It is that socialist values and socialist welfare objectives
> can only be realised in any foreseeable future by struggling within capitalism to
> reform it in the interests of human needs. It is also that this struggle now has as
> an urgent priority a transnational and global dimension in the interests of
> socialist welfare objectives East and West, North and South. (Deacon, 1992: 191)

This study of the contending influences of supranational organizations on
the making of post-communist social policy has only served to reinforce
this conclusion. There is now a global social policy, constituted of global
redistributive mechanisms, global regulatory mechanisms, elements of
global provision and empowerment, and a shifting discourse concerning the
future of national social policy. Within this expanded framework of policy
making those with socialist values have to play a part and assert a project.
Implicit throughout this text has been our preference for a global social
reformist project which would call for more rather than less redistribution
of resources between states, for more rather than less global social and
labour regulation as a framework for the operation of corporations, for
more rather than less authority to be given to supranational bodies to
intervene in the affairs of states when those states fail their citizens, and for
the prescriptions being offered countries concerning their social policy by
global organizations to reflect the values of solidarity, inclusion and justice
rather than individualism and competitiveness. This global social reformist
project recognizes the interconnectedness of the different elements. There
should be no free trade without global social regulation. There should
be no global social regulation without global social redistribution. To
ensure global citizens (and not their governments) benefit there should be
no global social redistribution without the empowerment of citizens before
a global court of social rights. Trade, regulation, redistribution and
empowerment go hand in hand.

Such a global social reformist project has to be defended against its
critics. The challenges would seem to come in five guises. First, the socialist
fundamentalists see it merely as a project for the legitimation of an
exploitative and imperialist global capitalism and as having nothing to do

with a socialist challenge to it. Secondly, the post-modern relativists see it as a denial of difference and diversity and the imposition of a western set of prejudices upon dissenting others. Thirdly, the deep-entrist technicians of the global epistemic communities prefer to reform from within by stealth rather than explicate the political value choices being made in the practice of their skills. Fourthly, a variety of sources implicitly or explicitly believe that the globalization case has been overstated and that the immediate priorities of political economy and political movements remain national in both North and South. Fifthly, there are those who believe, to the contrary, that globalism has not been overstated but rather that its logic is now so strong that it will in its wake destroy any remnant of a civilizing project based on the belief in the possibilities of transnational citizenship. In exploring the positions of these critics some attempt is made below to theorize the supranational and global social forces and processes that might enable us to analyse the possibilities for the making of a global reformist social policy. Ideas introduced in Chapter 2 are developed further.

Vaclav Havel (1994) has argued that

> Today more than ever before in the history of mankind, everything is inter-related. Therefore the values and prospects of contemporary civilization are everywhere subject to great tensions . . . the future of Europe is being decided in the suffering in Sarajevo . . . in the wretched poverty in Bangladesh . . . Theor-etically almost everybody knows this. But how does this knowledge find expression in practical policies? . . . People today know that they can only be saved by a new type of global responsibility.

From within the framework of a Gramscian analysis Cox has argued that for a global counter-hegemonic project to be built (counter, that is to the ravages of liberal global capitalism) 'the existing globalisation grounded in the economic logic of markets would have to be countered by a new globalisation re-embedding the economy in global society' (1993: 273). In the same volume he reminds us that 'world hegemony is described as a social structure, an economic structure, and a political . . . structure . . . and is expressed in universal norms, institutions and mechanisms which lay down general rules of behaviour for states and those forces of civil society, that act across national boundaries' (1993: 62). In a related essay on global hegemony and the structural power of capitalism it is suggested by Gill and Law (1993) that an embryo of a counter-hegemonic bloc exists in the form of Amnesty International, Greenpeace, Oxfam and the World Council of Churches. For this to be developed further Islamic involvement would, they argue, be essential but unlikely. In the same volume Arrighi (1993) con-cludes that each successive hegemonic state has become less capitalist: 'the next hegemone would have to be world social democracy.'

Within this framework the question about global social reformism could be reformulated:

1   Is the prospect of a global hegemonic social democratic project desirable?

2   Is it feasible? What are the obstacles?
3   Where does the discourse within and between the global institutions fit in?

Is the prospect of a global social democratic project desirable?

One of the founding fathers of Fabian social policy analysis and long standing campaigner for social democracy within the UK clearly believes the project is necessary and desirable. Townsend argues:

> The problems of the industrial revolution and exploitative forms of capitalism led in the late nineteenth century to the establishment of the welfare state in one country after another. The problems in the late twentieth century of the international market and the replacement of sovereignty and empire by international hierarchical power will demand the establishment of forms of an international welfare state. (1995: 20)

While the form that this international welfare state might take can and is being argued about (a citizenship income model versus a safety net and provident fund model) its defenders are many. Van Parijs has similarly concluded that the

> Key issues for the future are rather whether, when, and how one should introduce an unconditional basic income, attribute redistributive powers to supranational authorities, or constrain the organisation of social life so as to nurture feelings of solidarity. These are the issues around which the crucial struggles of the future will be fought. (1995: 232)

The epistemological framework of this book, of Townsend, of van Parijs and of others is clearly one that is situated within the camp of the liberal seekers after truth, as distinct from the relativists and the fundamentalists (Gellner, 1992). It is a framework that implies that, far from having been exhausted, the modernist project should and will continue and that, in the spirit of Margaret Archer's address to the International Sociological Association in 1992, this project is on the side of enlightened humanity not relativism (McGrew et al., 1993). If postmodernism has drawn our attention to diversity and difference and fractured our fundamentalist belief in the inevitable social progress accompanying the defence of working class interests, it has equally obliged us to rediscover our values (Squires, 1993).

In the concluding essay in *Gramsci, Historical Materialism, and International Relations* (Gill, 1993) the case appears to be put by Cox (1993) for departing from this search for a progressive global hegemony. Europe, he argues, 'could be a proving ground for a new form of world order: post-hegemonic in its recognition of co-existing universalistic civilisations; post-Westphalian in its restructuring of political authority into a multi-level system; and post-globalisation in its acceptance of legitimacy of different paths towards the satisfaction of human needs' (1993: 286). Duffield (1996a) has noticed also how the celebration of difference and the focus on the politics of identity among western intellectuals has led to a questioning of the very idea of an agreed path of future social development. The response to this has to be that respect for cultural diversity, and respect for the right to seek different paths towards human needs, does not, we believe, mean endorsing inhumanity, accepting injustice, or denying people's rights to a creative and full life. To uphold these things in a globalized world calls precisely for a global ethic, a global regulatory authority, a global process of ironing out injustice, and the right of legitimate global authority to intervene when cultural differences become an excuse for the blocking for individuals of access to the emerging rights of global citizens. The global social reformist project stands or falls by these universal values.

Is it feasible? What are the obstacles?

For some the globalization process destroys any possibility of reconstructing social citizenship bonds at a supranational level and weakens those at a national level. Jordan (forthcoming) concludes that

> Far from implying further collectivisation in transnational units, globalisation might instead signal serious problems for existing collective institutions, at the international as well as the national level, and especially over social policy issues. The global citizen of the next century might be a sovereign bargain hunter in search of his or her most favoured bundle of collective goods, available through the development of private sites by landlords in partnership with minimalist local authorities. Such contractual communities would allow comfortable households to move between self selecting, homogeneous income zones, leaving a residuum in 'communities of fate' under the authoritative regime of private contractors of a Benthamite complexion. The result would be a mediaeval landscape of free (but walled) citadels, separated by a wasteland of panopticons and predation.

A weaker version of this pessimistic scenario is provided by Duffield (1996a) who suggests the world is becoming divided into zones of stability where normal social policy reigns and zones of instability where globalized NGOs now substitute for normal social policy.

Ranged against this pessimism is only theory that still posits a place for collective social actors at a transnational level constraining individualism, for global discourses that embody international and transnational obligations and for the hope that a transnational political will, capable of overcoming the preoccupations of narrow national populist political leaders and uniting the diversity of different cultures, can prevail. Democracy when giving expression to national self-interest subglobal regional trading competition fostering cost cutting and exclusion, diversity and difference problematizing global social progress, and the limits of ecologically sustainable development are all part of the web and substance of contemporary global politics. Their existence does not necessarily preclude transnational rational solutions.

Comparative social policy has, as we discussed in Chapter 2, made a significant contribution to understanding the forces and discourses shaping diversity in national social policy through its use of the analytical frame-work of class, nation and family (Williams, 1987; 1995). Ginsburg's (1992) account that the diversity of developed western welfare states reflected different dynamics within a racially structured and patriarchal capitalism was plausible. Welfare settlements of different kinds emerged, as Williams argues, from 'the state's relationship to the specific and interrelated organisations, conditions, current and historic social relations of *power, discursive practices*, and forms of *mobilization* associated with *family, nation*, and *work*' (1995: 148). The emerging new global welfare settlement, whether it is to take the form of a social liberal safety net with provident funds or of a purchasing power parity citizenship income, will emerge out of comparable power struggles, discursive practices and forms of mobilization at the supranational level. The settlement will reflect global power relations of capital and labour (Lipow, 1994), even if global labour can now be fractionalized into the over-consumers, the sustainables and the marginals (Brown, 1995); the global gender struggles that could unite northern female consumers and southern female workers even as they wrestle with diversity (Grant and Newland, 1991); and the globalized ethnic conflicts reflected in stronger migration pressures and tightening asylum regulations (Harris, 1996). The emerging global discursive practices and movements around labour and its future (together with ecologically associated issues); around family and the global limits that might be set to its diversity on the way it treats its members; and around nation and the extent to which its rights to sovereignty over its citizens should be subsumed to a greater global civil ethic will also shape this future global welfare settlement. This, as we shall note in the last section, is a rich field for future analysis and research, and transnational political practice. The prospects for the global social reformist project will be settled by these power struggles, discourses, and movements.

Where does the discourse within and between global organizations fit in?

For some (Gowan, 1996) global financial institutions remain the un-ashamed accomplices of global economic imperialism, helping to subjugate the whole of humanity to the demands of markets and accumulation. Their contribution to the post-communist transition boiled down to imposition of neo-liberal theory and practice on Eastern Europe. The heated contest of policy alternatives between an old-style cut-throat liberalism, a more humane social safety net liberalism, and the solidaristic orientations of a European social policy passed such commentators by. Global capitalism is evil, and it makes little difference whether it is humanely regulated or not. Challenging this kind of fundamentalism, we argue that in the wake of the collapse of 'communism' socialist transformation is not on the foreseeable practical political agenda, and even if it were, it does make a difference as to what kind of capitalism we live under. The contest for the kind of global capitalism we are to inhabit in the next century *is* being struggled over not only by labour and social movements but also with the tools of discursive practice employed by global human resource specialists, global social security experts and the global poverty/development lobby (Figure 6.1).

A challenge, argued Cox as we noted earlier, to the hegemony of global liberal capitalism cannot be built within the existing international organizations: 'One tactic for bringing about change in the structure of world order can be ruled out as total illusion. There is very little likelihood of a war of movement at the international level . . . These superstructures are inadequately connected with any popular political base' (1993: 62–4). The empirical evidence of this book suggests to the contrary, that a war of positions (albeit only positions between cut-throat and humane capital – but what else matters right now?) *is* being fought within and between international organizations; that through the support given to labour movements and their representatives in ministries of labour in some post-communist countries by those, certainly in the ILO and to some extent in the World Bank, a connection to local social forces can be developed; and that international non-governmental organizations and their complex connections to local civil society are part of this war of positions. Whereas Cox would, for example, write off the ILO in that 'by advocating tripartism [it] legitimates the social relations evolved in the core countries as the desirable model for emulation' (1993: 63), this study has shown how the ILO acts as a bulwark against the fiscalization of welfare precisely because it builds tripartite forms of governance. That is not, of course, to set aside the problems the ILO has in generalizing its ideas in a new flexible global economy. For Cox (1993: 65) the task of changing world orders begins with the long laborious effort to build new historic blocks within national boundaries. For us the task of socializing the capitalist world order requires this project of alliance building to be also transnational and for it to utilize the tactic of struggle within and against the emerging institutions of global governance.

In sum, we can give the following answers to the five kinds of criticism of the global social reformist project. To the socialist fundamentalists, we argue that a socially regulated global capitalism is preferable to an unregulated one and those with socialist values should work for such regulation. To post-modern relativists, we merely assert socialist values above those of the celebration of diversity and difference when this becomes an excuse for the denial of human social rights. To the global epistemic communities who would want to confine their discussions within the international organiz-ations they inhabit, we argue the need to build alliances and make connec-tions between their discursive practices and transnational power struggles and social movements. To those who believe that the locus of the struggle of interests and ideas continues to be primarily at the national level, we offer the evidence of the research reported in this book. Finally, to those who believe globalism will destroy any remnant of a civilizing project, we ask what motivates their work.

A research agenda for supranational social policy analysis

This book has drawn attention to the ways in which social policy within countries is shaped by economic forces, social actors, political and financial institutions, and discursive practices that are global in their reach. It has conceptualized the emerging subject area of global social policy constituted of the practices of global redistribution, global regulation and global provision and empowerment.

It has not argued that this expanded terrain of social policy analysis has to jettison the conceptual and analytic tools that have served the subject area well. Concepts such as social citizenship merely become more multi-layered when analysed within a transnational framework. Struggles and discourses around class, gender and nation merely become that much more complex to observe and make sense of at a global level. The analysis of policy decisions merely becomes complicated by the addition of supranational layers and spheres of influence involved. The dialogue that social policy as a subject has always had with political science, sociology, and political economy needs to encompass development studies and international relations. The value choices that many in social policy writing have always identified with need to be recast onto a global terrain. The battle between and the search for any common ground between individualism, social reformism, Marxism, feminism and black perspectives remain relevant to the emerging political project of regulating global capital.

If, as we have seen, the framework within which future comparative social policy analysis might be structured is that of the 'state's relationship to the . . . social relations of power, discursive practices, and forms of mobilization associated with family, nation, and work' (Williams, 1995: 148) then the framework within which future global social policy analysis might be structured is that of the supranational organization's relationships to the global social relations of power, global discursive practices and global forms of mobilization associated with family, nation and work.

Global struggles between capital and labour, between genders and between different ethnicities, global mobilizations around these conflicts of interest, and global discourses regarding the globally acceptable forms of family life, the globally accepted divisions of power between nations, and the supranational, globally contested conceptions of the future of work would form part of the analytic framework. A study begun in early 1996 at the University of Sussex, which is researching the relations between international feminism and the World Bank, between international labour movements and the World Trade Organization, and between other transnational social movements and the IMF, would seem to be of the kind that is required.

A rich future for global and supranational social policy research and analysis lies ahead. With appropriate interdisciplinary collaboration with those in development studies, international relations and political economy, all of the following ideas, which develop aspects of the work reported in this book, commend themselves as worthy of urgent attention.

1   Conflicting discourses concerning work, family and nation and the implications for social policy as articulated by western liberalism and Islam need to be examined. A major omission in the book has been the contending influences on social policy of liberal and Islamic influenced supranational institutions. A study in a region such as the southern Balkans or Central Asia could overcome this lacuna.

2   The emergent supranational social policy of regional trade blocs requires investigation. While a sharp contrast between the socially regulatory approach of the EU and the deregulatory approach of NAFTA has been focused on in Chapter 3, little has been researched systematically about competing ideas regarding the level of transnational social regulation appropriate in East and South East Asia and elsewhere.

3   The implicit and explicit policy proposals in the sphere of income maintenance, health, education and other social policies of the increasingly important international NGOs require codification. Their role, especially in zones of instability and their contribution to the global policy discourse have been noted but the content of their social policy prescriptions has been little analysed and even less regulated.

4   Given the tendency, noted in this book, for transnational social policy to become depoliticized because of the role played by consultancy companies in advising government, a major study is required of the value frameworks and policy prescriptions of the major international firms and consortia active in this field. Their role in PHARE and TACIS especially deserve attention.

5   Increased migration for economic and political reasons has generated a set of pressures on citizenship laws, and a set of problems concerning the rights to and social consequences of asylum seeking. Social policy analysts need to work with refugee studies experts to divine the emerging practices in this field. At the same time the impact on national social policy making of the diaspora is an under-researched topic. The emerging practice of funding repatriation is clearly a new transnational social policy of importance and equally under-researched.

6   The value scale associated with the analytical and policy continuum from apartheid, through assimilation and multiculturalism, to anti-racism which has dominated social policy analysis has come under sharp challenge in the post-Yugoslav case studies highlighted in this book. In working for a cosmopolitan multiculturalism, western international agencies have chosen not to work for a peaceable ethnic separation. The detailed social policy measures associated with a renewed ethnical nationalism call for further study and evaluation.

7   The tools of actuarial analysis so far used to fashion income transfer and maintenance schemes within one country should now be put to

better use in fashioning transnational income transfer schemes. The scale of global taxation needed to ensure such rich country to poor country transfers to fund minimum income entitlements should not be unrealistic. The political pressures for such reforms are being generated by migration. The altruistic wish to alleviate poverty is evidenced by charitable schemes that adopt a child or a granny. The science of actuarial analysis would help bring this element of transnational social policy out of the era of fluctuating charitable dependence and into the era of global social citizenship entitlement.

Global social policy research and analysis and the fashioning of global social justice should commend themselves to the emerging generation of social policy scholars.

Bibliography

Adams, R. and Kingsbury, B. (eds) (1993) *United Nations, Divided World*. Oxford: Clarendon Press.

Adiin-Yaanshah, E. (1995) *An Analysis of Domestic Legislation to Regulate the Activities of Local and Foreign NGOs in Croatia, Kenya, Rwanda and Uganda*. Oxford: RSP and Centre for Socio-Legal Studies.

Adiin-Yaanshah, E. and Harrell-Bond, B. (1995) 'Regulating the Non-Governmental Sector', *Refugee Participation Network*, 19: 4–9.

Adler, E. and Haas, P. (1992) 'Epistemic Communities, World Order and the Creation of a Reflective Research Programme', *International Organisation*, 46(1).

African Rights (1994) 'Humanitarianism Unbound? Current Dilemmas Facing Multi-National Relief Organisations in Political Emergencies'. African Rights Discussion Paper 5.

Ahmad, S.E. (1993) 'Poverty, Demographic Characteristics and Public Policy in C.I.S. Countries'. IMF Working Paper WP/93/9, IMF, Washington.

Ahmad, S.E. and Schneider, J.-L. (1993) 'Alternative Social Security Systems in C.I.S. Countries'. IMF Working Paper WP/93/8, IMF, Washington.

Alexandrova, D. (1992) 'The World Bank Sets Terms', *The Insider*, Bulgarian Monthly Digest, no. 5.

Allcock, J. et al. (1992) 'Introduction', in J. Allcock, J. Horton and M. Milivojevic (eds), *Yugoslavia in Transition: Essays in Honour of Fred Singleton*. New York: Berg.

Andor, L. (1995) 'The Role of the Debt Crisis in Hungary's Transition', *Labour Forum on Eastern Europe*, no. 54.

Archer, M. (1991) 'Sociology for One World: Unity and Diversity', *International Sociology*, 6(2).

Arrighi, G. (1993) 'The Three Hegomones of Historical Capitalism', in S. Gill (ed.), *Gramsci, Historical Materialism and International Relations*. Cambridge: Cambridge University Press.

Atkinson, A.B. (1995) *Incomes and the Welfare States: Essays on Britain and Europe*. Cambridge: Cambridge University Press.

Atkinson, A.B. and Micklewright, J. (1992) *Economic Transformation in Eastern Europe and the Distribution of Income*. Cambridge: Cambridge University Press.

Atkinson, A.B. and Morgensen, G.V. (1993) *Welfare and Work Incentives*. Oxford: Clarendon Press.

Baehr, D.R. and Gordenker, L. (1994) *The United Nations in the 1990s*. London: Macmillan.

Barr, N. (ed.) (1994) *Labour Markets and Social Policy in Central and Eastern Europe: The Transition and Beyond*. Oxford: Oxford University Press.

Barratt Brown, M. (1993) *Fair Trade: Reform and Realities in the International Trading System*. London and New Jersey: Zed.

Barre, R., Luers, W.H., Solomon, A. and Ners, K.J. (1992) *Moving Beyond Assistance*. Final Report of the IEWS Task Force on Western Assistance to Transition in the Czech and Slovak Federal Republic, Hungary and Poland. Institute of East–West Studies, European Studies Center, New York and Prague.

Baubock, R. (1994) *Transnational Citizenship*. Cheltenham: Edward Elgar.

Bauman, Z.(1991) *Intimations of Postmodernity*. London: Routledge.

Bauman, Z. (1993) *Postmodern Ethics*. Oxford: Blackwell.

Beattie, R. and McGillivray, W. (1995) 'A Risky Strategy: Reflections on the World Bank Report *Averting the Old Age Crisis*', *International Social Security Review*, 48(3/4).

Beck J. (1995) 'Winners and Losers of the Transition: Roma in the Czech Republic', *HCA Quarterly*, no. 13.

Beleva, I., Bobeva, D., Dilova, S. and Mitchkovski, A. (1991) 'Labour Market, Social Policy and Industrial Relations: A Report on Bulgaria'. OCDE/ILO/GD(91)131, ILO, Geneva.

Beleva, I.S. et al. (1993) *Bulgaria and the European Community: The Transformation of the Labour Market and Social Policy: A View towards Europe*. ACE Programme of the European Commission.

Benson, C. and Clay, E. (1992) *Eastern Europe and the Former Soviet Union: Economic Change, Social Welfare and Aid*. ODI Special Report. London: Overseas Development Institute.

Bienkowski, W. (1992) 'Can Poland Deviate from IMF Requirements?', *RFE/RL Research Report*, 1(31).

Bird, G. (1991) *The IMF in the 1990s: Forward to the Past or Back to the Future?* ODI Working Paper 46. London: Overseas Development Institute.

Bird, G. (1992) *Economic Reform in Eastern Europe*. Cheltenham: Edward Elgar.

Blackburn, R. (ed.) (1990) *Restructuring the Labour Market*. London: Macmillan.

Blaho, A. (1994) *Russian Transition – Chinese Reforms: A Comparative View*. Helsinki: WIDER of United Nations University.

Blank, R.M. (1994) *Social Protection versus Economic Flexibility*. Chicago: University of Chicago Press.

Boardman, R. (1994) *Post-Socialist World Orders: Russia, China and the UN System*. London: Macmillan.

Bobeva, D. (1993) 'Labour Market Policy in Bulgaria'. Paper contributed to Technical Workshop on the Persistence of Unemployment in Central and Eastern Europe, OECD CCET, 30 September to 2 October.

Boeri, T. and Sziraczki, G. (1993) 'Labour Market Developments and Policies in Central and Eastern Europe: A Comparative Analysis', in OCED CCET, *Structural Change in Central and Eastern Europe: Labour Market and Social Policy Implications*. Paris: OECD.

Bohm, A. and Simoneti, M. (1993) *Privatization in Central and Eastern Europe*. Central and Eastern European Privatization Network with UNDP, PHARE and the Economic Development Institute of the World Bank, Ljubljana, Slovenia.

Bojcun, M. (1995) 'Ukraine under Kuchma', *Labour Focus on Eastern Europe*, no. 54.

Bonanate, L. (1995) *Ethics and International Politics*. Cambridge: Polity.

Brandt, W. (chairman) (1980) *North–South: A Programme for Survival*. Brandt Report. London: Pan.

Brown, B.S. (1991) *The US and the Politicization of the World Bank*. London: Kegan Paul.

Brown, L.R. (1995) *State of the World 1995: A World Watch Institute Report on Progress toward Sustainable Society*. London: Earthscan.

Bruno, M. (1992) *Stabilization and Reform in Eastern Europe: A Preliminary Evaluation*. IMF Staff Papers, vol. 39, no. 4.

Bruszt, L. (1992) 'Transformative Politics: Social Costs and Social Peace in East Central Europe', *East European Politics and Societies*, 6(1).

Burley, A.-M. (1993) 'Regulating the World: Multilateral International Law and the Protection of the New Deal Regulatory State', in J.G. Ruggi (ed.), *Multilateralism Matters*. New York: Columbia University Press.

Burrows, R. and Loader, B. (eds) (1994) *Towards a Post-Fordist Welfare State*. London. Routledge.

Buus Jensen, S. (1994) 'Psycho-Social Stress and Protective Factors in Families under War Conditions and Peace-Building in former Yugoslavia', in L. Archel (ed.), *War Victims, Trauma and Psycho-Social Care*. Zagreb: ECTF.

Camdessus, M. (1995) Address to the World Summit on Social Development by M. Camdessus, Managing Director of IMF. 7 March.

Camillieri, J.A. and Falk, J. (1992) *The End of Sovereignty*. Cheltenham: Edward Elgar.

Carnoy, M. et al. (1993) *The New Global Economy: Reflections on Our Changing World*. Pennsylvania: Pennsylvania State University Press.

Castles, F. (1993) *Families of Nations*. Aldershot: Dartmouth.

Castles, F. and Mitchell, D. (1990) *Three Worlds of Welfare Capitalism or Four?* Public Policy Discussion Paper no. 21. Canberra: Australia National University.

Castles, S. and Miller, M. (1993) *The Age of Migration: International Population Movements in the Modern World*. London: Macmillan.

Cavanagh, J. et al. (eds) (1994) *Beyond Bretton Woods: Alternatives to the Global Economic Order*. London: Pluto.

Chadha, B., Coricelli, F. and Krajnyak, K. (1993) 'Economic Restructuring, Unemployment and Growth in a Transition Economy'. IMF Working Paper WP/93/16, IMF, Washington.

Chand, S.K. and Shome, P. (1995) 'Poverty Alleviation in a Financial Programming Framework: an Integrated Approach'. IMF Working Paper WP/95/29, Fiscal Affairs Department, IMF, Washington.

Chandler, D. (1996) 'The Internationalisation of Minority Rights Protection in East Europe: an example of How the Globalisation Thesis recreates the East/West Divide'. Paper presented to the Annual Conference of the UK Political Studies Association, March.

Chomsky, A.N. (1993) *Year 501: the Conquest Continues*. London and New York: Verso.

Chu, K. and Gupta, S. (1993) 'Protecting the Poor: Social Safety Nets during Transition', *Finance and Development*, 30(2).

Cichon, M. (1994a) 'Financing Social Protection in Central and East Europe: Safeguarding Political and Economic Change', in *Restructuring Social Security in Central and Eastern Europe*. Geneva: ILO.

Cichon, M. (1994b) 'Social Protection in Transition Economies: From Improvisation to Social Concepts'. Policy Discussion Paper, ILO, Geneva.

Cichon, M. (ed.) (1995) 'Social Protection in the Visegrad Countries: Four Country Profiles'. ILO CEET Report 13, Budapest.

Cichon, M. (1996) 'The Ageing Debate in Social Security: Barking Up the Wrong Tree'. Unpublished manuscript, ILO, Geneva.

Cichon, M. and Samuel, L. (eds) (1995) *Making Social Protection Work: The Challenge of Tripartism in Social Governance for Countries in Transition*. Budapest: ILO CEET.

Clark, J. (1991) *Democratizing Development*. London: Earthscan.

Cleary, S. (1996) 'The World Bank and NGOs', in P. Willets, (ed.), *The Conscience of the World*. Washington: Brookings Institute.

Closa, C. (1995) 'Some Sceptical Remarks on the Solidarity Dimension of the Citizenship of the E.U.'. Paper presented to Conference, 'A New Social Contract?', Robert Schuman Centre, European University Institute, 5–6 October.

Close, P. (1995) *Citizenship, Europe and Change*. London: Macmillan.

Coble, R. (1995) 'The Role of Non Profit Organisations in Emerging Democracies'. Mimeo, North Carolina Center for Public Policy Research.

Coenen, H. and Leisink, P. (1993) *Work and Citizenship in the New Europe*. Cheltenham: Edward Elgar.

Cohen, L. (1993) *Broken Bonds: The Disintegration of Yugoslavia*. Boulder, CO: Westview.

Collingworth, T. et al. (1994) 'Time for a New Global Deal', *Foreign Affairs*, 73(1).

Commander, S. and Coricelli, F. (eds) (1995) *Unemployment, Restructuring and the Labour Market in Eastern Europe and Russia*. Washington: World Bank.

Commission on Global Governance (1995) *Our Global Neighbourhood*. Oxford: University Press.

Cornia, G. (1994) 'Income Distribution, Poverty and Welfare in Transitional Economies: A comparison between Eastern Europe and China'. UNICEF Occasional Papers, Economic Policy Series 44.

Cornia, G., Jolly, R. and Stewart, F. (1987) *Adjustment with a Human Face*. Oxford: Clarendon Press.

Cornia, G. and Sipos, S. (1991) *Children and the Transition to the Market Economy: Safety Nets and Social Policies in Central and Eastern Europe*. Aldershot: Avebury.

Council of Europe (1992a) *The European Social Charter*. Strasbourg: Council of Europe.

Council of Europe (1992b) *European Co-operation on Social and Family Policy*. RS-Inf (92) 1 rev. Strasbourg: Council of Europe.

Council of Europe (1992c) *Project III.8 'Childhood Policies'*. CDPS III.8 (93) 21. Strasbourg: Council of Europe.

Council of Europe (1992d) *Parliamentary Assembly Report on the Application by the Republic of Bulgaria for Membership of the Council of Europe*. Doc. 6591. Strasbourg: Council of Europe.

Council of Europe (1992e) *The Council of Europe's Co-operation and Assistance Programmes with Central and Eastern European Countries in the Human Rights Field: Annual Report for 1991*. SG/INF(91)4. Strasbourg: Council of Europe.

Council of Europe (1993a) *Specific Recommendations as to How a European Report on Poverty and Social Exclusion Might Be Carried Out*. Report by Hugh Frazer, Director of the Combat Poverty Agency, Dublin, CDPS III.5 (93)2. Strasbourg: Council of Europe.

Council of Europe (1993b) *Parliamentary Assembly Report on the Application by the Czech Republic for Membership of the Council of Europe*. Doc. 6855. Strasbourg: Council of Europe.

Council of Europe (1993c) *Parliamentary Assembly Report on the Application by the Slovak Republic for Membership of the Council of Europe*. Doc. 6864. Strasbourg: Council of Europe.

Council of Europe (1993d) *The Council of Europe's Co-operation and Assistance Programmes with Central and Eastern European Countries in the Human Rights Field*. H(93)1. Strasbourg: Council of Europe.

Council of Europe (1993e) *The Council of Europe's Co-operation and Assistance Programmes with Central and Eastern European Countries in the Human Rights Field: Synopsis of Projects*. SG/INF (93)1. Strasbourg: Council of Europe.

Council of Europe (1993f) *The Council of Europe's Co-operation and Assistance Programmes with Central and Eastern European Countries in the Human Rights Field: Annual Report for 1992*. SG/INF (93)1. Strasbourg: Council of Europe.

Council of Europe (1995a) *The Council of Europe: Achievements and Activities*. Strasbourg: Council of Europe.

Council of Europe (1995b) *Draft European Convention on the Exercise of Children's Rights and Explanatory Report*. DIR/JUR (95)12. Strasbourg: Council of Europe.

Council of Europe (1995c) 'Committee of Experts on the Promotion of Standard Setting Instruments'. EM PIN (95)5, Directorate of Social and Economic Affairs. Council of Europe, Strasbourg.

Cox, R.W. (1993) 'Structural Issues of Global Governance: Implications for Europe', in S. Gill (ed.), *Gramsci, Historical Materialism and International Relations*. Cambridge: Cambridge University Press.

Cox, R.W. et al. (1995) *Understanding Global Disorder*. London and New Jersey: Zed.

Davidson, S. (1993) 'The European System for Protecting Human Rights', in S. Davidson (ed.), *Human Rights*. Oxford: Oxford University Press with the Open University.

Davis, H. and Scase, R. (1985) *Communist Political Systems*. New York: St Martin's.

Deacon, B. (1983) *Social Policy and Socialism: The Struggle for Socialist Relations of Welfare*. London: Pluto.

Deacon. B. (1992) *The New Eastern Europe: Social Policy – Past, Present and Future*. London: Sage.

Deacon, B. (1994) 'Global Social Policy and the Shaping of Post-Communist Social Policy', in A. de Swann (ed.), *Social Policy beyond Borders*. Amsterdam: Amsterdam University Press.

Deacon, B. (1995) 'The Experience of Social Security Reform in Eastern Europe and the Former Soviet Union: Some Considerations of its Relevance to China'. Paper presented to a Workshop on the Reform of the Labour System of China, Beijing, October.

Deacon, B. et al. (1996) 'Action for Social Change: A New Facet of Preventative Peace Keeping'. Report for UNPREDEP, Helsinki: National Research and Development Centre for Welfare and Health, STAKES.

Deacon, B., Stubbs, P. and Soroya, B. (1994) 'Globalizacija, Postkuminizam i Socijalna

Politka: teme na Hrvatskoj', (Globalization, Post-communism and Social Policy: Issues in Croatia), *Revija za Socijalnu Politiku*, 1(4): 33–8.

Deacon, B. and Szalai, J. (eds) (1990) *Social Policy in the New Eastern Europe: What Future for Socialist Welfare?* Aldershot: Avebury.

Deacon, B. and Vidinova, A. (1992) 'Social Policy in Bulgaria', in Deacon, B. (ed.), *The New Eastern Europe: Social Policy – Past, Present and Future.* London: Sage.

Dean H. and Khan, Z. (1995) 'Muslim Perspectives on Welfare'. Paper presented at the Annual Conference of the Social Policy Association, Sheffield Hallam University, 18–20 July.

Denitch, B. (1994) *Ethnic Nationalism: The Tragic Death of Yugoslavia.* Minneapolis: University of Minneapolis Press.

Denitch, B. (1995) 'National Identity Politics and Democracy'. Paper presented to Conference on Identity, the Other and Democracy, Ljubljana, May.

de Senarclens, P. (1993) 'Regime Theory and the Study of International Organizations', *International Social Science Journal*, 138 (November).

de Swann, A. (1994) 'Perspectives for Transnational Social Policy in Europe: Social Transfers from West to East', in A. de Swann (ed.), *Social Policy Beyond Borders.* Amsterdam: Amsterdam University Press.

de Swann, A. (undated) 'The Sociological Study of Transnational Society'. Paper in progress, PdIS, Amsterdam School for Social Research.

de Vries, B.A. (1996) 'The World Bank's Focus on Poverty', in J.M. Griesgraber and B.G. Gunter (eds), *The World Bank.* London: Pluto.

Deutsch, K.W. (1981) 'From the National Welfare State to the International Welfare System', in W.J. Mommsen (ed.), *The Emergence of the Welfare State in Britain and Germany.* London: Croom Helm.

Doyal, L. and Gough, I. (1991) *A Theory of Human Needs.* London: Macmillan.

Doyal, L. and Gough, I. (1994) Isaac Deutscher Memorial Lecture, LSE.

Duffield, M. (1994) *Complex Political Emergencies: An Exploratory Report for UNICEF with Reference to Angola and Bosnia.* Birmingham: School of Public Policy, University of Birmingham.

Duffield, M. (1996a) 'The Symphony of the Damned: Racial Discourse, Complex Political Emergencies and Humanitarian Aid'. Occasional Paper 2, School of Public Policy, University of Birmingham.

Duffield, M. (1996b) 'The Globalisation of Public Policy'. Mimeo, University of Birmingham, Centre for Urban and Regional Studies.

Elkins, P. (1992) *New World Order: Grass Roots Movements for Global Change.* London: Routledge.

Elliott, S. (1993) 'Local and Western NGOs: Partnerships or Exploitation?', *War Report*, no. 22.

Esping-Andersen, G. (1990) *The Three Worlds of Welfare Capitalism.* Cambridge: Polity.

Esping-Andersen, G. (1994) 'After the Golden Age: The Future of the Welfare State in the New Global Order'. Synthesis paper for UNRISD for the World Summit on Social Development, March 1995.

Esping-Andersen, G. (1996) *Welfare States in Transition.* London: Sage.

Esty, D.C. (1994) *Greening the Gatt: Trade, Environment and the Future.* Washington: Institute for International Economics.

European Centre Vienna (1993) *Welfare in a Civil Society.* Report for the Conference of European Ministers Responsible for Social Affairs, Bratislava, 28 June to 2 July.

European Commission (1992a) *PHARE 1992 Operational Programmes: Hungary.* Brussels: European Commission.

European Commission (1992b) *PHARE 1992 Employment and Social Development: Financing Memorandum: Hungary.* Brussels: European Commission.

European Commission (1993a) *Growth, Competitiveness and Employment: The Challenges and Ways Forward into the 21st Century.* Brussels: European Commission.

European Commission (1993b) *European Social Policy: Options for the Union*. Green Paper COM (93) 551. Brussels: European Commission.

European Commission (1993c) *PHARE 1992 Indicative Programmes: Hungary*. Brussels: European Commission.

European Commission (1994a) *European Social Policy: A Way Forward for the Union*. White Paper COM (94) 333. Brussels: European Commission.

European Commission (1994b) *PHARE Hungary Orientations Paper*. Brussels: European Commission.

European Commission (1994c) 'TACIS Activities in Ukraine'. Report by the TACIS Information Office, Kiev.

European Commission (1995a) *The Future of Social Protection: A Framework for Debate*. COM/95/466. Brussels: European Commission.

European Commission (1995b) *Social Protection in Europe*. Brussels: European Commission.

European Commission (1995c) *Co-operation Programme between the European Union and the Republic of Hungary*. PHARE. Brussels: European Commission.

European Commission (1996) 'TACIS'. Report of the Tacis Conference on Employment, Brussels, 1995. Brussels.

European Community (1990) *Framework Agreement between the Commission of the E.C. and the Government of the Republic of Hungary for the PHARE Assistance Programme by the E.E.C. to the Republic of Hungary*. Brussels: European Commission.

European Union (1995) Contribution to the World Summit on Social Development, March, 1995. Doc 94/669. Brussels.

Fajth, G. (1994) 'Family Support Policies in Transitional Economies: Challenges and Contrasts'. UNICEF International CDC, Economic Policy Series 43.

Featherstone, M. (1990) *Global Culture: Nationalism, Globalization and Modernity*. London: Sage.

Ferge, Z. (1991) 'Recent Trends in Social Policy in Hungary', in J. Adam (ed.), *Economic Reforms and Welfare Systems in the USSR, Poland and Hungary: Social Contract in Transformation*. London: Macmillan.

Ferge, Z. (1993) 'Winners and Losers Following the Collapse of State Socialism', in J. Baldock and R. Page (eds), *Social Policy Review 5*. Canterbury: Social Policy Association.

Field, G.M. (1995) 'The Health Crisis in the Former Soviet Union: A Reflection of Social Crisis'. Paper presented to the fifth World Congress of Central and East European Studies, Warsaw, 6–11 August.

Fischer, G. and Standing, G. (1991) 'Restructuring in Eastern and Central Europe: Labour Market and Social Policy Issues'. OCDE/ILO/GD(91)144, ILO, Geneva.

Fischer G. and Standing, G. (1993) 'Structural Change in Central and Eastern Europe: Labour Market and Social Policy Implications'. OECD, Paris.

Fitzgerald, E.V.K. (1991) 'Economic Reform and Citizen Entitlements in Eastern Europe: Some Social Implications of Structural Adjustment in Semi-Industrialized Economies'. UNRISD Discussion Papers 27.

Flynn, P. (1995) Address to the World Summit by Mr P. Flynn, Member of the European Commission responsible for Employment and Social Affairs. 6–12 March. Copenhagen.

Foster-Carter, A. (1993) 'Development', in M. Haralambos (ed.), *Developments in Sociology*, vol. 9. Ormskirk: Causeway Press.

Foucher, M. (1994) *Minorities in Central and Eastern Europe*. Strasbourg: Council of Europe Press.

Fox, L. (1994a) 'Old Age Security in Transition Economies'. Policy Research Working Paper 1257, World Bank Research Division, Washington.

Fox, L. (1994b) 'What to Do? Pensions in Transition Economies'. *Transition: World Bank Newsletter*, 15(2–3).

Garrett, G. and Mitchell, D. (1995) 'Globalization and the Welfare State: Income Transfers in the Industrial Democracies, 1965–1990'. Paper presented to Conference on Comparative Research on Welfare State Reforms, Pavia, 14–17 September.

Gellner, E. (1992) *Post-Modernism, Reason and Religion*. London: Routledge.

Gellner, E. (1994) *Conditions of Liberty: Civil Society and its Rivals*. London: Hamish Hamilton.

George, S. (1988) *A Fate Worse than Debt*. Harmondsworth: Penguin.

George, V. (1993) 'Poverty in Russia: From Lenin to Yeltsin', in J. Baldock and R. Page (eds), *Social Policy Review 5*. Canterbury: Social Policy Association.

George, S. and Sabelli, F. (1994) *Faith and Credit: The World Bank's Secular Empire*. London: Penguin.

Ghai, D. (1991) *The I.M.F. and the South: Social Impact of Crisis and Adjustment*. London and New Jersey: Zed.

Giddens, A. (1995) *Beyond the Left and Right*. Stanford: Stanford University Press.

Gill, S. (1993) *Gramsci, Historical Materialism and International Relations*. Cambridge: Cambridge University Press.

Gill, S. and Law, D. (1993) 'Global Hegemony and the Structural Power of Capital', in S. Gill (ed.), *Gramsci, Historical Materialism and International Relations*. Cambridge: Cambridge University Press.

Gillion, C. (1991) *Social Protection in East and Central European Countries: Before, During and After their Transition from a Centrally Planned Economy*. OCDE/ILO/GD (91)140. Geneva: ILO.

Gilpin, R. (1984) 'The Richness of the Tradition of Political Realism', *International Organisation*, 38(2): 285–304.

Ginsburg, N. (1992) *Divisions of Welfare*. London: Sage.

Girvan, N. (1995) 'Empowerment for Development: From Conditionality to Partnership', in J.M. Griesgraber and B.G. Gunter (eds), *Promoting Development*. London, East Haven: Pluto.

Gleckman, H. and Krut, R. (1995) *The Social Benefits of Regulating Transnational Corporations*. Benchmark Environmental Consulting.

Glenny, M. (1992) *The Fall of Yugoslavia*. London: Penguin.

Godfrey, M. (1995) 'The Struggle against Unemployment: Medium-Term Policy Options for Transitional Economies', *International Labour Review*, 134(1).

Goldstein, J. (1993) 'Creating the GATT Rules: Politics, Institutions and American Policy', in J.G. Ruggie (ed.), *Multilateralism Matters*. New York: Columbia University Press.

Goodman, P. and Peng, I. (1996) 'The East Asian Welfare States Peripatetic Learning, Adaptive Change and Nation Building', in G. Esping-Andersen (ed.), *Welfare States in Transition*. London: Sage.

Gora, M. (1993) 'Labour Market Policies in Poland'. Paper presented at the OECD CCET Technical Workshop on the Persistence of Unemployment in Central and Eastern Europe, Paris, 30 September to 2 October.

Gotovska-Popova, T. (1993) 'Bulgaria's Troubled Social Security System', *RFE/RL Research Report*, 2(17).

Gotting, U. (1993) 'Welfare State Development in Post-Communist Bulgaria, Czechoslovakia and Hungary: A Review of Problems and Responses (1989–1992)'. Paper 6/93, Centre for Social Policy Research, University of Bremen.

Gotting, U. (1994) 'Destruction, Adjustment and Innovations: Social Policy Transformation in Eastern and Central Europe', *Journal of European Social Policy*, 4(3).

Gotting, U. (1995) 'In Defense of Welfare: Social Protection and Social Reform in Eastern Europe'. Paper prepared for Conference, 'A New Social Contract?', Florence, Badia Fiesolana, 5–6 October.

Gough, I. (1993) 'Auditing Well Being in Central/Eastern Europe'. Paper presented at an International Conference on Privatization and Socioeconomic Policy in Central and Eastern Europe, Krakow, Poland, 18–21 October.

Gough, I. (1995) 'Diverse Systems, Common Destinations? A Comparative Study of Social Assistance in OECD Countries'. Paper contributed to ISA RC19 Conference on Comparative Research on Welfare State Reforms, University of Pavia, Italy, 14–17 September.

Gough, I. (1996) 'Social Welfare and Competitiveness', in J. Millar and J. Bradshaw (eds),

Social Welfare Systems: Towards a Research Agenda. Bath Social Policy Paper 24. Bath: Centre for the Analysis of Social Policy.

Gough, I. with Thomas, T. (1993) 'Cross-National Variations in Need Satisfaction'. Paper presented to the Fourth Comparative Research Programme on Poverty Conference, Paris, 16–18 April.

Gould, A. (1993) *Capitalist Welfare Systems*. London: Longman.

Gowan, P. (1991) 'New Wine in Old Bottles: Western Policy towards Eastern Europe', *World Policy Journal*, winter.

Gowan, P. (1992) 'The E.C. and Eastern Europe', *Labour Focus on Eastern Europe*, no. 3.

Gowan, P. (1993) 'The CIS and the World Economy: The Politics of Integration', *Labour Focus on Eastern Europe*, no. 3.

Gowan, P. (1996) 'Analysing Shock Therapy', *New Left Review*, 213.

Graham, C. (1994a) 'Comparing Experiences with Safety Nets during Market Transitions: New Coalitions for Reform? Latin America, Africa, Eastern Europe'. Mimeo, UNRISD.

Graham, C. (1994b) *Safety Nets, Politics and the Poor*. Washington: Brookings Institute.

Grant, R. and Newland, K. (eds) (1991) *Gender and International Relations*. London: Oxford University Press.

Grant, S. (1994) 'Paying in the Hague?', *War Report*, no. 28.

Green, R.H. (1995) 'Reflections on Attainable Trajectories: Reforming Global Economic Institutions', in J.M. Griesgraber and B.G. Gunter (eds), *Promoting Development*. London, East Haven: Pluto.

Greenberg, M.E. with Heintz, S.B. (1994) *Removing the Barriers: Strategies to Assist the Long-Term Unemployed*. A Report of an Expert Working Group in Central and Eastern Europe. New York and Prague: Institute of East–West Studies.

Griesgraber, J.M. and Gunter, B.G. (eds) (1995) *Promoting Development*. London: Pluto.

Griesgraber, J.M. and Gunter, B.G. (eds) (1996) *The World Bank*. London: Pluto.

Griesgraber, J.M. and Gunter, B.G. (eds) (1977) *The World Bank*. London: Pluto.

Griffith-Jones, S. (1992) 'Cross-Conditionality or the Spread of Obligatory Adjustment: A Review of the Issues and Questions for Research', in E. Rodriguez (ed.) (1992), *Cross-Conditionality Banking Regulation and Third World Debt*. UN Commission for Latin America and the Caribbean.

Griffiths, A. and Wall, S. (1993) *Applied Economics*. London: Macmillan.

Grinspin, C. and Cameron, M.A. (eds) (1993) *The Political Economy of North American Free Trade*. London: Macmillan.

Grosh, M. (1995) 'Targeting: Lessons from the Experience of Latin America with Ponderings on their Application in Ukraine'. Draft working paper (unpublished), World Bank, Washington.

Group of Seven (1996) *Sommet de Lyons. Economic Communiqué: Making a success of Globalization for the Benefit of All*. Lyons.

Haas, P. (1992) 'Epistemic Communities and International Policy Co-ordination', special issue of *International Organization*, 46 (Winter).

Haggard, S. and Kaufman, R.R. (1992) *The Politics of Economic Adjustment*. Princeton, NJ: Princeton University Press.

Halliday, F. (1994) *Rethinking International Relations*. London: Macmillan.

Hansenne, M. (1995) Statement to the World Summit on Social Development by M. Hansenne, Director General of ILO. 9 March. Copenhagen.

Hanson, P. (1993) 'Western Aid to the Soviet Union's Successor States', *RFE/RL Research Report*, 1(18).

Hardy, D.C. (1991) *Soft Budget Constraints, Firm Commitments and the Social Safety Net*. Washington: IMF.

Harrell-Bond, B. (1986) *Imposing Aid: Emergency Assistance to Refugees*. Oxford: Oxford University Press.

Harrell-Bond, B. (1993) 'Relief: From Dependency to Development', *War Report*, no. 2.

Harris, N. (1996) *The New Untouchables: Immigration and the New World Order*. Manchester: I.B. Tauris.

Havel, V. (1994) 'A Call for Sacrifice', *Foreign Affairs*, 73(2).

Healy, J. and Robinson, M. (1992) *Democracy, Governance and Economic Policy*. London: ODI.

Held, D. (1991) *Political Theory Today*. Cambridge: Polity.

Held, D. (1995) *Democracy and the Global Order: From the Modern State to Cosmopolitan Governance*. Cambridge: Polity.

Henderson, A. (1992) 'The International Monetary Fund and the Dilemmas of Adjustment in Eastern Europe: Lessons from the 1980s and Prospects for the 1990s', *Journal of International Development*, 4(3).

Hirsl, M. et al. (1995) 'Market Reforms and Social Welfare in the Czech Republic: A True Success Story?' UNICEF Occasional Papers, Economic Policy Series 50.

Hirst, P. and Thompson, G. (1996) *Globalization in Question*. Cambridge: Polity.

Hodges, M. and Woolcock, S. (1993) 'Atlantic Capitalism versus Rhine Capitalism in the European Community', *West European Politics*, 16: 3.

Holm, H.H. (1995) *Whose World Order?* Oxford: Westview.

Holzmann, R. (1991) *Adapting to Economic Change: Reconciling Social Protection with Market Economies*. ILO CTASS/1991/6. Geneva: ILO.

Holzmann, R. (1992) 'Adapting to Social Change: Social Policy in Transition from Plan to Market', *Journal of Public Policy*, 12(1).

Horsman, M. and Marshall A. (1994) *After the Nation State: Citizens, Tribalism and the New World Disorder*. London: HarperCollins.

Howse, R. and Trebilcock, M. (1995) *The Regulation of Free Trade*. London: Routledge.

Huber, E. (1996) 'Options for Social Policy in Latin America: Neoliberal versus Social Democratic Models', in G. Esping-Andersen (ed.), *Welfare States in Transition*. London: Sage.

Huber, E. and Stephens, J.D. (1993) 'The Future of the Social Democratic Welfare State: Options in the Face of Economic Internationalization and European Integration'. Paper prepared for the Conference on Comparative Research on Welfare States in Transition, International Sociological Association, 9–12 September.

Hughes, M. (1992) 'Can the West Agree on Aid to Western Europe?' *RFE/RL Research Report*, 13 March.

Hughes, M. (1993) 'Eastern Pain and Western Promise: The Reaction of Western Governments to the Economic Plight of the "New Eastern Europe"', *International Relations*.

Hulse, M. (1995) 'The Council of Europe's Role in Influencing Post-Communist Social Policy'. Paper presented to the Fifth World Congress of East European Studies, Warsaw, 6–11 August.

Humana, C. (1992) *World Human Rights Guide, 3rd edn*. Oxford: Oxford University Press.

ILO (1991a) 'Labour Market Transitions in Eastern Europe and the USSR', special issue of *International Labour Review*, 130(2), Geneva.

ILO (1991b) *Technical Assistance to the Social Security Sector: Family Benefits and Social Assistance: Czechoslovakia*. Draft Report, ILO with PHARE. Geneva: European Commission.

ILO (1992a) *World Labour Report 5*. Geneva: ILO.

ILO (1992b) *Technical Assistance to the Social Security Sector*. Czechoslovakia PHR/T9107/GTAF/TEN/005. Report by M. Castle-Kanerova and B. Deacon, ILO with PHARE. Geneva: European Commission.

ILO (1994a) *The Ukrainian Challenge: Reforming Labour Market and Social Policy*. Budapest: ILO CEET with UNDP.

ILO (1994b) 'Bulgaria: Comments on the Strategy of Social Security Reform'. Draft White Paper. Geneva: ILO with UNDP.

ILO (1994c) *Labour Market Dynamics in Ukrainian Industry in 1992–1994: Results from the ULFS*. Budapest: ILO CEET.

ILO (1994d) *Labour Market Developments in Hungary*. Budapest: ILO CEET.

ILO (1994e) *The Bulgarian Challenge: Reforming Labour Markets and Social Policy*. ILO CEET with PHARE. Budapest: European Commission.

ILO (1995a) 'Ukraine: Review of Social Protection Forms and Issues of Implementation'. Draft White Paper, ILO with UNDP, Geneva.

ILO (1995b) *World Employment 1995: An ILO report*. Geneva: ILO.

ILO (1995c) *Report of the Director-General: Fifth European Regional Conference*, Warsaw, ILO, Geneva.

ILO (1995d) *Perspectives for Labour Market and Social Policy Reform in the Russian Federation in the Mid-1990s*. Budapest: ILO CEET Report 12.

IMF (1992) Statement by IMF on the Realization of Economic, Social and Cultural Rights. UN Doc. E/CN.4/Sub.2/1992/57 of 14 September.

IMF (1993) 'Social Security Reforms and Social Safety Nets in Reforming and Transforming Economies'. Paper presented by IMF and World Bank to the Development Committee on the UN no. 32, Washington, 27 September.

IMF (1994) *Annual Report 1994*. Washington: IMF.

IMF (1995a) *Social Dimensions of Change: the IMF's Policy Dialogue*. Contribution to the World Summit on Social Development. Washington: IMF.

IMF (1995b) 'Social Safety Nets for Economic Transition: Options and Recent Experiences'. Paper on Policy Analysis and Assessment by Expenditure Policy Division Staff, PPAA/95/3, February. IMF, Washington.

IMF (1995c) *Economic Review of the Ukraine*. Washington: IMF.

Isakovič, Z. (1993) 'Croatia: The Refugee Flood', *War Report*, no. 22: 14–15.

ISSA (1993a) *Responding to Changing Needs: Developments and Trends in Social Security Throughout the World 1990–1992*. Geneva: ISSA.

ISSA (1993b) *The Implications for Social Security of Structural Adjustment Policies*. Studies and Research 43. Geneva: ISSA.

ISSA (1994a) *Restructuring Social Security in Central and Eastern Europe: a Guide to Recent Developments, Policy Issues and Options*. Geneva: ISSA.

ISSA (1994b) *Financing of Social Insurance in Central and Eastern Europe*. European Series 20. Geneva: ISSA.

ISSA (1995) *Social Security Tomorrow: Permanence and Change*. Studies and Research 36. Geneva: ISSA.

Jackman, R. and Layard, J. (1990) 'Social Policy and Unemployment'. Paper for Conference on the Transition to a Market Economy in Central and Eastern Europe, OECD.

Jessop, B. et al. (1991) *The Politics of Flexibility*. Aldershot: Edward Elgar.

Jolly, R. (1991) 'Adjustment with a Human Face: A UNICEF Record and Perspective on the 1980s', *World Development*, 19(12).

Joly, D. (1992) *Refugees: Asylum in Europe*. London: Minority Rights Group.

Jones, C. (ed.) (1993a) *New Perspectives on the Welfare State in Europe*. London: Routledge.

Jones C. (1993b) 'The Pacific Challenge: The Confucian Welfare States', in C. Jones (ed.), *New Perspectives on the Welfare State in Europe*. London: Routledge.

Jonsson, C. (1993) 'International Organization and Co-operation: An International Perspective', *International Social Science Journal*, November: 138.

Jordan, B. (1985) *The State: Authority and Autonomy*. Oxford: Blackwell.

Jordan, B. (forthcoming) 'European Social Citizenship: Why a New Social Contract Will (Probably) Not Happen', in Y. Meny and M. Rhodes (eds), *A New Social Contract? Charting the Future of European Welfare*. London: Macmillan.

Kahler, M. (1992) 'External Influence: Conditionality and the Politics of Adjustment', in S. Haggard and P.R. Kaufman (eds), *The Politics of Economic Adjustment*. Princeton, NJ: Princeton University Press.

Kaldor, M. and Kumar, (1993) 'New forms of Conflict', in Helsinki Citizen's Assembly (eds), *Conflicts in Europe*. Prague: HCA.

Kamerman, S. (1995) 'Social Security Has Proved its Worth: Now It Must Adapt', in *Social Security Tomorrow: Permanence and Change*. Studies and Research 36. Geneva: ISSA.

Karatnycky, A. (1992) 'The Ukrainian Factor' *Foreign Affairs*, 71(3).

Katwari, N. (1995) 'Income Inequality, Welfare and Poverty in Ukraine'. World Bank Research Project on Income Distribution during the Transition, Paper 7.

Keane, J. (1996) *Reflections on Violence*. London: Verso.

Kelly, R. (1992) 'Eastern Promise by Two Different Routes', *Guardian*, 27 April, quoting from 'Macroeconomics of Transition in Eastern Europe', *Oxford Review of Economic Policy*, 8(1).

Kenen, P.B. (ed.) (1994) *Managing the World Economy: Fifty Years after Bretton Woods*. London: Longman.

Kessides, C. (1992) *Hungary: Reform of Social Policy and Expenditures*. Washington: World Bank.

Killick, T. et al. (1991) *What Can We Know about the Effects of IMF Programmes?* ODI Working Paper 47. London: Overseas Development Institute.

Killick, T. and Malik, M. (1991) *Country Experiences with IMF Programmes in the 1980s*. ODI Working Paper 48. London: Overseas Development Institute.

Killick, T. And Stevens, C. (1991a), 'Eastern Europe: Lessons on Economic Adjustment from the Third World', *International Affairs*, 67(4).

Killick, T. and Stevens, C. (1991b), *Economic Adjustment in Eastern Europe: Lessons from the Third World*. ODI Working Paper. London: Overseas Development Institute.

Kirder, U. and Silk, L. (1995) *People: From Impoverishment to Empowerment*. New York: New York University Press.

Kleinman, M. and Piachaud, D. (1993) 'European Social Policy: Conceptions and Choices', *Journal of European Social Policy*, 3(1): 1–19.

Knor, M. (1997) 'WTO Battles over Labour Standards', <twn@igc.apc.org>, in Unreform newsgroup (26 January 1997).

Koivusalo, M. and Ollila, E. (1997) *International Organisations and Health Policy*. London: Zed.

Kolarič, Z. et al. (eds) (undated) 'The Development of Non Profit and Voluntary Organisations in Slovenia'. Mimeo, University of Ljubljana, Faculty of Social Sciences.

Kolarič, Z. and Svetlik, I. (1987) 'Jugoslavanske Sistem Blaginje v Pogojih Ekonomske Krize', *IB Revija za Planiranje*, 21(8–9).

Kopits, G. (1993) 'Towards a Cost-Effective Social Security System', in *The Implications for Social Security of Structural Adjustment Policies*. Studies and Research 34. Geneva: ISSA.

Kopits, G. (1994) 'Social Security in Economies in Transition', in *Restructuring Social Security in Central and Eastern Europe: A Guide to Recent Developments, Policy Issues and Options*. Geneva: ISSA.

Kopits, G. and Offerdal, E. (1994) 'Fiscal Policy in Transition Economies: A Major Challenge', *Finance and Development*, December.

Korpi, W. (1993) 'Economists as Policy Experts and Policy Advocates: On Problems of Values and Objectivity in the Welfare State — Economic Growth Debate'. Paper presented at the Conference on Comparative Research on Welfare States in Transition organized by ISSA's Research Committee on Poverty, Social Welfare and Social Policy at Wadham College, Oxford, 9–12 September.

Kosonen, P. (1995) 'Competitiveness, Welfare Systems and the Debate on Social Competition'. Paper contributed to ISA RC19 Conference on Comparative Research on Welfare State reforms, University of Pavia, Italy, 14–17 September.

Koves, A. (1992) *Central and Eastern European Economies in Transition: The International Dimension*. Oxford: Westview.

Krawchenko, B. (1993) 'Ukraine: the Politics of Independence' in I. Bremmer and R.C. Taras (eds), *Nations and Politics in the Soviet Successor States*. Cambridge: Cambridge University Press.

Kroč, J. (1996) 'Untying Macedonia's Gordian Knot: Preventative Diplomacy in the Southern Balkans', in J. Letterman, W. Demas, P. Galley and R. Vayrynes (eds), *Preventative and Inventive Action in Interstate Crisis*. Draft.

Krumm, K. et al. (1994) 'Transfers and the Transition from Socialism: Key Tradeoffs'. World Bank Policy Research Working Paper 1380.

Ksiezopolski, M. (1993a) 'Social Policy in Poland in the Period of Political and Economic Transition', *Journal of European Social Policy*, 3(3).

Kuchma, L. (1995) Address to the World Summit on Social Development by L. Kuchma, President of Ukraine. 12 March. Copenhagen.

Kuzio, T. (1992) *Ukraine: The Unfinished Revolution*. European Security Study 16, Institute for European Defence and Strategic Studies.

Kužmanič, T. (1995) 'New Social Movements and a New State', *War Report*, no. 30: 38–9.

Lado, M. Szalai, J. and Sziraczki, G. (1991) 'Recent Labour Market and Social Developments in Hungary'. OCDE/ILO/GD(91) 134, ILO, Geneva.

Lang, T. and Hines, C. (1995) *The New Protectionism*. London: Earthscan.

Lang, T. and Hines, C. (1996) 'The "New Protectionist" Position', *New Political Economy*, 1(1).

Lee, P. and Raban, C. (1990) *Welfare Theory and Social Policy*. London: Sage.

Leibfried, S. (1990) 'The Classification of Welfare State Regimes in Europe'. Plenary Session Paper, Social Policy Association Annual Conference, University of Bath, July.

Leibfried, S. (1994) 'The Social Dimensions of the EU: En Route to Positively Joint Sovereignty', *Journal of European Social Policy*, 4(4).

Liebfried, S. and Pierson, P. (1995) *Fragmented Social Policy*. Washington: Brookings Institute.

Lewis, J. (1992) 'Gender and the Development of European Welfare Regimes', *Journal of European Social Policy*, 2(3).

Lieven, A. (1993) *The Baltic Revolution: Estonia, Latvia, Lithuania and the Path to Independence*. New Haven, CT: Yale University Press.

Lind, J. and Moller, I.H. (1995) *Unemployment and Basic Income: Is There a Middle Road?* Copenhagen: CID Studies.

Lipow, A. (1994) 'Internationalism and Social Policy: Trade Unions in Central/Eastern Europe'. Paper presented to the Third International Prague Conference on Social Transformation in Central/Eastern Europe, May.

Lipshultz, P. (1992) 'Reconstructing World Politics: The Emergence of Global Civil Society', *Millennium: Journal of International Relations*, 21(3).

Loescher, G. (1993) *Beyond Charity*. Oxford: Oxford University Press.

Luard, E. (1990) *The Globalisation of Politics*. London: Macmillan.

Lumsdaine, D.H. (1993) *Moral Vision in International Politics: The Foreign Aid Regime 1949–1989*. Princeton, NJ: Princeton University Press.

Lyons, G.M. (1993) 'International Intervention, State Sovereignty and the Future of International Society', *International Social Science Journal*, November: 138.

MacPherson, S. and Midgley, J. (1987) *Comparative Social Policy and the Third World*. Brighton: Wheatsheaf.

Madzar, L. (1992) 'The Economy of Yugoslavia', in J. Allcock, J. Horton and M. Milivojevic (eds), *Yugoslavia in Transition: Essays in Honour of Fred Singleton*. New York: Berg.

Magas, B. (1993) *The Destruction Of Yugoslavia*. London: Verso.

Manning, N. (1994) 'Social Policy and the Welfare State in Russia'. Paper presented to the Conference on Russia in Transition: Elites, Classes and Inequalities, Emmanuel College, Cambridge, 15–17 December.

Maret, X. and Schwartz, G. (1993) 'Poland: The Social Safety Net during the Transition'. IMF Working Paper WP/93/42, IMF, Washington.

Marnie, S. (1992) 'How Prepared is Russia for Mass Unemployment?', *RFE/RL Research Report*, 1(48).

Marnie, S. (1993a) 'Economic Reform and the Social Safety Net', *RFE/RL Research Report*, 2(17).

Marnie, S. (1993b) 'The Social Safety Net in Russia', *RFE/RL Research Report*, 2(17).

Mayo, M. and Craig, G. (1995) 'Community Participation and Empowerment: The Human Face of Structural Adjustment or Tools for Democratic Transformation', in G. Craig and M. Mayo (eds), *Community Empowerment*. London: Zed.

McAuley, M. (1992) *Soviet Politics 1917–1991*. Oxford: Oxford University Press.

McAuley, A. (1994) 'Social Welfare in Transition: What Happened in Russia'. World Bank Research Project on Income Distribution, Paper 6.

McGrew, A. et al. (1993) *Global Politics*. Milton Keynes: Open University Press.

Meehan, E. (1993) *Citizenship and the European Community*. London: Sage.

Merrit, G. (1991) *Eastern Europe and the USSR: The Challenge of Freedom*. Brussels: European Commission.

Mesič, M. (1992) 'External Migration in the Context of the Post-War Development of Yugoslavia', in J. Allcock, J. Horton and M. Milivojevic (eds), *Yugoslavia in Transition: Essays in Honour of Fred Singleton*. New York: Berg.

Mesič, M. (1993) 'Fluchtlingstypen in Fall Kroatians', *Migration*, 19(3): 41–59.

Mestrovič, S. (1994) *The Balkanization of the West*. London: Routledge.

Meyer, A.G. (1994) 'The End of Communism? A Review of Several "Post-Communist Texts"', *Slavic Review*, Summer.

Meznarič, S. and Winter, J. (1993) 'Forced Migration and Refugee Flows in Croatia, Slovenia and Bosnia-Hercegovina', *Refugee* (Canada), 12(7): 3–5.

Meznarič, S. and Winter, J. (1995) 'Negotiating the Future: Return and Community Revitalization Strategies of Croatian Displacees'. Paper presented to Refugees in Europe Meeting, Amsterdam, May.

Mickey, R. (1995) 'Macedonia: Unstable in a Stable Way', in *Transition 1994*, Review, Part 1. Prague: OMRI.

Micklewright, J. and Nagy, G. (1994) 'How Does the Hungarian Unemployment Insurance System Really Work?' EUI Working Paper ECO 94/11, Florence.

Mies, M. (1986) *Patriarchy and Accumulation on a World Scale: Women in the International Division of Labour*. London and New Jersey: Zed.

Milanovic, B. (1992) 'Review of Social Safety Net Chapters in Reports on the Former Soviet Union'. Unpublished paper, World Bank, Washington.

Milanovic, B. (1995) 'Poverty in Transition', in 'Income, Inequality and Poverty during the Transition'. World Bank Research Project on Income Distribution, Paper 9.

Miles, I. (1985) *Social Indicators for Human Development*. London: Frances Pinter.

Milwood, D. (ed.) (1996) *The International Response to Conflict and Genocide: Synthesis Report*. Copenhagen: Steering Committee of the Joint Evaluation of Emergency Assistance to Rwanda.

Minev, D. (1993) 'Pension Provision in Bulgaria, Problems of Reform in the Context of the Transition to a Market Economy', in I.S. Beleva et al. (eds), *Bulgaria and the European Community: The Transformation of the Labour Market and Social Policy: A View Towards Europe*. Sofia: Demos.

Minnear, L. (1994) *Humanitarian Action in the Former Yugoslavia: The UN's role 1991–1993*. Thomas J. Watson Institute for International Studies.

Mishra, R. (1990) *The Welfare State in Capitalist Society: Policies of Retrenchment and Maintenance in Europe, North America and Australia*. Hemel Hempstead: Harvester Wheatsheaf.

Moller, I.H. (1995) 'A Regulation Theoretical Perspective on Labour Market Marginalisation. Globalization and the Welfare State: Income Transfers in the Industrial Democracies, 1965–1990. Paper presented to ISA, RC19 Conference on Comparative Research on Welfare State Reforms, University of Italy, Pavia, Italy, 14–17 September.

Mommsen, W.J. (ed.) (1981) *Emergence of the Welfare States in Britain and Germany: 1850–1950*. London: Croom Helm.

Mosely, P. et al. (1991) *Aid and Power, Volume 1: The World Bank and Policy-Based Lending*, 2nd edn. London: Routledge and Kegan Paul.

Mros, J.E. (1993) *Securing the Euro-Atlantic Bridge: The Council of Europe and the United States*. Strasbourg: Institute of East–West Studies with the Council of Europe.

Nagel, S. (1991) *Global Policy Studies: International Action towards Improving Public Policy*. London: Macmillan.

Nagel, S. (ed.) (1994) *Eastern Europe: Development and Public Policy*. London: Macmillan.

Nahaylo, B. (1992) *The New Ukraine*. London: Royal Institute of International Affairs.

National Agency for Welfare and Health (1992) *Competitive Society in Central and Eastern*

Europe: The Social Dimension. Conference Report, Kellokaski, Finland. Finland: National Agency for Welfare and Health.

Nelson, J.M. (1992) 'Poverty, Equity and the Politics of Adjustment', in S. Haggard and P.R. Kaufman (eds), *The Politics of Economic Adjustment.* Princeton, NJ: Princeton University Press.

Nesporova, A. and Simonyi, A. (1994) *Labour Market Developments in Hungary.* Budapest: ILO CEET.

New Economics Foundation (1989) *Alternative Economic Indicators.* London: NEF.

ODA (1995a) *A Guide to Social Analysis for Projects in Developing Countries. Chapter 3.* HMSO: London.

ODA (1995b) 'Social Policy Research for Development'. Report prepared for the ODA's Economic and Social Committee for Overseas Development (ESCOR).

OECD (1981) *The Crisis of Welfare.* Paris: OECD.

OECD (1988a) *Reforming Public Pensions.* Social Policy Studies 5. Paris: OECD.

OECD (1988b) *The Future of Social Protection.* Social Policy Studies 6. Paris: OECD.

OECD (1990a) 'Policies for Manpower and Social Affairs: Labour Market Flexibility and Work Organization'. OECD, Paris.

OECD (1990b) *Health Care Systems in Transition: The Search for Efficiency.* Social Policy Studies 7. Paris: OECD.

OECD (1991a) 'Policies for Manpower and Social Affairs: Private Pensions and Public Policy'. Paris: OECD.

OECD (1991b) *The Transition to a Market Economy, Volume 1: The Broad Issues.* Paris: OECD CCET.

OECD (1991c) *The Transition to a Market Economy, Volume 2: Special Issues.* Paris: OECD.

OECD (1991d) 'Training Programme Schedule: Courses for 1993'. OECD CCET, Paris.

OECD (1991e) 'Revised 1991 Regional Programme of Activities Relating to Central and Eastern European Countries'. OECD CCET, Paris.

OECD (1991f) *A Study of the Soviet Economy.* Paris: OECD with IMF, EBRD and World Bank.

OECD (1992a) *Annual Report of the OECD.* Paris: OECD.

OECD (1992b) 'Programme of Work'. OECD CCET, Paris.

OECD (1992c) 'Innovation and Employment: Social Welfare Services delivered by the Private Sector'. Study Series Occasional Paper 10, OECD CCET, Paris.

OECD (1993a) *The Transition from Work to Retirement.* Social Policy Studies 16. Paris: OECD.

OECD (1993b) 'Challenge for the Mid 1990's: The Development Centre's Programme for 1993–1995'. OECD Development Centre, Paris.

OECD (1993c) *Structural Change in Central and Eastern Europe: Labour Market and Social Policy Implications.* Paris: OECD CCET.

OECD (1993d) *Economic Integration, OECD Economies, Dynamic Asian Economies and Central and Eastern European Countries.* Paris: OECD.

OECD (1993e) 'Scoreboard of Assistance Commitments to Central and Eastern Europe'. Doc. (CU)24/93, OECD and G24, Paris.

OECD (1993f) 'Employment/Unemployment Study'. Report by the Secretary-General, Doc. OEDE/GD(93)102, OECD, Paris.

OECD (1994a) *New Orientations for Social Policy.* Social Policy Studies 12. Paris: OECD.

OECD (1994b) *Economic Integration: OECD Economies, Dynamic Asian Economies and Central and Eastern European Countries.* Paris: OECD.

OECD (1995a) *The Transition from Work to Retirement.* Social Policy Studies 16. Paris: OECD.

OECD (1995b) *Social and Labour Market Policies in Hungary.* Paris: OECD.

OECD (1996) *Employment Outlook,* July. Paris: OECD.

Offe, C. (1991) 'Capitalism by Democratic Design? Democratic Theory Facing the Triple Transition in Eastern Central Europe', *Social Research,* 4.

Offe, C. (1993) *The Politics of Social Policy in East European Transitions: Antecedents, Agents and Agenda for Reform.* Bremen: Centre for Social Policy Research.

O'Keohane, R. (1991) 'International Relations Theory Contributions of a Feminist Standpoint', in R. Grant and K. Newland (eds), *Gender and International Relations.* Milton Keynes: Open University Press.

Okolicsanyi, K. (1993) 'Hungary's Misused and Costly Social Security System', *RFE/RL Research Report*, 2(17).

O'Neill, O. (1991) 'Transnational Justice', in D. Held (ed.), *Political Theory Today.* Cambridge: Polity.

Orloff, A.S. (1993) 'Gender and the Social Rights of Citizenship: The Comparative Analysis of Gender Relations and Welfare States', *American Sociological Review*, 58: 303–28.

Oxfam Supporter Services (1995) *Oxfam at Work Overseas: 1994–1995.* Oxford: Oxfam Supporter Services.

Panic, M. (1992) 'Managing Reforms in the East European Countries: Lessons from the Post-War experience of Western Europe'. UN ECE Discussion Paper, vol. 1, no. 3, United Nations, New York.

Panitch, A. and Mandel, E. (1992) 'Globalism and Socialism', in A. Panitch and E. Mandel (eds), *Socialist Register.* London: Merlin Press.

Parun-Kolin, M. (1996) 'Social Policy in Serbia: New Welfare Mix in Eastern Europe'. Mimeo, Institute of Social Sciences, Belgrade.

Paull, G. (1991) *Poverty Alleviation and Social Safety Net Schemes for Economies in Transition.* Washington: IMF.

Pauly, L.W. (1994) 'Promoting a Global Economy: The Normative Role of the I.M.F.', in R. Stubbs and G.R.D. Underhill (eds), *Political Economy and the Changing Global Order.* London: Macmillan.

Pfaller, A., Gough, I. and Therborn, G. (eds) (1991) *Can the Welfare State Compete? A Comparative Study of Five Advanced Capitalist Societies.* Basingstoke: Macmillan.

Picciotto, S. (1991) 'The Internationalization of the State', *Capital and Class*, 43.

Pierson, C. (1995) *Socialism after Communism: The New Market Socialism.* Cambridge: Polity.

Piirainen, T. (1994) *Change and Continuity in Eastern Europe.* Aldershot: Dartmouth.

Pik, K. (1994) 'The Emergence of Homelessness in Hungary'. Paper presented to the Third International Prague Conference on Social Transformation in Central/Eastern Europe, May.

Pinder, J. (1991) *The European Community and Eastern Europe.* London: RIIA, Pinter.

Pitt, D. and Weiss, T.G. (eds) (1986) *The Nature of the UN's Bureaucracies.* London: Croom-Helm.

Plant, R. (1994) 'Labour Standards and Structural Adjustment in Hungary'. Occasional Paper 7, Interdepartmental Project on Structural Adjustment, ILO, Geneva.

Potucek, M. (1993) 'Current Social Policy Developments in the Czech and Slovak Republics', *Journal of European Social Policy*, 3(3).

Puljiz, V. (1992) 'Refugees comme la consequence de la guerre en Croatie', *AWR Bulletin*, 30(4): 173–8.

Purdy, D. (1996) 'The Case for Basic Incomes', *New Left Review*, 208.

Ramet, P. (ed.) (1985) *Yugoslavia in the 1980's.* Colorado, CO: Westview.

Ramet, S. (1996) *Balkan Babel: the Disintegration of Yugoslavia from the Death of Tito to Ethnic War.* Boulder, CO: Westview.

Ramon, S. (1995) 'Slovenian Social Work: A Case Study of Unexpected Developments in the Post-1990 Period', *British Journal of Social Work*, 25.

Republic of Hungary (1993) *PHARE 1990–1993.* Budapest: Ministry of International Economic Relations.

Richard, P. et al. (1992) *States and Development in the Asian Pacific.* London: Sage.

Richmond, A.H. (1996) *Global Apartheid: Refugees and the New World Order.* Milton Keynes: Open University Press.

Rieff, D. (1995) *Slaughterhouse: Bosnia and the Failure of the West.* London: Vintage.

Rhodes, M. (1995) 'Globalization and West European Welfare States'. Paper presented to

Conference, 'A New Social Contract?', Robert Schuman Centre, European University Institute, 5–6 October.

Roberts, A. and Kingsbury, B. (1989) *UN, Divided World*. Oxford: Clarendon Press.

Robertson, J. (1996) 'Debate: Citizen's Income – Towards a New Social Compact: Citizen's Income and Radical Tax Reform', *The Political Quarterly*, 67(1).

Roche, M. (1992) *Rethinking Citizenship: Welfare Ideology and Change in Modern Society*. Cambridge: Polity.

Rodgers, G. (ed.) (1995) *The Poverty Agenda and the I.L.O.: Issues for Research and Action*. Geneva: ILO.

Rodriguez, E. and Griffith-Jones, S. (1992) *Cross Conditionality Banking Regulations and Third World Debt*. London: Macmillan.

Ruggie, J.G. (ed.) (1993) *Multilateralism Matters*. New York: Columbia University Press.

Sachs, J. (1995) 'Postcommunist Parties and the Politics of Entitlements', *Transition*, Policy Research Department of the World Bank, 6(3).

Sainsbury, D. (1995) *Gendering Welfare States*. London: Sage.

Salvatore, D. (ed.) (1993) *Protectionism and World Welfare*. Cambridge: Cambridge University Press.

Sampson, A. (1973) *Sovereign State*. London: Hodder and Stoughton.

Sandstrom, S. (1995) 'Economic Reform and Investment in People: The Keys to Development'. Address to the World Summit for Social Development by S. Sandstrom, Managing Director World Bank. Copenhagen.

Save the Children (1994) *Developing a Strategy for Central and Eastern Europe*. London: SCF.

Scarpetta, S. et al. (1993) 'Unemployment Benefit Systems and Active Labour Market Policies in Central and East Europe: An Overview'. Paper contributed to Technical Workshop on the Persistence of Unemployment in Central and Eastern Europe, CCET OECD, 30 September to 2 October.

Scharpf, F.W. (1995) 'Negative and Positive Integration in the Political Economy of European Welfare States'. Paper presented to Conference, 'A New Social Contract?', Robert Schuman Centre, European University Institute, October 5–6.

Senior Nello, S. (1991) *The New Europe: Changing Economic Relations between East and West*. New York: Harvester Wheatsheaf.

Shapiro, J. (1995a) 'The Russian Mortality Crisis and its Causes', in A. Aslund (ed.), *Russian Economic Reform at Risk*. London: Pinter.

Shapiro, J. (1995b) 'The Non-Making of Russian Social Policy'. Paper presented to SPA Annual Conference, Sheffield, 18–20 July.

Shaver, S. and Bradshaw, J. (1993) *The Recognition of Wifely Labour by Welfare States*. Sydney: Social Policy Research Centre, Sydney University.

Shaw, M. (1992) 'Global Society and Global Responsibility: The Historical and Political Limits of "International Society"', *Millennium: Journal of International Relations*, 21(3).

Shaw, M. (1994) *Global Society and International Relations*. Cambridge: Polity.

Shokin, A.N. (1991) 'Social Aspects of Economic Reform in the USSR'. Paper presented at International Institute for Labour Studies and Research Institute for Labour Conference on Social Institutions for Economic Reform, Balatonfured, Hungary.

Shopov, G. (1993) 'Impoverishment of the Population and Social Assistance', in I.S. Beleva et al. (eds), *Bulgaria and the European Community: The Transformation of the Labour Market and Social Policy – A View Towards Europe*. Sofia: Demos.

Siaroff, A. (1994) 'Work, Women and Gender Equality: A New Typology', in D. Sainsbury (ed.), *Gendering Welfare States*. London: Sage.

Siegel, D. and Yancey, J. (1992) *The Rebirth of Civil Society: The Development of the Non-Profit Sector in East Central Europe and the Role of Western Assistance*. New York: Rockefeller Brothers Trust.

Silber, L. and Little, A. (1995) *The Death of Yugoslavia*. London: Penguin.

Simmie, J. and Verlič-Dekleva, J. (eds) (1991) *Yugoslavia in Turmoil: After Self-Management?* London: Pinter.

Simpura, J. (ed.) (1995) *Social Policy in Transition Societies: Experience from the Baltic Countries and Russia*. Helsinki: Finnish ICSW.

Singer, H.W. (1995) 'Rethinking Bretton Woods from a Historical Perspective', in J.M. Griesgraber and B.G. Gunter (eds), *Promoting Development*. London, East Haven: Pluto.

Singer, M. and Wildavsky, A. (1993) *The Real World Order: Zones of Peace/Zones of Turmoil*. New Jersey: Chatham.

Singleton, F. (1979) 'Regional Economic Inequalities, Migration and Community Response, with Special Reference to Yugoslavia'. Bradford Studies on Yugoslavia 1, University of Bradford.

Sivanandan, A. (1993) 'European Commentary – Racism: The Road from Germany', *Race and Class*, 34(3).

Sklair, L. (1991) *Sociology of the Global System*. Brighton: Harvester.

Sklair, L. (1992) 'Globalization and Europe: Conceptual Framework and Research Agenda'. Paper presented at the British Sociological Association Conference, April.

Smith, A.D. (1995) *Nations and Nationalism in a Global Era*. Cambridge: Polity.

Smouts, M.-C. (1993) 'Some Thoughts on International Organizations and Theories of Regulation', *International Social Science Journal*, November: 138.

Snower, D.J. (1995) 'Evaluating Unemployment Policies: What Do the Underlying Theories Tell Us?' IMF Working Paper WP/95/7, IMF, Washington.

Solchanyk, R. (1994) 'The Politics of State Building Center–Periphery Relations in Post-Soviet Ukraine', *Europe–Asia Studies*, 46(1).

Sole, R. (1997) 'From Emergency to Reconstruction', *Eurohealth*, 3(1).

South Centre (1995) *Reforming the United Nations: A View from the South*. Geneva: South Centre.

Speth, J. G. (1995) 'The new Age of Equity'. Address to the World Summit on Social Development by J.G. Speth, Administrator UNDP. 6 March. Copenhagen.

Squires, J. (ed.) (1993) *Postmodernism and the Rediscovery of Values*. London: Lawrence and Wishart.

Standing, G. (1991) *In Search of Flexibility: The New Soviet Labour Market*. Geneva: ILO.

Standing G. (1992) 'Restructuring for Distributive Justice in Eastern Europe'. Document prepared for the Conference, 'Towards a Competitive Society in Central and Eastern Europe: Social Dimensions', Kellokoski, Finland, September. ILO, Geneva.

Standing, G. (1996) 'Social Protection in Central and Eastern Europe: A Tale of Slipping Anchors and Torn Safety Nets', in G. Esping-Andersen (ed.), *Welfare States in Transition*. London: Sage.

Standing, G. and Sziraczki, G. (1991) 'Labour Market Issues in Eastern Europe's transition', *International Labour Review*, 130: 2.

Strang, D. and Chang, P.M.Y. (1993) 'The ILO and the Welfare State: Institutional Effects on National Welfare Spending', *International Organisation*, 47(2).

Strange, S. (1994) 'Wake Up, Krasner: The World *has* Changed', *Review of International Political Economy*, 1.

Strange, S. and Sabelli, F. (1994) *Faith and Credit: The World Bank's Secular Empire*. Harmondsworth: Penguin.

Stern, N. (forthcoming) 'The World Bank as "International Actor"', in *The Official History of the Bank*. Vol. II. Washington DC: Brookings Institute.

Stevens, C. and Killick, T. (1989) 'Structural Adjustment and Lome IV', *Trocaire Development Review*.

Stewart, F. (1995) *Adjustment and Poverty: Options and Choices*. London: Routledge.

Stohl, M. and Targ, H.R. (1983) *Global Political Economy in the 1980s: The Impact of the New International Economic Crises*. New York: Schekman.

Stubbs, P. (1996a) 'Nationalisms, Globalization and Civil Society in Croatia and Slovenia', *Research in Social Movements, Conflict and Change*, 19: 1–26.

Stubbs, P. (1996b) 'Social Reconstruction and Social Development in Croatia and Slovenia: the Role of the NGO Sector'. Mimeo, Leeds Metropolitan University.

Stubbs, P. and Sertic, N. (1996) 'Nevladine Organizacije, Ulagaje Sredstva I Socijalno

Blagostanje: Neke Hipoteze o Hrvatskoj I Sloveriji' (Non-Governmental Organisations, Funding and Social Welfare: Some Hypotheses in Croatia and Slovenia), *Revija za Socijalnu Politku*, 3(1): 25–30.

Stubbs, R. and Underhill, G.R.D. (eds) (1994) *Political Economy and the Changing Global Order*. London: Macmillan.

Summerfield, D. (1996) 'The Impact of War and Atrocity on Civilian Populations: Basic Principles for NGO Interventions and a Critique of Psycho-Social Trauma Projects'. ODI Relief and Rehabilitation Network Paper 14.

Svetlik, I. (ed.) (1992b) *Social Policy in Slovenia: Between Tradition and Innovation*. Aldershot: Avebury.

Szalai, J. and Orosz, E. (1992) 'Social Policy in Hungary' in B. Deacon (ed.), *The New Eastern Europe*. London: Sage.

Tanzi, V. (ed.) (1992) *Fiscal Policies in Economies in Transition*. Washington: IMF.

Tanzi, V. (1993) *Transition to Market: Studies in Fiscal Reform*. Washington: IMF.

Taylor, P. (1994) *International Organisations in the Modern World*. London: Pinter.

Taylor-Gooby, P., Bonoli, G. and George, V. (1996) 'Welfare Futures: The Views of Key Influentials in Six European Countries on Likely Developments in Social Policy'. Preliminary Report from Squaring the Welfare Circle in Europe, University of Canterbury Research Project.

Thirlwall, A. (1993) *Growth and Development*, 3rd edn. London: Macmillan.

Thompson, J. (1992) *Justice and World Order: A Philosophical Inquiry*. London: Routledge.

Thompson, M. (1992) *A Paper House: The Ending of Yugoslavia*. London: Hutchinson.

Tickner, A. and Morgenthaus, H. (1991) 'Principles of Political Realism: A Feminist Reformulation', in R. Grant and K. Newland (eds), *Gender and International Relations*. Milton Keynes: Open University Press.

Tomasevski, K. (1993) *Development Aid and Human Rights Revisited*. London: Pinter.

Tomasevski, K. (1995) 'Human Rights Impact Assessment: Proposals for the Next 50 Years of Bretton Woods', in J.M. Griesgraber and B.G. Gunter (eds), *Promoting Development*. London, East Haven: Pluto.

Tomes, I. (1995) 'Progress Report 2'. Unpublished paper, World Bank.

Townsend P. (1993) *An International Analysis of Poverty*. Hemel Hempstead: Harvester Wheatsheaf.

Townsend, P. with Donkor, K. (1995) 'Global Restructuring and Social Policy: An Alternative Strategy: Establishing an International Welfare State'. Draft paper presented to ISA RC19 Conference on Comparative Research on Welfare State Reforms, University of Pavia, Italy, 14–17 September.

Trocaire Development Review (ed.) (1990) 'The World Bank and Development: An NGO Critique and World Bank Response', *Trocaire Development Review*, Dublin, 1990.

UN (1987) *The Social Impact of Housing*. New York: UN.

UN (1991) 'International Cooperation for the Eradication of Poverty in Developing Countries'. Report of the Secretary-General, A/46/454, UN General Assembly, New York.

UN (1992) 'United Nations System's Action in International Assistance to the Newly Independent States'. UN, New York.

UN (1993a) 'Integration of the Economies in Transition into the World Economy: The Role of the United Nations'. Report of the Secretary-General A/48/317, UN General Assembly, New York.

UN (1993b) *Report on the World Social Situation*. New York: UN, Department of Economic and Social Development.

UN (1995a) 'Report of the Preparatory Committee for the World Summit on Social Development, 16–28 January, 1995', A/CONF.166/PC/28, UN General Assembly, New York.

UN (1995b) 'Adoption of the Declaration and Programme of Action of the World Summit for Social Development, 6–12 March, 1995', (A/CONF.166), UN General Assembly, Copenhagen.

UNDP (1990) *Human Development Report 1990*. New York: Oxford University Press.

UNDP (1991) *Human Development Report 1991*. New York: Oxford University Press.
UNDP (1991–2) 'Eastern Europe: UNICEF Alarmed over Transition', *Development Forum*, 19(6); 20(1).
UNDP (1992) *Human Development Report 1992*. New York: Oxford University Press.
UNDP (1992a) *Human Development at Work*. New York: UNDP.
UNDP (1993a) *Human Development Report 1993*. New York: Oxford University Press.
UNDP (1993b) *Eastern Europe and the Countries of the Former Soviet Union: The Transition – UNDP's Perspectives*. New York: UNDP.
UNDP (1994) *Human Development Report 1994*. New York: Oxford University Press.
UNDP (1995a) *Human Development Report 1995*. New York: Oxford University Press.
UNDP (1995b) *Ukraine Human Development Report 1995*. Kiev: Blitz-Inform Press.
UNDP (1996) *Human Development Report 1996*. New York: Oxford University Press.
UNECE (1989–90) 'Economic Reform in the East: A Framework for Western Support', in *Economic Survey of Europe*. New York: UNECE.
UNECE (1990a) *Economic Survey of Europe in 1989–1990*. New York: UNECE.
UNECE (1990b) *Economic Bulletin for Europe, Volume 42/90*. New York: UNECE.
UNECE (1991a) *Economic Survey of Europe in 1990–1991*. New York: UNECE.
UNECE (1991b) *Economic Bulletin for Europe, Volume 43/91*. New York: UNECE.
UNECE (1991c) 'Managing Reforms in the East European Countries: Lessons from the Post-War Experience of Western Europe'. ECE Discussion Papers, vol. 1, no.3, New York.
UNECE (1992a) *Economic Survey of Europe in 1991–1992*. New York: UNECE.
UNECE (1992b) *Economic Bulletin for Europe, Volume 44/92*. New York: UNECE.
UNECE (1992c) 'The Conditions for Economic Recovery in Central and Eastern Europe'. ECE Discussion Papers, vol. 2, no. 3, New York.
UNECE (1992d) 'The Scope for Macroeconomic Policy to Alleviate Unemployment in Western Europe'. ECE Discussion Papers, vol. 2 no. 3, New York.
UNECE (1993a) *Economic Survey of Europe in 1992–1993*. New York: UNECE.
UNECE (1993b) *Economic Bulletin for Europe, Volume 45/93*. New York and Geneva: UNECE.
UNECE (1993c) 'Structural Change, Employment and Unemployment in the Market and Transition Economies'. ECE Discussion Papers, vol. 3, no.1, New York and Geneva.
UNECE (1993d) 'A Comparative View on Economic Reform in Poland, Hungary and Czechoslovakia'. ECE Discussion Papers, vol. 3, no. 1, New York and Geneva.
UNECE (1993e) 'Commissions Activities Designed to Assist Countries of the Region in Transition to a Market Economy and their Integration with the European and Global Economy'. E/ECE/1272, Geneva: UNECE.
UNECE (1994a) *Economic Survey of Europe in 1993–1994*. New York and Geneva: UNECE.
UNECE (1994b) *Economic Bulletin for Europe, Volume 46/94*. New York and Geneva: UNECE.
UNECE (1995a) *Economic Survey of Europe in 1994–1995*. New York: UNECE.
UNECE (1995b) *Economic Integration in Europe and America*. Economic Studies 5. New York and Geneva: UNECE.
UNESCO (1989) *Statistical Yearbook 1989*. Paris: UNESCO.
UNHCR (1993) *The State of the World's Refugees: the Challenge of Protection*. London: Penguin.
UNHCR (1994) 'Information Notes on Former Yugoslavia'. UNHCR Office of the Special Envoy for Former Yugoslavia, Zagreb.
UNICEF (1987) *The State of the World's Children*. Oxford: Oxford University Press.
UNICEF (1991a) *Mission Reports: Hungary*. Central and Eastern Europe Division, New York: UNICEF.
UNICEF (1991b) *Mission Reports: Bulgaria*. Central and Eastern Europe Division, New York: UNICEF.
UNICEF (1992a) *Bulgaria's Children and Families*. Central and Eastern Europe Division, New York: UNICEF.

UNICEF (1992b) 'UNICEF Activities in Central and Eastern Europe, the CIS and the Baltic States'. E/ICEF/1992/L.14, UNICEF, New York.

UNICEF (1992c) 'Ukraine: Crisis and Transition: Meeting Human Needs'. Report of UNICEF/WHO Mission, February 1992, New York.

UNICEF (1992d) 'Overview of Health, Education and Social Safety Nets and Assessment of Priority Needs'. Report of UNICEF Mission to Lithuania, 22–27 February 1992, New York.

UNICEF (1992e) 'Public Policy and Social Conditions: A Proposal for "The Monitoring of Social Conditions during the Transition to the Market Economy in Central and East Europe"'. UNICEF International Child Development Centre, Florence.

UNICEF (1993a) *Public Policy and Social Conditions*. Economies in Transition Regional Monitoring Report 1, November 1993. New York: UNICEF.

UNICEF (1993b) *Strategies for Children during the Transition: Developing National Programmes of Action*. Report of the Central and Eastern Europe Regional Seminar, 13–16 April, Budapest.

UNICEF (1994) *Crisis in Mortality, Health and Nutrition*. Economies in Transition Regional Monitoring Report 2, August 1994. UNICEF, New York.

UNICEF (1995a) *The State of the World's Children 1995*. New York: UNICEF.

UNICEF (1995b) *Poverty, Children and Policy: Responses for a Brighter Future*. Economies in Transition Regional Monitoring Report 3. UNICEF International Child Development Centre, Florence.

UNICEF (1995c) '20/20: Breaking the Poverty Cycle'. Brochure for the World Summit on Social Development, March.

UNICEF (1995d) 'Priorities for Children: What the World Summit on Social Development Can Do'. Brochure for the World Summit for Social Development, March.

UNICEF (1996) *The State of the World's Children 1996*. New York: UNICEF.

UNICEF (1997) *Central and Eastern Europe: Transition Public Policy and Social Conditions. Children at Risk in Central and Eastern Europe: Perils and Promises*. Florence: UNICEF International Child Development Centre.

UNRISD (1991) *Progress Report on UNRISD Activities 1990/1991*. Geneva: UNRISD.

UNRISD (1993a) *UNRISD: 30 Years of Research for Social Development*. Geneva: UNRISD.

UNRISD (1994) *The Crisis of Social Development in the 1990s: Preparing for the World Social Summit*. Report of UNRISD's 30th Anniversary Conference, Geneva, 7–8 July 1993. Geneva: UNRISD.

UNRISD (1995a) *Adjustment, Globalization and Social Development*. Report of the UNRISD/UNDP International Seminar on Economic Restructuring and Social Policy, New York, 11–13 January. Geneva: UNRISD.

UNRISD (1995b) *States of Disarray: the Social Effects of Globalization*. Report for the World Summit on Social Development. Geneva: UNRISD.

UNRISD (1995c) *Structural Adjustment in a Changing World*. Report for the World Summit of Social Development. Geneva: UNRISD.

US Committee for Refugees (1996) *World Refugee Survey 1995*. Washington: IRSA.

Van Brabant, J. (1993) *The New Easter Europe and the World Economy*. Oxford: Westview.

Van de Walle, D. et al. (1993) 'Poverty and Social Spending in Hungary'. Independent Discussion Paper, Policy Research Department, World Bank, Washington.

Van Parijs, P. (1995) *Freedom for All: What (If Anything) Can Justify Capitalism?* Oxford: Clarendon Press.

Van Parijs, P. (1996) 'Basic Income and the Two Dilemmas of the Welfare State', *The Political Quarterly*, 67(1).

Vecernik, J. (1995) 'Incomes in Central Europe: Distributions, Patterns and Perceptions'. Paper contributed to ISA RC19 Conference on Comparative Research on Welfare State Reforms'. University of Pavia, Italy, 14–17 September.

Vince, P. (1996) 'Transformation of the Hungarian Welfare System: Sovereign Decisions and External Influences'. Research consultancy report.

Vobruba, G. (1994) 'Transnational Social Policy in Processes of Transformation', in A. de

Swann (ed.), *Social Policy beyond Borders: The Social Question in Transnational Perspective*. Amsterdam, Amsterdam University Press.

Vodopivec, M. (1990) *The Labour Market and the Transition of Socialist Economies*. Washington: World Bank.

Vodopivec, M. (1992) 'Review of the Labour Market and Social Safety Net Sectors of CIS Country Economic Memorandum'. Unpublished report, World Bank, Washington.

Voirin, M. (1993) 'Social Security in Central and Eastern European Countries: Continuity and Change', *International Social Security Review*, 1.

Vojnič, D. (1995) 'Disparity and Disintegration: The Economic Dimension of Yugoslavia's Demise', in P. Akhavan and R. Howse (eds), *Yugoslavia: The Former and the Future*. Washington DC: Brookings Institute.

Wallerstein, E. (1991) *Geopolitics and Geoculture*. Cambridge: Cambridge University Press.

Waltz, K. (1986) 'Political Structures', in R. Keohane (ed.), *Neo-Realism and Its Critics*. New York: Columbia University Press.

Waters, M. (1995) *Globalization*. London and New York: Routledge.

Weale, A. (1994) 'Social Policy and the EU', *Social Policy and Administration*, 28(1): 5–19.

Weiss, T.G. (1994) *The UN and Changing World Politics*. Oxford: Westview.

Wheeler, M. (1993) 'The Unmaking of Yugoslavia', *Journal of Area Studies*, 3: 40–9.

Wheeler, N.J. (1996) 'Guardian Angel or Global Gangster: A Review of the Ethical Claims of International Society', *Political Studies*, XLIV: 123–35.

White, G. et al. (1983) *Revolutionary Socialist Development in the Third World*. Brighton: Wheatsheaf.

White, G. and Shang, X. (1995) 'Social Security Reforms in Urban China: A Preliminary Research Report'. Paper presented at a Workshop on Social Insurance Reforms: Issues and Answers, Beijing, October.

Whitfield, D. (1994) *Globalisation: The Future for the Welfare State and Public Services*. Sheffield: Centre for Public Services.

Whittaker, B. (1983) *A Bridge of People: A Personal View of Oxfam's First Forty Years*. London: Heinemann.

Wilensky, H. (1975) *The Welfare State and Equality*. Berkeley, CA: University of California Press.

Willets, P. (ed.) (1996) *The Conscience of the World*. Washington: Brookings Institute.

Williams, F. (1987) *Social Policy: A Critical Introduction*. Cambridge: Polity.

Williams, F. (1994) 'Social Relations, Welfare and the Post-Fordism Debate', in R. Burrows and B. Loader (eds), *Towards a Post-Fordist Welfare State*. London: Routledge.

Williams, F. (1995) 'Race/Ethnicity, Gender and Class in Welfare States: A Framework for Comparative Analysis', *Social Politics*, Summer.

Williams, S. et al. (1991) *Social Safety Nets in East/Central Europe*. Cambridge, MA: Harvard University Press.

Woodward, S.L. (1995) *Balkan Tragedy: Chaos and Dissolution after the Cold War*. Washington: Brookings Institute.

Woodward, S.L. (1996), *Implementing Peace in Bosnia and Herzegovina: A Post-Dayton Primer and Memo of Warning*. Brookings Discussion Paper. Washington: Brookings Institute.

Woolcock, S. (1995) 'The Trade and Labour Standards Debate: Overburdening or Defending the Multilateral System?'. Paper for the CRUSA/RIIA Study Group, October.

World Bank (1975) *Yugoslavia: Development with Decentralisation*. Baltimore: Johns Hopkins University Press.

World Bank (1987) *World Development Report*. Washington: World Bank.

World Bank (1989) *World Development Report*. Washington: World Bank.

World Bank (1990) *World Development Report: Poverty*. Washington: World Bank.

World Bank (1991a) *The Transformation of Economies in Eastern and Central Europe: Issues, Progress and Prospects*. Washington: World Bank.

World Bank (1991b) *Social indicators of Development 1990*. Baltimore: Johns Hopkins University Press.

World Bank (1991c) *Bulgaria: Crisis and Transition to a Market Economy, Volume I – The Main Report.* Washington: World Bank.

World Bank (1991d) *Assistance Strategies to Reduce Poverty.* Washington: World Bank.

World Bank (1992a) *Poverty Reduction: Operational Directives.* Washington: World Bank.

World Bank (1992b) *Hungary, Reform of Social Policy and Expenditures.* Washington: World Bank.

World Bank (1993a) *Ukraine: The Social Sectors during Transition.* Washington: World Bank Country Study.

World Bank (1993b) 'Support for Adjustments in Hungary'. Operations Evaluation Department Precis 51, Washington.

World Bank (1993c) *Implementing the World Bank's Strategy to Reduce Poverty: Progress and Challenges.* Washington: World Bank.

World Bank (1993d) *The East Asian Miracle.* Washington: World Bank.

World Bank (1993e) *Hungary: Performance Audit Report, Structural Adjustment Loan.* Report 12103, 29 June, Washington: World Bank.

World Bank (1993f) 'Development Issues'. Presentations to the 47th Meeting of the Development Committee, 27 September, Washington.

World Bank (1993g) *Annual Report.* Washington: World Bank.

World Bank (1994a) *Bulgaria: An Economic Update.* Country Operations Division, May, Washington.

World Bank (1994b) *Averting the Old Age Crisis: Policies to Protect the Old and Promote Growth.* World Bank Policy Research Report. New York: Oxford University Press.

World Bank (1994c) 'Reform Issues on Social Policy'. Manuscript, Budapest.

World Bank (1995b) *Hungary: Structural Reforms for Sustainable Growth.* Washington: World Bank Country Study.

World Bank (1995c) *Social Indicators of Development 1995.* Washington: World Bank.

World Bank (1995d) *Investing in People: the World Bank in Action.* Washington: World Bank.

World Bank (1995e) *World Development Report 1995: Workers in an Integrating World.* Washington: World Bank.

World Bank (1995f) 'Priedlog reforme hrvatskog mirovinskog sustava' (A Proposal for a Reform of the Croatian Pension System), Revija za Socijalnu Politiku, 2(4): 315-22.

World Bank (1995g) *Staff Appraisal Report: The Former Yugoslav Republic of Macedonia: Social Reform and Technical Assistance Project.* Washington: World Bank.

World Bank (1995h) *Advancing Social Development.* World Bank Contribution to the World Summit on Social Development, March. Washington.

World Bank (1996) *World Development Report: from Plan to Market.* Washington: World Bank.

World Bank (1997) Social Assistance Strategy Meeting of Resident Mission in Bosnia and Herzegovina. Mimeo, 27 May, Sarajevo.

World Health Organization (1989) *World Health Statistics Annual 1989.* WHO: Geneva.

Yugofax (1992) *Breakdown: War and Reconstruction in Yugoslavia.* London: IWPR.

Zavirsek, D. (1995) 'Social Innovations: A New Paradigm in Central European Social Work', *International Perspectives in Social Work*, 1.

Index